Algebra Readiness

Guided Practice Book

Name ______________________________

Teacher Created Materials PUBLISHING

Authors
Carol Edgar and Jamie Robin

Editor
Karie Feldner Gladis, M.S.Ed.

Assistant Editor
Torrey Maloof

Associate Editor
Christina Hill, M.A.

Editorial Assistant
Kathryn R. Kiley

Publisher
Rachelle Cracchiolo, M.S.Ed.

Editor-in-Chief
Sharon Coan, M.S.Ed.

Editorial Director
Emily R. Smith, M.A.Ed.

Editorial Manager
Gisela Lee, M.A.

Creative Director
Lee Aucoin

Illustration Manager/Designer
Timothy J. Bradley

Designer
Neri Garcia

Imaging
Don Tran
Sandra Riley
Phil Garcia

Foreword Author
Dr. Debi Mink

Introduction Author
Shelly Frei

Mathematics Consultants
Lori Barker
Brenda Bourque
Wendy Conklin, M.A.
Pamela H. Dase, M.A.Ed.
Melanie Easterday, M.A.Ed.
Donna Erdman, M.Ed.
Briita L. Halonen, M.A.
Sharon Ice
Rachel Rimpel
Robert F. Smith

Teacher Created Materials
5301 Oceanus Drive
Huntington Beach, CA 92649
http://www.tcmpub.com
ISBN: 978-1-4333-0000-4

Reprinted 2011

Table of Contents

Student Letter

Dear Student,

You are starting a math program that will prepare you for Algebra I. The program is called *Active Algebra—Algebra Readiness*. Up to this point in school, you have learned many mathematical skills. This program will help you focus on what you already know how to do in math and what you need to learn. You will learn the important mathematical concepts, skills, and vocabulary that you will need next year in the Algebra I classroom.

Sometimes students have trouble learning algebra concepts because it is an area of math that has many brand new objectives, skills, and formulas. However, passing an Algebra I class is an important part of your high school requirements. Also, algebra concepts are the key for continuing on in mathematics in high school and college. Algebra skills are used in everyday life as people solve various problems that arise. The program has many ties to real life so that you can easily see this important connection.

It is not a good idea to simply memorize formulas and use the right ones. You need to truly understand the concepts and the vocabulary behind the formulas. That way, you understand when to use the right skills to solve a wide variety of problems in your math books and tests as well as in real-life situations. The lessons in this program will help you to fully understand the math concepts and know when to use the right formulas and skills to solve problems.

As you are working on the assignments in this program, you are responsible for letting your teacher know whether you are struggling with some of the concepts and need more practice. On the following pages, there is a list of all the key mathematics objectives we will be covering in this course. It might be interesting to read through the list to find out what skills you will be learning. You can also use these to let your teacher know which skills she or he may need to reexplain.

Please sign the bottom of this letter and keep it in this book as a reminder of the goals of this mathematics program. Have fun getting algebra ready!

____

Student Signature

NCTM Mathematics Standards

Number and Operations—Grades 6–8

Targeted Standards

Students will understand the meaning and effects of arithmetic operations with fractions, decimals, and integers.

Students will develop and analyze algorithms for computing with fractions, decimals, and integers and develop fluency in their use.

Students will use factors, multiples, prime factorization, and relatively prime numbers to solve problems.

Students will use the associative and commutative properties of addition and multiplication and the distributive property of multiplication over addition to simplify computations with integers, fractions, and decimals.

Students will understand and use the inverse relationships of addition and subtraction, multiplication and division, and squaring and finding square roots to simplify computations and solve problems.

Students will understand and use ratios and proportions to represent quantitative relationships.

Students will develop meaning for integers and represent and compare quantities with them.

Students will work flexibly with fractions, decimals, and percents to solve problems.

Students will develop an understanding of large numbers and recognize and appropriately use exponential, scientific, and calculator notation.

Algebra—Grades 6–8

Targeted Standards

Students will develop an initial conceptual understanding of different uses of variables.

Students will use symbolic algebra to represent situations and to solve problems, especially those that involve linear relationships.

Students will recognize and generate equivalent forms for simple algebraic expressions and solve linear equations.

Students will represent, analyze, and generalize a variety of patterns with tables, graphs, words, and, when possible, symbolic rules.

Students will identify functions as linear or nonlinear and contrast their properties from tables, graphs, or equations.

Standards are listed with the permission of the National Council of Teachers of Mathematics (NCTM). NCTM does not endorse the content or validity of these alignments.

NCTM Mathematics Standards *(cont.)*

Algebra—Grades 6–8 *(cont.)*

Targeted Standards

Students will relate and compare different forms of representation for a relationship.

Students will explore relationships between symbolic expressions and graphs of lines, paying particular attention to the meaning of intercept and slope.

Students will use graphs to analyze the nature of changes in quantities in linear relationships.

Students will model and solve contextualized problems using various representations, such as graphs, tables, and equations.

Geometry—Grades 6–8

Targeted Standards

Students will use geometric models to represent and explain numerical and algebraic relationships.

Students will use two-dimensional representations of three-dimensional objects to visualize and solve problems such as those involving surface area and volume.

Students will create and critique inductive and deductive arguments concerning geometric ideas and relationships, such as congruence, similarity, and the Pythagorean relationship.

Measurement—Grades 6–8

Targeted Standards

Students will develop and use formulas to determine the circumference of circles and the area of triangles, parallelograms, trapezoids, and circles and develop strategies to find the area of more-complex shapes.

Students will develop strategies to determine the surface area and volume of selected prisms, pyramids, and cylinders.

Data Analysis and Probability—Grades 6–8

Targeted Standards

Students will use proportionality and a basic understanding of probability to make and test conjectures about the results of experiments and simulations.

Students will make conjectures about possible relationships between two characteristics of a sample on the basis of scatter plots of the data and approximate lines of fit.

Standards are listed with the permission of the National Council of Teachers of Mathematics (NCTM). NCTM does not endorse the content or validity of these alignments.

NCTM Mathematics Standards *(cont.)*

Algebra—Grades 9–12

Targeted Standards

Students will understand the meaning and effects of arithmetic operations with fractions, decimals, and integers.

Students will develop and analyze algorithms for computing with fractions, decimals, and integers and develop fluency in their use.

Students will use factors, multiples, prime factorization, and relatively prime numbers to solve problems.

Students will use the associative and commutative properties of addition and multiplication and the distributive property of multiplication over addition to simplify computations with integers, fractions, and decimals.

Students will understand and use the inverse relationships of addition and subtraction, multiplication and division, and squaring and finding square roots to simplify computations and solve problems.

Students will understand and use ratios and proportions to represent quantitative relationships.

Students will develop meaning for integers and represent and compare quantities with them.

Students will work flexibly with fractions, decimals, and percents to solve problems.

Students will develop an understanding of large numbers and recognize and appropriately use exponential, scientific, and calculator notation.

Number and Operations—Grades 3–5

Foundational Skills

Students will understand the place-value structure of the base-ten number system and be able to represent and compare whole numbers and decimals.

Students will recognize equivalent representations for the same number and generate them by decomposing and composing numbers.

Students will understand various meanings of multiplication and division.

Students will understand the effects of multiplying and dividing whole numbers.

Students will develop fluency in adding, subtracting, multiplying, and dividing whole numbers.

Students will identify and use relationships between operations, such as division as the inverse of multiplication, to solve problems.

Students will develop understanding of fractions as parts of unit wholes, as parts of a collection, as locations on number lines, and as divisions of whole numbers.

Students will use visual models, benchmarks, and equivalent forms to add and subtract commonly used fractions and decimals.

Standards are listed with the permission of the National Council of Teachers of Mathematics (NCTM). NCTM does not endorse the content or validity of these alignments.

NCTM Mathematics Standards *(cont.)*

Number and Operations—Grades 3–5 *(cont.)*

Foundational Skills

Students will select appropriate methods and tools for computing with whole numbers from among mental computation, estimation, calculators, and paper and pencil according to the context and nature of the computation and use the selected method or tools.

Algebra—Grades 3–5

Foundational Skills

Students will identify such properties as commutativity, associativity, and distributivity and use them to compute with whole numbers.

Students will represent the idea of a variable as an unknown quantity using a letter or a symbol.

Students will express mathematical relationships using equations.

Students will model problem situations with objects and use representations such as graphs, tables, and equations to draw conclusions.

Students will investigate how a change in one variable relates to a change in a second variable and then identify and describe situations with constant or varying rates of change and compare them.

Geometry—Grades 3–5

Foundational Skills

Students will make and use coordinate systems to specify locations and to describe paths.

Students will find the distance between points along horizontal and vertical lines of a coordinate system.

Problem Solving, Connections, Representations—Grades K–12

Foundational Skills

Students will build new mathematical knowledge through problem solving; solve problems that arise in mathematics and in other contexts; apply and adapt a variety of strategies to solve problems; monitor and reflect on the process of mathematical problem solving.

Students will recognize and use connections among mathematical ideas; understand how mathematical ideas interconnect and build on one another to produce a coherent whole; and recognize and apply mathematics in contexts outside of mathematics.

Students will create and use representations to organize, record, and communicate mathematical ideas. Students will select, apply, and translate among mathematical representations to solve problems. Students will use representations to model and interpret physical, social, and mathematical phenomena.

Standards are listed with the permission of the National Council of Teachers of Mathematics (NCTM). NCTM does not endorse the content or validity of these alignments.

Place Value Chart

Billions Period			Millions Period			Thousands Period			Ones Period			Less Than Zero		
hundred billions	ten billions	billions	hundred millions	ten millions	millions	hundred thousands	ten thousands	thousands	hundreds	tens	ones	tenths	hundredths	thousandths

Teacher Created Materials PUBLISHING

Mathematics Chart

AREA	circle	$A = \pi r^2$		
	rectangle	$A = lw$	or	$A = bh$
	trapezoid	$A = \frac{1}{2}(b_1 + b_2)h$	or	$A = \frac{(b_1 + b_2)h}{2}$
	triangle	$A = \frac{1}{2}bh$	or	$A = \frac{bh}{2}$
CIRCUMFERENCE	circle	$C = 2\pi r$	or	$C = \pi d$
PERIMETER	rectangle	$P = 2l + 2w$	or	$P = 2(l + w)$
SURFACE AREA	cone (lateral)	$S = \pi rl$		
	cone (total)	$S = \pi rl + \pi r^2$	or	$S = \pi r(l + r)$
	cube	$S = 6s^2$		
	cylinder (lateral)	$S = 2\pi rh$		
	cylinder (total)	$S = 2\pi rh + 2\pi r^2$	or	$S = 2\pi r(h + r)$
	sphere	$S = 4\pi r^2$		
VOLUME	prism or cylinder	$V = Bh$		
Note: B represents the area of the base of the solid figure.	pyramid or cone	$V = \frac{1}{3}Bh$	or	$V = \frac{Bh}{3}$
	sphere	$V = \frac{4}{3}\pi r^3$	or	$V = \frac{4\pi r^3}{3}$

Density Formula	$d = \frac{m}{v}$
Direct Variation Formula	$y = kx$
Distance Formula	$d = rt$
Formula for Total Output	rate · time = total output
Pi (π)	$\pi \approx 3.14$ or $\pi \approx \frac{22}{7}$
Pythagorean Theorem	$a^2 + b^2 = c^2$
Simple Interest Formula	$I = prt$
Slope of a Line	$m = \frac{y_2 - y_1}{x_2 - x_1}$
Slope-Intercept Form of an Equation	$y = mx + b$

Mathematics Chart *(cont.)*

CAPACITY AND VOLUME		
	Metric	1 liter = 1,000 milliliters
	Customary	1 gallon = 4 quarts 1 gallon = 128 ounces 1 quart = 2 pints 1 pint = 2 cups 1 cup = 8 ounces
LENGTH		
	Metric	1 centimeter = 10 millimeters 1 meter = 100 centimeters 1 kilometer = 1,000 meters
	Customary	1 foot = 12 inches 1 yard = 3 feet 1 mile = 5,280 feet 1 mile = 1,760 yards
MASS AND WEIGHT		
	Metric	1 gram = 1,000 milligrams 1 kilogram = 1,000 grams
	Customary	1 pound = 16 ounces 1 ton = 2,000 pounds
TIME		
		1 minute = 60 seconds 1 hour = 60 minutes 1 day = 24 hours 1 week = 7 days 1 year = 365 days 1 year = 52 weeks 1 year = 12 months

Practicing with a Purpose

- Try each and every problem on the activity sheet(s).
- After solving a problem, look to see if your answer is reasonable or try checking your answer using another strategy.
- If you cannot figure out how to solve a problem, review your notes from class or ask a friend or teacher to assist.
- After your work has been checked or graded, review the problems to see which ones were incorrect.
- Determine why the problem is incorrect by reviewing your work on the page or by resolving the problem. Refer to your notes to ensure that you are carrying out the procedure correctly.
- When reviewing for a quiz or test, practice solving different types of problems from your notes and *Guided Practice Book* activities.

Name ______________________________

Understanding Whole Numbers

Directions: Solve each problem.

1. Write in words the value of each underlined digit.

<u>5</u>,222,222 ____________________ 222,22<u>5</u> ____________________

2<u>5</u>2,222 ____________________ 22,2<u>5</u>2 ____________________

2,<u>5</u>22 ____________________ <u>5</u>,222 ____________________

2. Explain how you know the value of each 5.

____

____

Directions: Fill in each blank with the correct period name for the following numbers.

3. 5,246,842

5 ______________ 246 ______________ 842 ______________

4. 900,735,215

900______________ 735 ______________ 215 ______________

Directions: Write in words the name of the place value of each underlined digit. Then, identify in words the value of that digit.

5. 34,<u>5</u>27

Place value: ____________________

Value of digit: ____________________

6. 832,5<u>7</u>6,104

Place value: ____________________

____

Value of digit: ____________________

7. 91<u>2</u>,620,215

Place value: ____________________

Value of digit: ____________________

8. 264,<u>1</u>73,003

Place value: ____________________

____

Value of digit: ____________________

Understanding Whole Numbers *(cont.)*

Directions: Write each number in standard form.

9. ten thousand, seven hundred thirty-two ______

10. seven hundred forty-five thousand, two hundred fifty-five ______

11. four hundred five thousand, three ______

12. two million, fifty-seven thousand, three hundred five ______

13. fifty-seven million, two hundred four thousand, sixty ______

14. 500 + 30 + 2 ______

15. 6,000 + 200 + 3 ______

16. 400,000 + 20,000 + 50 ______

Directions: Write each number in expanded form.

17. 485,253 ______

18. 7,215,000 ______

19. 5,002,000 ______

20. 3,056,023 ______

Directions: Read and answer each question.

21. Write the smallest 8-digit number in which each digit is used only once. Do not use zero and do not use decimals.

______

22. Saturn has a diameter of about one hundred twenty thousand kilometers. Write this diameter in standard form. ______

23. Venus has a diameter of about twelve thousand, one hundred kilometers. Write this diameter in standard from.

______

Bonus

24. By taking expanded form one step further, a number such as 2,304 may be written as $2 \cdot 1{,}000 + 3 \cdot 100 + 4 \cdot 1$. Write 402,370 in the same sort of expanded form.

______

Name ______________________________

Understanding Decimals

Directions: Write each number in expanded form.

1. 42.175 ______________________________

2. 0.9316 ______________________________

3. 500.028 ______________________________

4. 90,000.0004 ______________________________

Directions: Place >, <, or = between each set of two numbers so that there is a true statement of the form **a** > **b**, **a** < **b**, or **a** = **b**.

5. 48.219 __________ 48.292

6. 0.385 __________ 0.098

7. 1.285 __________ 1.275

8. 99.989 __________ 99.999

Directions: Place the numbers in increasing order.

9. 0.816; 0.429; 15.624; 15.426; 2.947

____

Apply It!

Directions: Let *a* represent the money in Anton's checking account and let *b* represent the money in Bo-Bae's checking account. Use *a* and *b* to write inequalities that compare their accounts for each situation below.

10. Anton has \$135.97 and Bo-Bae has \$248.62. ______________

11. Anton has \$1,638.97 and Bo-Bae has \$1,638.79. ______________

12. Anton has \$529.48 and Bo-Bae has \$628.47. ______________

Name ______________________________

Adding and Subtracting

Directions: Answer each question fully. Use complete sentences.

1. Describe how to add 175 + 183 + 546 in columns. Why do we align the digits the way we do?

____

____

2. Explain how addition and subtraction are related. Use an example to help your explanation.

____

____

Directions: Solve. Show your work on another sheet of paper.

3. 485 + 1,732 = ____________
4. 47.942 + 8.779 = ____________
5. 3,293 – 765 = ____________
6. 5.472 – 4.927 = ____________
7. 738,262 – 547,985 = ____________
8. 1,893 + 26,427 + 3,871 + 56 + 2,746 = ____________
9. 432 + 78 + 2,304 + 32,591 = ____________
10. 27,602 – 13,465 = ____________
11. 702.465 – 23.982 = ____________
12. 7.25 + 8.3 – 3 = ____________
13. 2.9 + 4.71 = ____________
14. 4.5 – 2.74 = ____________

Directions: Translate and simplify each problem.

15. 3.5 plus 3.7 ____________
16. 6.32 greater than 47.242 ____________
17. the difference of 5.24 and 0.234 ____________
18. 4.7 less than 9.1 ____________
19. 9.03 more than 23.63 ____________

Adding and Subtracting *(cont.)*

Directions: Read and answer each question. Show your work and label your answers.

20. Cassie is 5 years older than her sister. Cassie is 17 years old. How old is her sister?

____

21. The temperature at noon is 12 °F hotter on Tuesday than it was on Monday. The temperature at noon on Monday was 65 °F. What is the temperature at noon Tuesday?

____

22. Kiley downloaded 132 songs in January, 78 songs in February, 34 songs in March, 142 songs in April, 18 songs in May, 179 songs in June, 154 songs in July, 120 songs in August, 72 songs in September, 30 songs in October, 18 songs in November, and 116 songs in December. How many songs did she download all year?

____

23. Complete the balances for the checkbook record below.

Check #	Date	Description	Amount	Balance
——		Starting Balance	——	$1,058
202	9/1	Lunch	$3	
——	9/2	Deposit	+ $198	
203	9/3	Helmet	$28	
204	9/4	Gift	$79	
——	9/7	Deposit	+ $260	
205	9/10	Computer Repair	$188	
206	9/11	Gloves	$22	

Directions: Translate into a mathematical equation, and solve. Show your work.

24. If you owe $423.97 on a credit card and you pay $128.34, how much do you still owe?

____

Name ______________________________

Multiplying Multidigit Numbers

Directions: Solve the following problems.

1. 284 · 48 = ____________

2. 2,784 · 13 = ____________

3. 1,199 · 21 = ____________

4. 1,469 · 23 = ____________

5. 610 · 32 = ____________

6. 1,965 · 41 = ____________

7. 2,436 · 62 = ____________

8. 743 · 53 = ____________

Directions: Read and answer each question. Show your work and label your answers.

9. An elephant in the wild needs about 400 pounds of food a day. How many pounds of food does it need in 2 weeks?

____

10. What is the area of the rectangle? ____________________

A = *lw*

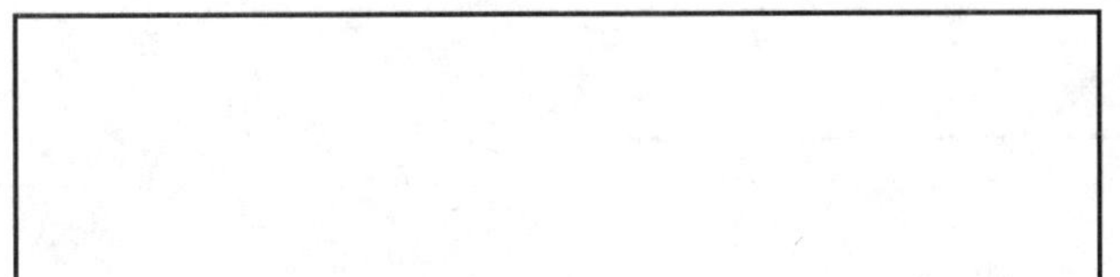

Name ______________________________

Dividing Multidigit Numbers

Directions: Divide. Write each remainder in fraction form. Show your work.

1. $841 \div 7 =$ ____________

2. $652 \div 3 =$ ____________

3. $751 \div 5 =$ ____________

4. $850 \div 4 =$ ____________

5. $398 \div 8 =$ ____________

6. $317 \div 9 =$ ____________

7. $339 \div 6 =$ ____________

8. $853 \div 4 =$ ____________

Directions: Find the missing factor.

9. $a \cdot 6 = 5{,}178$

$a =$ ______________________

10. $b \cdot 5 = 5{,}115$

$b =$ ______________________

Name ______________________

Multiplying and Dividing Decimals

Directions: Multiply or divide. Round to the nearest thousandth. Show your work.

1. $42.8 \cdot 0.06 =$ __________

2. $2.203 \cdot 0.27 =$ __________

3. $9.655 \cdot 8.33 =$ __________

4. $428 \cdot 0.0002 =$ __________

5. $0.204 \cdot 0.03 =$ __________

6. $0.22 \cdot 0.33 =$ __________

7. $38.35 \div 6.5 =$ __________

8. $1.548 \div 0.06 =$ __________

9. $3.751 \div 6.2 =$ __________

10. $37.2 \div 1.5 =$ __________

11. $0.7042 \div 0.007 =$ __________

12. $0.00657 \div 0.6 =$ __________

Directions: Solve.

13. Jeannie worked at the Pizza Shack for 23.7 hours one week and was paid $146.94. How much did she earn per hour?

____

Name ______________________

Understanding Fractions

Directions: Reduce each fraction to its lowest term.

1. $\frac{45}{20}$ ______________

3. $\frac{84}{144}$ ______________

2. $\frac{16}{24}$ ______________

4. $3\frac{28}{40}$ ______________

Directions: Compare each pair of numbers.

5. $\frac{49}{60}$ ______________ $\frac{28}{45}$

6. $4\frac{13}{15}$ ______________ $4\frac{11}{12}$

7. $\frac{43}{8}$ ______________ $\frac{89}{20}$

Directions: Change each mixed number into an improper fraction.

8. $3\frac{2}{9}$ ______________

10. $6\frac{1}{6}$ ______________

9. $60\frac{11}{40}$ ______________

11. $1\frac{23}{24}$ ______________

Directions: Change each improper fraction into a mixed number.

12. $\frac{431}{100}$ ______________

13. $\frac{62}{13}$ ______________

Directions: Solve.

14. José serves soda to 5 friends, but the fifth cup is only $\frac{3}{4}$ full. Write a mixed number to show the number of cups of soda that José poured.

____

Name ____________________

Multiplying and Dividing Fractions 1

Directions: Solve. Reduce each answer to its lowest terms, but it is not necessary to change improper fractions to mixed numbers. Show your work.

1. $\frac{50}{27} \cdot \frac{45}{20} =$ ____________

2. $\frac{11}{24} \cdot \frac{16}{33} =$ ____________

3. $3\frac{3}{8} \cdot 2\frac{5}{9} =$ ____________

4. $6\frac{2}{3} \div 2\frac{4}{5} =$ ____________

5. $\frac{32}{45} \cdot \frac{18}{42} =$ ____________

6. $3\frac{5}{9} \div \frac{32}{9} =$ ____________

7. $\frac{12n}{hk} \cdot \frac{kmp}{15n} =$ ____________

8. $\frac{72kp}{az} \div \frac{10mk}{zd} =$ ____________

9. $\frac{abc}{def} \cdot \frac{djl}{bop} =$ ____________

10. $\frac{54pd}{25qr} \div \frac{64ps}{30rt} =$ ____________

Directions: Evaluate the expressions for the following values:

	$\frac{8xy}{3mn} \cdot \frac{15m}{4y}$	$\frac{8xy}{3mn} \div \frac{12x}{9y}$
11. x = 5, y = 6, m = 10, and n = 1	____________	____________
12. x = 15, y = 2, m = 3, and n = 4	____________	____________
13. x = 2, y = 1, m = 8, and n = 3	____________	____________

Directions: Translate as a mathematical statement and then solve.

14. A.J. and Sherita are filling bottles with lemonade to sell at their school track meet. Each bottle holds $5\frac{1}{6}$ ounces of lemonade. A.J. has 120 bottles. How many ounces of lemonade does he need? ____________________

Name ________________________________

Adding and Subtracting Fractions 1

Directions: Solve. Reduce each answer to its lowest terms, but it is not necessary to change improper fractions to mixed numbers. Show your work.

1. $\frac{11}{12} + \frac{7}{12} =$ ____________

2. $\frac{1}{15} - \frac{1}{15} =$ ____________

3. $\frac{11}{12} + \frac{1}{5} =$ ____________

4. $\frac{2}{3} - \frac{5}{8} =$ ____________

5. $\frac{23}{40} + \frac{5}{8} =$ ____________

6. $\frac{29}{36} - \frac{7}{9} =$ ____________

7. $\frac{11}{36} + \frac{7}{45} =$ ____________

8. $\frac{9}{10} - \frac{8}{45} =$ ____________

9. $\frac{a}{b} + \frac{c}{d} =$ ____________

10. $\frac{de}{gh} - \frac{p}{qr} =$ ____________

11. $2\frac{5}{8} + 1\frac{1}{4} =$ ____________

12. $5\frac{7}{9} - 2\frac{2}{3} =$ ____________

13. $9\frac{3}{5} - 2\frac{19}{20} =$ ____________

14. $8\frac{7}{12} + 6\frac{9}{16} =$ ____________

Directions: Translate as a mathematical statement and then solve.

15. The city plans to put a fence around a retention pond. The four sides measure $35\frac{1}{8}$ feet, 27 feet, $32\frac{3}{8}$ feet, and $31\frac{1}{8}$ feet. How many feet of fencing will be needed?

____

Name ________________________________

Understanding the Properties

Directions: Identify whether each property is the commutative, associative, or distributive.

1. $5 \cdot 6 = 6 \cdot 5$ ________________________________

2. $(6 \cdot 3) \cdot 2 = 6 \cdot (3 \cdot 2)$ ________________________________

3. $9 + 4 = 4 + 9$ ________________________________

4. $3(5 + 6) = 15 + 30$ ________________________________

5. $a + b = b + a$ ________________________________

6. $(a \cdot b) \cdot c = a \cdot (b \cdot c)$ ________________________________

7. $3(x + 5) = 3x + 15$ ________________________________

8. $(x + y) + z = x + (y + z)$ ________________________________

Directions: Give the value of the unknown.

9. $60 + \square = 97 + 60$ ________________________________

10. $\square \cdot 34 = 34 \cdot 75$ ________________________________

11. $(58 \cdot \square) \cdot 32 = 58 \cdot (45 \cdot 32)$ ________________________________

12. $(48 + 51) + \square = 48 + (51 + 61)$ ________________________________

Directions: Write mathematical statements to illustrate the correct property for each.

13. associative property of addition, $7 + 8 + 5 =$ ________________________________

14. associative property of multiplication, $6 \cdot 2 \cdot 9 =$ ________________________________

15. distributive property, $3(7 + x) =$ ________________________________

16. associative property of addition, $12 + 19 + 21 =$ ________________________________

Understanding the Properties *(cont.)*

Directions: Solve. Show your work on another sheet of paper.

17. $4(5 + 7) =$ ____________________

18. $5(3 + 4) =$ ____________________

19. $8(4 + 7) =$ ____________________

20. $9(2 + 6) =$ ____________________

21. $2(9 + 17) =$ ____________________

22. $6(10 - 4) =$ ____________________

23. $3(11 - 9) =$ ____________________

24. $7(12 - 5) =$ ____________________

25. $\frac{1}{2}(50 + 30) =$ ____________________

26. $0.3(7 + 8) =$ ____________________

27. $\frac{1}{4}(100 + 200) =$ ____________________

28. $0.75(350 + 125) =$ ____________________

Directions: Write each expression using the distributive property.

29. $4(x + 5)$ ____________________

30. $12(x - 3)$ ____________________

31. $7(15 + x)$ ____________________

32. $6(x + 7)$ ____________________

33. $11(x - 9)$ ____________________

34. $9(9 + x)$ ____________________

35. $5(x + 10)$ ____________________

36. $2(12 + x)$ ____________________

37. $9(17 - x)$ ____________________

38. $3(x + 25)$ ____________________

39. $3(15 + x)$ ____________________

40. $8(12 - x)$ ____________________

Name ______________________________

Understanding Equals

Directions: Determine what is needed to balance the equation if you have the following denominations of money.

1. 4 quarters + 5 nickels + 5 pennies = 1 dollar + 1 quarter + __________ pennies

2. 2 dollars + 1 50-cent piece = 7 quarters + 10 nickels + __________ nickels

Directions: Determine if each statement is true, and explain why or why not.

3. $(103.4 + 33.25) + 64.2 = 136.65 + (71.5 - 7.3)$ ______________________

____

4. $(103 \cdot 4) + 107 = 421 + (103 + 4)$ ______________________

____

Directions: Write both statements as one equal statement.

5. $15 + 16 = 31$ and $40 - 9 = 31$ ______ + ______ = ______ – ______

6. $9 \cdot 3 = 27$ and $10 + 17 = 27$ ______ • ______ = ______ + ______

7. $1.3 \cdot 2.4 = 3.12$ and $5.1 - 1.98 = 3.12$ ______ • ______ = ______ – ______

8. $\frac{1}{4} + \frac{2}{4} = \frac{3}{4}$ and $3 \div 4 = \frac{3}{4}$ ______ + ______ = ______ ÷ ______

Directions: Find the value for the circle or square in each equation.

9. $135 + 65 + 160 = \square + 200 - 40$

10. $(533 + 249) + \bigcirc = 20 \cdot (10 \cdot 5)$

11. $63.65 + 14.5 + 49.5 = \square + 105 - 55.5$

12. $\frac{4}{5} + \frac{1}{2} + \bigcirc = 1\frac{3}{10} + 1\frac{2}{3} - \frac{3}{6}$

Name ______________________________

Number Sense and Operations Unit Review

1. Write in words the value of each underlined digit.

32,507 ______________________________

7,170,054 ______________________________

2. Fill in the blank with the correct period name for each part of this number: 65,813,057

65 ______________________________

813 ______________________________

057 ______________________________

3. Write each number in standard form.

900,000,000 + 30,000,000 + 200,000 + 10,000 + 500 + 2 ______________

eighteen and four hundred seventy-two thousandths ______________

4. Write each number in expanded form.

34,781 ______________________________

13.502 ______________________________

5. The diameter of Earth is about seven thousand, nine hundred twenty-six miles. Write this in standard form.

____

Directions: Place >, <, or = between the two numbers so there is a true statement of the form *a* > *b*, *a* < *b*, or *a* = *b*.

6. 5,243 __________ 5,234

7. 8.09 __________ 8.9

8. 2.0 __________ 2.000

Number Sense and Operations Unit Review *(cont.)*

Directions: Solve. Show your work.

9. Damon is building a skateboard ramp. He needs pieces of wood that are between 3.78 and 4.21 feet long. He finds six boards in his garage. Their lengths are 3.92 feet, 4.4 feet, 3.6 feet, 4.01 feet, 4.2 feet, and 3.819 feet. List the boards that he can use in order from smallest to largest. Explain why the other boards cannot be used.

10. 5,612 + 33 + 410,532 = ____________

11. 22,109 – 364 = ____________

12. Justin is five years older than his youngest brother. If his youngest brother is 12, how old is Justin?

____

13. Lori had $55.32 in her bank account on Monday. By Friday, her account was down to $17.09. How much money did she spend that week?

____

Number Sense and Operations Unit Review *(cont.)*

Directions: Solve. Show your work.

14. $4{,}312 \cdot 76 =$ ______________________

15. $818 \cdot 919 =$ ______________________

16. $0.91 \cdot 76.5 =$ ______________________

17. $513 \div 9 =$ ______________________

18. $35 \div 0.04 =$ ______________________

19. The sides of a square are 3.52 cm. What is the area of the square? ($A = lw$)

____

20. Find the missing value: $6 \cdot \bigcirc = 87$ ______________________

21. Reduce the fraction to its lowest terms.

$\frac{15}{50} =$ ______________________

22. Change to an improper fraction.

$2\frac{3}{11} =$ ______________________

23. Change to a mixed number.

$\frac{140}{6} =$ ______________________

Number Sense and Operations Unit Review *(cont.)*

Directions: Solve. Reduce each answer to its lowest terms, but it is not necessary to change improper fractions to mixed numbers. Show your work.

24. $\frac{21}{4} \cdot \frac{3}{7} =$ ________________________

25. $\frac{19}{20} \div \frac{5}{8} =$ ________________________

26. Every day, Alphonse carries his backpack to school and back. If the average weight of his backpack is $10\frac{7}{10}$ pounds, how much weight has he carried during a 5-day school week? Explain your answer.

____

____

27. Evaluate $\frac{2xy}{3mn} \cdot \frac{12m}{7y}$ if the values of the variables are $x = 2$, $y = 7$, $m = 3$, $n = 5$.

____

28. $\frac{3}{9} + \frac{2}{3} =$ ________________________

29. $\frac{9}{12} - \frac{9}{48} =$ ________________________

30. Mr. Worden's bedroom needs new baseboards. The sides of the room are 14.2 feet, 20.5 feet, 19.26 feet, and 16.81 feet. What is the perimeter of the room? Explain your answer.

____

____

Number Sense and Operations Unit Review *(cont.)*

Directions: Identify whether the property being used is commutative or associative.

31. $3 \cdot 5 = 5 \cdot 3$ ______________________________

32. $(4 \cdot 8) \cdot 12 = 4 \cdot (8 \cdot 12)$ ______________________________

Directions: Write each expression using the distributive property.

33. $0.3(15 - 10)$ ______________________________

34. $2(3 + x)$ ______________________________

35. $0.5(11 - x)$ ______________________________

Directions: Find the value for the circle.

36. $56 \div 4 = 2 \cdot \bigcirc$ ______________________________

Directions: Determine whether each statement is true or false. Explain your answer.

37. $8 \cdot 4 = 40 - 6$ ______________________________

____

38. $5 + 5 - 3 = 4 + 4 + 2$ ______________________________

____

Problem Solving Strategy Notes: Part A
Using Simpler Numbers

What can you do if you come across a problem that seems too difficult to solve? If it has large numbers or complicated number concepts, you can use simpler numbers to help you understand what you need to do. Then, you'll be ready to tackle the hard problem!

Using simpler numbers can help in several ways. One way is that you will understand what operations you need to use to solve the problem. Try replacing the large numbers in the problem with smaller numbers. Then, solve the problem. If the answer makes sense for the smaller numbers, then you can use the same operations with the larger numbers.

Another way to use simpler numbers is to break down the problem into smaller parts. As you solve each part, keep track of your answers by drawing pictures or a table. Soon, you may see a pattern that will help you solve the big problem.

The following information and examples will help you understand how using simpler numbers in some problems is a very handy problem-solving strategy.

Find a Starting Point

Begin by using simpler numbers to work out a solution. You may find the operations and pattern that can be used to solve the more difficult problem.

Sample Problem: Finish the Mural
A total of 16 artists worked for 10 hours to paint half of a mural. Only 4 of the artists could stay to finish the other half. How long did it take the 4 artists to complete the other half?

Start with a Simpler Example

If it takes 4 artists 8 hours to paint half a mural, how long will it take 2 artists to paint the other half?

First, find out how long it would take 1 artist to paint half the mural alone.

He would have to work 4 times longer to do the job of the original four artists, so he would take 32 hours.

4 x 8 = 32 hours

If 2 artists work on the other half, each will only have to work half as much time as 1 artist, so it would take them only 16 hours.

32 ÷ 2 = 16 hours

Solve the Original Problem

Again, start by working out how long it will take 1 artist to complete the work.

We know that 16 artists take 10 hours, so 1 artist would have to work 16 times longer to do the job of 16 artists. So, 1 artist would take 160 hours.

16 x 10 = 160 hours

If 4 artists work on the other half, they would each have to work only one-fourth as much time as 1 artist, so they would each work 40 hours.

160 ÷ 4 = 40 hours

Part B Problem Solving Strategy Notes: Using Simpler Numbers *(cont.)*

Sample Problem

If the houses on your street are numbered from 1 to 150, how many houses will have the digit 8 as part of their house addresses?

Understanding the Problem

What do I know?

- The houses are numbered from 1 to 150.
- Some of the houses have an 8 in the addresses.

What do I need to find out?

- How many houses have 8 as part of their addresses?

Planning and Communicating a Solution

Begin by breaking the problem down into smaller parts. How many 8s are in the house numbers from 1 to 9? How many 8s are in the house numbers from 10 to 19? Continue this process through 150.

Put your results into a table. Plan your table so you can record all the information you will need to solve the problem. Ask yourself where in the numbers you could find 8s? (You can find an 8 in the ones place and the tens place, but not in the hundreds because you are only dealing with one hundred.) So, for this problem you will need table columns for the house numbers, the ones place, and the tens place.

What was the pattern? And, what happened when you came to the 80s?

Sample Table

House Numbers	Eights in Ones Place	Eights in the Tens Place
1–9	1 (8)	0
10–19	1 (18)	0
20–29	1 (28)	0
and so on	5 (38, 48, 58, 68, 78)	0
80–89	1 (88)	10 (80–89)
90–99	1 (98)	0
100–109	1 (108)	0
110–119	1 (118)	0
and so on	3 (128, 138, 148)	0
150	0	0
Totals	15	10
	Grand Total	25

Reflecting and Generalizing

By breaking the problem into pieces, it is easy to look for the number of 8s in a series of numbers.

Recording the results in a table made it possible to find the pattern more easily. It also made it easier to check your work.

Extension

You can extend this problem by asking the following questions:

How many 8s would be in a set of house numbers from 1 to 200?

How often will 3 and 1 appear in the sequence of numbers from 1 to 150?

Real-Life Problem Solving: Part A

Are You a Winner?

Music is everywhere—on car radios, at the ballpark, at stores, in elevators, in restaurants, on television, and in the movies. From records to cassettes, compact discs to MP3 players, the music industry has advanced.

- In 1877, Thomas Edison recorded his voice on a cylinder phonograph. The recording was made on a cylinder of tinfoil that was rotated by hand.
- Around 1948, the vinyl record was born. Early record players included an amplifier and speaker in the same cabinet as the turntable.
- In the late 1970s, digital audiotape recording technology was introduced to recording studios. In the early 1980s, small audiotape recorders were made for home use.
- In 1983, the compact disc introduced digital recordings for domestic use. In 1986, 53 million CDs were sold. By 1990, 200 million CDs were sold in the United States.
- By 1999, portable MP3 players appeared in the marketplace. Today, many people can be seen in stores, airports, schools, and on the street listening to their music on MP3 players.

Artists sell millions of CDs yearly. A local artist, Sammy D., wants to promote his new album by placing a special coupon in two out of every 25 CDs shipped. The winning coupons can be redeemed for tickets to one of his concerts. ABC Records will be distributing the CDs. You work for ABC Records and have been given the job of distributing the coupons.

Part B

Real-Life Problem Solving:

Are You a Winner? *(cont.)*

Directions: Use the information on page 35 and in the problems below to answer the questions. Before you begin solving the problems, be sure to locate the key information you will need.

What Is the Problem?

Your boss at ABC Records has asked you to estimate how many coupons will be distributed. In each box there are two special coupons. Answer the following questions for each problem.

- How many boxes of CDs are there?
- How many boxes are on each truck?
- How many coupons are there per truck?
- How many coupons are there in all?

Hint: To help you solve the problem, use simpler numbers by rounding.

Problem-Solving Strategy: Using Simpler Numbers

Problem A

The record company is using 62 trucks to distribute 1,550,000 CDs. A total of 25 CDs can fit in one box.

Answer: ______________________

____

____

____

Problem B

The record company is using 90 trucks to distribute 1,575,000 CDs. A total of 25 CDs can fit in one box.

Answer: ______________________

____

____

____

Problem C

The record company is using 61 trucks to distribute 2,251,439 CDs. A total of 25 CDs can fit in one box.

Answer: ______________________

____

____

____

Class Challenge

Research how many CDs your favorite artist sold in a year. If 25 CDs fit in a box, how many boxes were needed to ship them?

Real-Life Problem Solving: What Does an Architect Do?

Part A

Who designs a new home? Who makes plans for a new skyscraper? An architect does. Architects decide what a building will look like and how it will be built. They make drawings, or plans, that show how to build the structure. They also decide what rooms the building will have. Architects have the task of creating attractive, safe buildings for people.

The drawing below is a floor plan. It shows the different rooms in a house and how large each room will be. Use this drawing to answer the problems on the following page.

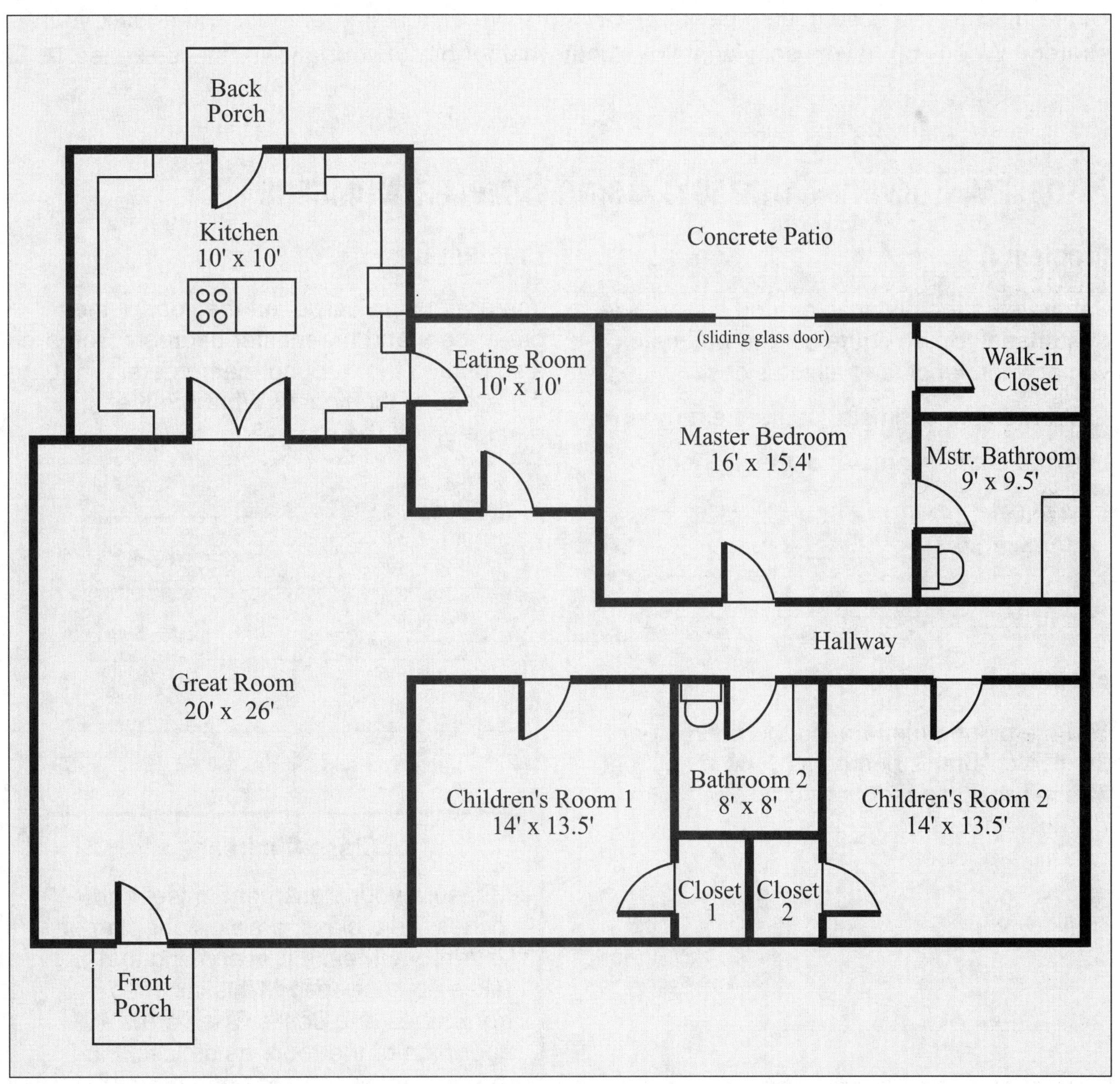

Part B Real-Life Problem Solving:

What Does an Architect Do? *(cont.)*

Directions: Use the information on page 37 and in the problems below to answer the questions. Before you begin solving the problems, be sure to locate the key information you will need.

What Is the Problem?

Imagine that you are studying to be an architect. Can you read the floor-plan drawing of the house and help solve the problems below?

Remember: If you have trouble planning ways to solve a problem, reread it and rethink your strategy. When you have a solution, think about whether or not your answer makes sense.

Problem-Solving Strategy: Using Simpler Numbers

Problem A

Perimeter is the distance around the outside of a shape. So, to figure out the perimeter, you add the lengths of all the sides.

- What is the perimeter of the great room?
- What is the perimeter of the kitchen?

Answer: ______________________________

____

Problem B

You are putting trim around the perimeter of the two children's bedrooms. How many feet of trim will you need?

Answer: ______________________________

Problem C

You are putting carpet on the floor of the great room and the master bedroom. You are also putting trim around the borders. What are the areas of the floors? What are the perimeters of the rooms?

Answer: ______________________________

____

____

____

Class Challenge

Measure your classroom in feet and inches. As a class, draw a floor plan of your room. Measure everything that takes up floor space. This includes bookcases and desks. Then draw a floor plan of the room as a class. Find the perimeter and area of the room.

Name ______________________________

Real-Life Problem Solving:
Using Simpler Numbers

Directions: Use the strategy to solve each problem. Then, explain each answer.

The Problem

There are a total of 12 tricycles, bicycles, and quadcycles at the local bike shop. There are a total of 40 wheels in all. How many of each kind of bike are at the shop?

Using the Strategy—Show Your Work

Explain Your Answer

Real-Life Problem Solving:
Using Simpler Numbers *(cont.)*

The Problem

Maria randomly took 24 candy hearts out of a bag of candy. She found $\frac{1}{4}$ of those hearts were purple, $\frac{1}{8}$ were white, 3 were green, and 12 were pink. If a full bag of candy has 192 pieces in it, how many of each color can Maria expect to find in the whole bag?

Using the Strategy—Show Your Work

Explain Your Answer

Name ______________________

Adding Integers 1

Directions: Solve.

1. $-1 + 6 =$ ________
2. $-2 - 3 =$ ________
3. $4 - 2 =$ ________
4. $4 - 6 =$ ________
5. $2 - 1 =$ ________
6. $3 + 2 =$ ________
7. $4 - 1 =$ ________
8. $-3 + 2 =$ ________
9. $-4 - 1 =$ ________
10. $-1 - 1 =$ ________
11. $-2 + 3 =$ ________
12. $-4 - 2 =$ ________
13. $-2 - 3 =$ ________
14. $6 - 5 =$ ________
15. $3 - 4 =$ ________
16. $-4 + 9 =$ ________
17. $-2 - 2 =$ ________
18. $-5 - 1 =$ ________
19. $1 - 3 =$ ________
20. $2 - 2 =$ ________
21. $3 - 1 =$ ________
22. $1 - 3 =$ ________
23. $-2 - 4 =$ ________
24. $-3 + 5 =$ ________
25. $6 - 2 =$ ________
26. $5 - 6 =$ ________
27. $3 - 4 =$ ________
28. $-3 - 4 =$ ________
29. $-1 + 4 =$ ________
30. $-3 - 5 =$ ________
31. $-3 + 6 =$ ________
32. $8 - 7 =$ ________

Name ______________________________

Adding Integers 2

Directions: Solve.

1. $5 - 9 =$ ________
2. $3 + 4 =$ ________
3. $-6 - 1 =$ ________
4. $-3 + 4 =$ ________
5. $-2 - 1 =$ ________
6. $-3 + 8 =$ ________
7. $8 - 1 =$ ________
8. $-2 + 4 =$ ________
9. $-6 - 2 =$ ________
10. $-3 - 5 =$ ________
11. $-1 - 1 =$ ________
12. $-6 + 5 =$ ________
13. $-8 + 3 =$ ________
14. $6 - 10 =$ ________
15. $-8 - 2 =$ ________
16. $-3 + 4 =$ ________
17. $-5 - 8 =$ ________
18. $-3 + 5 =$ ________
19. $-3 + (-5) =$ ________
20. $-6 + 4 =$ ________
21. $-4 - 2 =$ ________
22. $8 - 7 =$ ________
23. $-5 - 3 =$ ________
24. $3 - 8 =$ ________
25. $2 - 10 =$ ________
26. $9 - 12 =$ ________
27. $-4 - 5 =$ ________
28. $-3 + 10 =$ ________
29. $-5 - 1 =$ ________
30. $-7 - 3 =$ ________
31. $-2 - 1 =$ ________
32. $-2 + 7 =$ ________

Name ______________________________

Multiplying and Dividing Integers

Directions: Solve.

1. $-12 \div 3 =$ ____________
2. $6(-4) =$ ____________
3. $-8(-5) =$ ____________
4. $\frac{-24}{6} =$ ____________
5. $-2(-1)(-1) =$ ____________
6. $-20 \div 2 =$ ____________
7. $\frac{-3}{5} \cdot \frac{2}{3} =$ ____________
8. $-6(-3) =$ ____________
9. $-10(-3)(-2) =$ ____________
10. $\frac{-40}{8} =$ ____________
11. $-32 \div 4 =$ ____________
12. $-1(-1)(-1)(-1)(-1) =$ ____________
13. $\frac{-100}{-10} =$ ____________
14. $-6(7) =$ ____________
15. $-300 \div 10 =$ ____________
16. $\frac{-2}{3} \div \frac{1}{6} =$ ____________
17. $-5(-3)(-2) =$ ____________
18. $\frac{-3}{4} \cdot \frac{2}{3} =$ ____________
19. $-3(5)(-2) =$ ____________
20. $\frac{-60}{-5} =$ ____________
21. $-48 \div 6 =$ ____________
22. $72 \div -9 =$ ____________
23. $-5(6) =$ ____________
24. $\frac{-2}{5} \div \frac{1}{10} =$ ____________
25. $-6 \cdot \frac{2}{3} =$ ____________
26. $(-1.2)(3.4) =$ ____________
27. $\frac{-3}{4} \cdot \frac{1}{5} =$ ____________
28. $\frac{1}{3} \div (\frac{-2}{5}) =$ ____________
29. $(-2)(-3) + (4)(-8) =$ ____________
30. $(3)(-6) - 18 =$ ____________

Names ______________________________

Group Activity 1

Directions: Simplify.

1. $-3 + 8 =$ ________
2. $-7(-4) =$ ________
3. $6 - 10 =$ ________
4. $11 - 5 =$ ________
5. $-2 - 6 =$ ________
6. $14 - 18 =$ ________
7. $-24 \div 3 =$ ________
8. $\frac{16}{-8} =$ ________
9. $4 \div 0 =$ ________
10. $6 \div 0 =$ ________
11. $-2 + 5 =$ ________
12. $6 - 8 =$ ________
13. $-3 - 5 =$ ________
14. $-2(5) =$ ________
15. $-6 \cdot -9 =$ ________
16. $4 - 8 =$ ________
17. $-6 - 10 =$ ________
18. $-3(-7) =$ ________
19. $-4 + 10 =$ ________
20. $-4 - 8 =$ ________
21. $-6 \div 2 =$ ________
22. $-32 \div -8 =$ ________
23. $16 - 20 =$ ________
24. $-3 - 4 =$ ________
25. $-2 - 2 =$ ________
26. $0 - 8 =$ ________
27. $-3(-4)(2) =$ ________
28. $(-2)(-3)(-6) =$ ________
29. $-4 \cdot 3 + 5 =$ ________
30. $\frac{1}{3} \cdot \frac{-2}{5} =$ ________
31. $\frac{-3}{4} \cdot \frac{-6}{7} =$ ________
32. $\frac{-3}{5} \div \frac{2}{5} =$ ________
33. $-6(-3) - 20 =$ ________
34. $\frac{-4}{5} \div \frac{-2}{3} =$ ________
35. $\frac{-6 - 2}{-3 + 7} =$ ________
36. $-2 - 7 =$ ________
37. $-2(-7) =$ ________
38. $6 - 13 =$ ________
39. $6 - 2 =$ ________
40. $\frac{-28}{-7} =$ ________
41. $-6(-2) + (-3)(7) =$ ________
42. $-6 \div (-3) + 7 - 10 =$ ________
43. $-10(3) + 4(-2) =$ ________
44. $-8 - 3 =$ ________
45. $-9(6)(-3) =$ ________
46. $\frac{108}{-12} =$ ________
47. $-2 - 3 =$ ________
48. $-6 + 3 =$ ________
49. $-4 - 7 =$ ________
50. $-2 + 5 =$ ________
51. $(-2)(-5) =$ ________
52. $-7 - 10 =$ ________
53. $-4(-10) =$ ________
54. $11 - 7 =$ ________
55. $-4 - 12 =$ ________
56. $7 - 10 =$ ________
57. $(-3)(-4)(-6) =$ ________
58. $-14 - 20 =$ ________
59. $-3 + 8 =$ ________
60. $0 - 4 =$ ________

Names ______________________________

Group Activity 2

Directions: Simplify.

1. $-14 - 20 =$ ____________
2. $(-3)(-4)(-3) =$ ____________
3. $7 - 10 =$ ____________
4. $-4 - 12 =$ ____________
5. $11 - 7 =$ ____________
6. $4(-10) =$ ____________
7. $-7 - 10 =$ ____________
8. $(-2)(-5) =$ ____________
9. $-2 + 5 =$ ____________
10. $-4 - 7 =$ ____________
11. $-6 + 3 =$ ____________
12. $-2 - 3 =$ ____________
13. $-4 + 6 =$ ____________
14. $-6(-3) =$ ____________
15. $5 - 10 =$ ____________
16. $10 - 4 =$ ____________
17. $-2 - 6 =$ ____________
18. $13 - 17 =$ ____________
19. $-28 \div 7 =$ ____________
20. $\frac{24}{-3} =$ ____________
21. $0 \div 5 =$ ____________
22. $\frac{7}{0} =$ ____________
23. $-3 + 6 =$ ____________
24. $7 - 9 =$ ____________
25. $-3 - 6 =$ ____________
26. $-3(6) =$ ____________
27. $-7(-8) =$ ____________
28. $5 - 9 =$ ____________
29. $-6 - 10 =$ ____________
30. $-3(-7) =$ ____________
31. $-4 + 10 =$ ____________
32. $-4 - 8 =$ ____________
33. $-6 \div 2 =$ ____________
34. $-32 \div -8 =$ ____________
35. $16 - 20 =$ ____________
36. $-5 - 6 =$ ____________
37. $-1 - 1 =$ ____________
38. $0 - 7 =$ ____________
39. $(-3)(-2)(-1) =$ ____________
40. $-3(7) + 5 =$ ____________
41. $\frac{1}{2} \div \frac{-3}{5} =$ ____________
42. $\frac{-6}{7} \div \frac{-3}{5} =$ ____________
43. $\frac{-2}{3} \cdot \frac{3}{5} =$ ____________
44. $-7(-4) - 20 =$ ____________
45. $\frac{-6}{2} \div \frac{-12}{8} =$ ____________
46. $\frac{-7 - 8}{-4 + 3} =$ ____________
47. $-3 - 4 =$ ____________
48. $-2(-7) =$ ____________
49. $6 - 13 =$ ____________
50. $6 - 2 =$ ____________
51. $\frac{-30}{-6} =$ ____________
52. $-8 - 3 =$ ____________
53. $-7(6)(-3) =$ ____________
54. $\frac{108}{-12} =$ ____________
55. $10(4) + 6(-2) =$ ____________
56. $-8 \div (-2) + 8 - 11 =$ ____________
57. $-7(-3) - 24 =$ ____________
58. $-6 - 20 =$ ____________
59. $-3 + 8 =$ ____________
60. $7 - 14 =$ ____________

Name ________________________________

Collecting Like Terms

Directions: Simplify.

1. $-3x + 4x - 6x =$ ____________________
2. $-3m - 3m =$ ____________________
3. $-6x + 5k - 4x - k =$ ____________________
4. $-3p + 4m - 4m - 6p =$ ____________________
5. $-8 + 5m - 6m =$ ____________________
6. $3p - 6a - 6a - 6p =$ ____________________
7. $-8x + 4y - 6x - 4y =$ ____________________
8. $-a - a =$ ____________________
9. $-4x^2 - 4x^2 + 8y - 10y =$ ____________________
10. $-x + 4y + 3y - 7x =$ ____________________
11. $-3m + 4m - 3m =$ ____________________
12. $-2x - 2x + 4y - 4y =$ ____________________
13. $-3p - 8p + 4x - p =$ ____________________
14. $6k + k - 3k =$ ____________________
15. $-8mn + 4mn - 3p - 2p =$ ____________________
16. $-2xy + 4x - 6y - 3xy =$ ____________________
17. $-2mn + 8mn - 6x - 3x =$ ____________________
18. $-3x + x =$ ____________________
19. $p + p =$ ____________________
20. $-6y - 6y =$ ____________________

Name ______________________________

Distributing and Collecting

Directions: Simplify.

1. $7(x + 2) - 4$
2. $-3(m - 4) - 2m$
3. $-2(3k + 2) - 6k$
4. $7 + 3(2x - 6) - 3x$
5. $-2(2p - 4) - 6p - 3$
6. $-5(3n - 7) + 2n$
7. $-3(2x - 7) - 2x + 6$
8. $-6a - 4(2a + 7) - 7a$
9. $3x - (2x - 4) - 6x$
10. $3(4p - 7) - (2p + 3)$
11. $6m - (2m + 5) - 4m$
12. $3 - 4(6m + 1) - 5m$
13. $-4(2x - 7) - (3x - 7)$
14. $3 - 5(2p + 7) - 8p + 2$
15. $-(3x + 9) + 6x - x$
16. $2x - 7 - 3(5x + 6)$
17. $-7k - 3(2k + 3) - 2k$
18. $3(5m - 1) - 7m$

Name ______________________________

Writing Equations Packet

Directions: Assign the variable and write an equation for each of the following. **Do not solve.**

1. The first of two numbers is 3 times the second. Their sum is 88. Find the numbers.

   Let ________ = ______________________________

   ________ = ______________________________

   Equation: ______________________________

2. The length of a rectangular field is 10 meters less than 9 times the width. The perimeter is 140 meters. Find the length.

   Let ________ = ______________________________

   ________ = ______________________________

   Equation: ______________________________

3. The larger of two numbers is 10 less than 5 times the smaller. Their sum is 146. Find the smaller number.

   Let ________ = ______________________________

   ________ = ______________________________

   Equation: ______________________________

4. The perimeter of a rectangle is 482 cm. The length is 6 cm greater than 4 times the width. Find the length.

   Let ________ = ______________________________

   ________ = ______________________________

   Equation: ______________________________

5. Together, a football and a basketball cost $65. A football costs $5 more than $\frac{1}{2}$ of what a basketball costs. How much does a football cost?

   Let ________ = ______________________________

   ________ = ______________________________

   Equation: ______________________________

Writing Equations Packet *(cont.)*

6. The sum of three numbers is 75. The second number is 5 more than 4 times the first, and the third is 2 times the first. Find the second number.

   Let ________ = ______________________________

   ________ = ______________________________

   ________ = ______________________________

   Equation: ______________________________

7. If 7 less than 4 times a number is 29, find the number.

   Let ________ = ______________________________

   Equation: ______________________________

8. Juana and Jada made \$58 babysitting. Juana made \$6 more than 3 times as much money as Jada made. How much money did Juana make?

   Let ________ = ______________________________

   ________ = ______________________________

   Equation: ______________________________

9. José and Isabel went running. José ran 2 miles less than $\frac{1}{2}$ as many miles as Isabel. José ran 6 miles. How many miles did Isabel run?

   Let ________ = ______________________________

   ________ = ______________________________

   Equation: ______________________________

10. Together, a dresser, a nightstand, and a vanity cost \$1,605. The dresser costs 3 times as much as the nightstand, and the vanity costs \$300 more than the nightstand. Find the cost of the vanity.

    Let ________ = ______________________________

    ________ = ______________________________

    ________ = ______________________________

    Equation: ______________________________

Writing Equations Packet *(cont.)*

11. Mrs. Lin cut a piece of wire that was 125 cm long into two pieces. The first piece was 10 cm less than 4 times the second. Find the length of both pieces of wire.

Let ________ = ______________________________

________ = ______________________________

Equation: ______________________________

12. Chester, the dog, loves to eat treats. He has eaten twice as many today as yesterday. He has eaten a total of 15 dog treats in both days. How many treats has he eaten today?

Let ________ = ______________________________

________ = ______________________________

Equation: ______________________________

13. The price for 2 student tickets and 4 adult tickets to a play is $50. Adult tickets are $5 more than student tickets. How much does each ticket cost?

Let ________ = ______________________________

________ = ______________________________

Equation: ______________________________

14. The sum of two numbers is 73. One number is 3 greater than the other number. Find each number.

Let ________ = ______________________________

________ = ______________________________

Equation: ______________________________

15. Together, a pair of shorts, jeans, and a T-shirt cost $37. The shorts cost $2 more than the jeans, and the shirt costs $3 less than the shorts. Find the cost of the shorts.

Let ________ = ______________________________

________ = ______________________________

________ = ______________________________

Equation: ______________________________

Writing Equations Packet *(cont.)*

16. Jasper High School has 47 drill team members. This is 18 less than 5 times the number of twirlers in the school. How many twirlers does the school have?

Let ________ = ______________________________

________ = ______________________________

Equation: ______________________________

17. A rectangle has a length that is 4 meters more than the width. The perimeter is 184 meters. Find the length.

Let ________ = ______________________________

________ = ______________________________

Equation: ______________________________

18. Bae bought one twin pack of video games for $42. This is $6 less than $\frac{2}{3}$ the cost of a triple pack of video games. What is the price of a triple pack of video games?

Let ________ = ______________________________

________ = ______________________________

Equation: ______________________________

19. Maria is 240 cm tall. This is 3 cm less than 3 times her height at birth. Find her height at birth.

Let ________ = ______________________________

________ = ______________________________

Equation: ______________________________

20. The electric wheelchair is $600 more than the manual wheelchair. The total cost of 1 manual and 1 electric wheelchair is $3,200. Find the price of an electric wheelchair.

Let ________ = ______________________________

________ = ______________________________

Equation: ______________________________

Writing Equations Packet *(cont.)*

21. Jawan's wheelchair weighs 8 pounds more than Natasha's wheelchair. Together, they weigh 100 pounds. Find the weight of Jawan's wheelchair.

    Let ________ = ______________________________

    ________ = ______________________________

    Equation: ______________________________

22. At the fair, Jing and Miguel played a game of throwing darts at balloons. Jing popped 4 more balloons than Miguel did. Together, they popped 8 balloons. How many balloons did Jing pop?

    Let ________ = ______________________________

    ________ = ______________________________

    Equation: ______________________________

23. Jamal earned $4 more than 6 times what Dulce earned. Together, they earned $53. How much money did Jamal earn?

    Let ________ = ______________________________

    ________ = ______________________________

    Equation: ______________________________

24. Jacinta worked 8 hours more than 6 times the number of hours Jake worked. Shamika worked 2 hours less than Jacinta worked. Shamika worked 30 hours. How many hours did Jacinta work?

    Let ________ = ______________________________

    ________ = ______________________________

    ________ = ______________________________

    Equation: ______________________________

25. A boom box costs $10 more than half the price of a CD player. How much is the CD player if the boom box costs $60?

    Let ________ = ______________________________

    ________ = ______________________________

    Equation: ______________________________

Writing Equations Packet *(cont.)*

26. Lacey has 6 more than 7 times the number of marbles Rasheed has. Together, Lacey and Rasheed have 70 marbles. How many marbles does Lacey have?

Let ________ = ______________________________

________ = ______________________________

Equation: ______________________________

27. Javier made $83 less than 7 times what Bo made. The sum of their earnings is $381. How much money did Bo make?

Let ________ = ______________________________

________ = ______________________________

Equation: ______________________________

28. The number of CDs that CeDaniel owns is 6 less than 6 times the number of CDs that Carla owns. Altogether, they own 78 CDs. How many CDs does CeDaniel own?

Let ________ = ______________________________

________ = ______________________________

Equation: ______________________________

29. Kwan and Marco went on a 16-mile bike ride. Kwan finished in 60 minutes. Kwan finished 2 minutes less than $\frac{1}{5}$ of Marco's time. Find Marco's time.

Let ________ = ______________________________

________ = ______________________________

Equation: ______________________________

30. Damon and Ruben ran 14 miles. Ruben ran 2 miles more than 3 times the distance Damon ran. How many miles did each boy run?

Let ________ = ______________________________

________ = ______________________________

Equation: ______________________________

Writing Equations Packet *(cont.)*

31. Heather and Jeong Kim attended school a total of 183 days. Heather attended 9 days less than $\frac{1}{2}$ the days Jeong Kim attended. How many days did Heather attend school?

    Let ________ = ______________________________
    ________ = ______________________________
    Equation: ______________________________

32. There are 90 rare birds from South Africa at the Houston Zoo. This is 3 times as many as the number of rare birds from Tanzania. How many Tanzanian rare birds are there at the Houston Zoo?

    Let ________ = ______________________________
    ________ = ______________________________
    Equation: ______________________________

33. If you add $\frac{3}{4}$ of a number back to the number itself, you get 49. Find the number.

    Let ________ = ______________________________
    Equation: ______________________________

34. Darnell has 26 farm animals. The number of cows is 5 more than twice the number of horses. How many of each animal does he have?

    Let ________ = ______________________________
    ________ = ______________________________
    Equation: ______________________________

35. Janna ran 2 miles more than $\frac{3}{8}$ the distance Takara ran. Janna ran 5 miles. How many miles did Takara run?

    Let ________ = ______________________________
    ________ = ______________________________
    Equation: ______________________________

Writing Equations Packet *(cont.)*

36. Laron bowled two games. His first score was $\frac{1}{2}$ of his second score. He scored 330 points in the two games combined. How many points did he score in each game?

Let ________ = ______________________________

________ = ______________________________

Equation: ______________________________

37. Jazmin, Tashika, and Diego went to the candy store. Together, they purchased a case of Super Sticky Candy. Diego pitched in $5 more than Tashika, and Jazmin pitched in twice the money Diego did. The case of candy costs $27. How much money did Jazmin pitch in for the candy?

Let ________ = ______________________________

________ = ______________________________

________ = ______________________________

Equation: ______________________________

38. Together, a bracelet and a ring cost $200. Find the price of each item if the bracelet costs 3 times as much as the ring.

Let ________ = ______________________________

________ = ______________________________

Equation: ______________________________

39. LaRhonda and Nikki went to buy Braille books at the bookstore. LaRhonda brought $\frac{2}{3}$ the amount of money that Nikki brought. LaRhonda brought $80. How much money did Nikki bring to the bookstore?

Let ________ = ______________________________

________ = ______________________________

Equation: ______________________________

40. There were a total of 72 geese in two flocks. One flock was 3 times greater than the other. How many geese were in each flock?

Let ________ = ______________________________

________ = ______________________________

Equation: ______________________________

Writing Equations Packet *(cont.)*

41. Stephanie and Ming Lee earned a total of $52 for mowing lawns this summer. Ming Lee earned $10 more than $\frac{1}{5}$ of what Stephanie earned. How much money did Ming Lee earn?

Let ________ = ______________________________

________ = ______________________________

Equation: ______________________________

42. The perimeter of a triangle is 44 meters. Side one is 8 meters longer than side two, and side three is twice as long as side one. Find the length of each side.

Let ________ = ______________________________

________ = ______________________________

________ = ______________________________

Equation: ______________________________

43. The perimeter of a rectangle is 42 cm. The width is 7 cm less than the length. Find the dimensions of the rectangle.

Let ________ = ______________________________

________ = ______________________________

Equation: ______________________________

44. Last week, Pedro and Julio walked 17 miles together. Julio walked 1 mile less than 2 times the distance Pedro walked. How many miles did each boy walk?

Let ________ = ______________________________

________ = ______________________________

Equation: ______________________________

45. Josefa spent $7.61 on a new hearing aid battery. This is $3.50 more than 3 times the amount of money that Erin spent. How much money did Erin spend?

Let ________ = ______________________________

________ = ______________________________

Equation: ______________________________

Writing Equations Packet *(cont.)*

46. Keenan, Lexy, and Lupe went to a popular clothing store and spent a total of $500.00. Lupe spent $5 more than $\frac{1}{2}$ of what Lexy spent, and Keenan spent three times what Lupe spent. Find the amount of money each one spent.

Let ________ = ______________________________

________ = ______________________________

________ = ______________________________

Equation: ______________________________

47. There are 20 apples and oranges in the grocery store. There are 6 more apples than oranges. How many apples are in the store?

Let ________ = ______________________________

________ = ______________________________

Equation: ______________________________

48. Oriana spent $16 at the concession stand. This is $4 less than twice what her friend Amber spent. How much money did Amber spend at the concession stand?

Let ________ = ______________________________

________ = ______________________________

Equation: ______________________________

Part A

Problem Solving Strategy Notes: Working Backwards

Working backwards can help you solve problems that have a lot of events or several steps where some information is missing. Many times this information is missing at the beginning of the problem. To solve these problems, you can usually start with the answer and work your way backwards to fill in the missing information.

This strategy is very helpful in dealing with a sequence of events or when each piece of information is related to the one before it. For example, Paul is four years older than Ali, but Kaya is two years younger than Ali. If Kaya is eight, how old is Paul? In this case, everyone's age is related to everyone else's age. Working backwards will help you solve this problem.

Before you begin solving problems using this strategy, read the following information to help you.

Using the Opposite Operation when Working Backwards

When you are solving a problem by starting at the end and working backwards, any mathematical operations you come across will need to be reversed. This means if the problem requires you to add something, then you must subtract when working backwards.

This is how you would solve the problem above about Paul's age.

Kaya is eight. Kaya is two years younger than Ali. (Ali's age – 2 = 8) So, when using the opposite operation, subtraction becomes addition. (8 + 2 = Ali's age) Ali is 10. Pablo is four years older than Ali, so Pablo is 10 + 4 = 14. So, Pablo is 14 years old.

Starting with the Answer and Working Backwards

In a problem where you know the final answer, but do not know the starting point, you can begin at the end and work your way backwards to the beginning.

Problem: Mrs. Garcia's class had a spelling bee and all of the students were at the front of the room together. After three minutes, five of the students had made mistakes and sat down. In the next five minutes, four more spellers sat down. One minute later, two more children sat down. In the final few minutes, one more student made a mistake, and one student was left as the winner of the spelling bee. How many children were originally in the spelling bee?

Start at the end and reverse the process.

At the end there was one winner.	1 speller
In the final few minutes, there was one more speller. (1 + 1 = 2)	2 spellers
One minute earlier there were two more spellers. (2 + 2 = 4)	4 spellers
In the previous five minutes, there were four more spellers. (4 + 4 = 8)	8 spellers
In the first three minutes there were five more spellers. (8 + 5 = 13)	13 spellers

There were 13 students in the spelling bee.

Problem Solving Strategy Notes: Working Backwards (cont.)

Part B

Sample Problem

Arnold baked cupcakes over the weekend. Each day during the week he took three cupcakes to school to share with his friends. On Saturday he counted the cupcakes, and there were 18 left. How many cupcakes had he baked?

Understanding the Problem

What do I know?

- Arnold had 18 cupcakes left.
- Each day he took 3 cupcakes to school.

What do I need to find out?

- How many cupcakes did Arnold make in the beginning?

Planning and Communicating a Solution

Begin with the information you know, the number of cupcakes Arnold ended with, and work backwards.

Arnold had 18 cupcakes by the end of the week.

On Friday, he brought 3 cupcakes to school. (18 + 3 = 21)

On Thursday, he brought 3 cupcakes to school. (21 + 3 = 24)

On Wednesday, he brought 3 cupcakes to school. (24 + 3 = 27)

On Tuesday, he brought 3 cupcakes to school. (27 + 3 = 30)

On Monday, he brought 3 cupcakes to school. (30 + 3 = 33)

Arnold originally made 33 cupcakes.

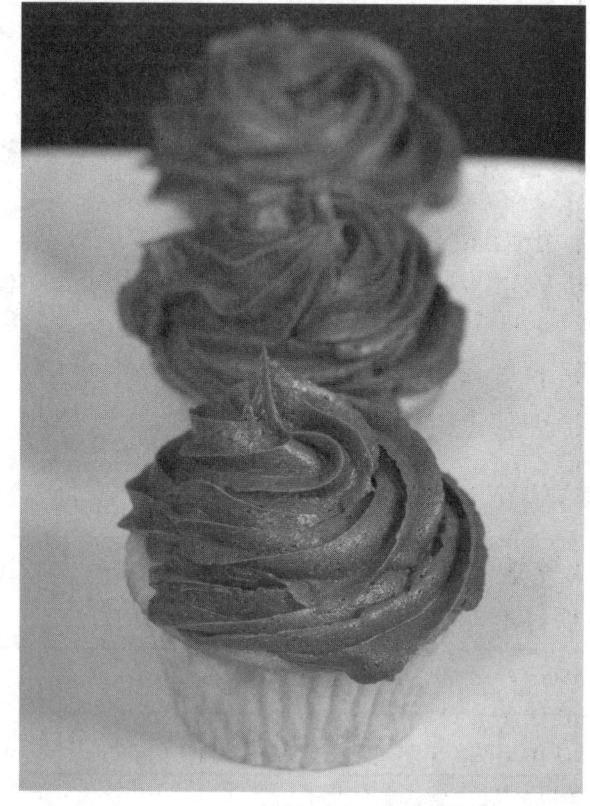

Source: David P. Smith/Shutterstock, Inc.

Reflecting and Generalizing

By starting with the known number of cupcakes Arnold had in the end, we were able to work backwards to find the answer. This strategy can be applied to problems that include a sequence of events where we know the end result, but we do not know the starting point. You can check your answer by working forward through the problem to see if you reach the correct number.

Extension

What if Arnold kept bringing cupcakes to school? How many more days could he bring cupcakes to school? What day of the week would be the last day he brought cupcakes to school?

Part A

Real-Life Problem Solving:
Keep Your Car Like New

Source: Hemera Technologies

Service Department
Price List

Service	Price
Change Automatic Transmission Fluid (includes labor and disposal fee)	$149.95
Replace Battery/Cables (includes cable inspection and labor)	$135.95
Replace Timing Belt (includes labor and engine inspection)	$172.58
Replace Brakes	$125.00
Wash Car (with 8 gallon gas purchase)	$5.00
Polish Car (includes complete inside and outside detailing)	$95.00
Change Coolant (includes labor and disposal fee)	$114.70
Air Filter Replacement	$15.99
Change Oil (includes labor, filter replacement, disposal fee, and engine cleaner additive)	$34.96
Engine Tune-Up (includes spark plug replacement and gap adjustment)	$169.95
Replace Tires	
Tires	$46.99 each
Old Tire Recycle Fee	$14.00
Mount and Balance	$60.00
Alignment	$39.99
Fill Windshield Washer Fluid	$2.99
Replace Wiper Blades	$6.99

Auto Service Schedule

Special Services	When
Change Automatic Transmission Fluid	every 24,000 miles
Replace Battery and Cables	every three years
Replace Timing Belt	at 80,000 miles
Replace Brakes	every two years
Regular Services	**When**
Wash Car	at least once a month
Polish	every six months
Change Coolant	every year
Replace Engine Air Filter	every year
Replace Engine Oil and Filter	every three months or 3,000 miles
Replace Spark Plugs (Tune-up Engine)	every 50,000 miles
Replace Tires	every 50,000 miles
Fill Windshield Washer Fluid	every 6,000 miles
Replace Wiper Blades	every six months

Source: Hemera Technologies

Real-Life Problem Solving: Part B
Keep Your Car Like New *(cont.)*

Directions: Use the information on page 60 and in the problems below to answer the questions. Before you begin solving the problems, be sure to locate the key information you will need.

What Is the Problem?

Your family just bought a fancy sports car. The car is one-year-old and you want to keep it looking and running like new for a long time.

Hint: Think about what operations are needed to find the answers to the problems. When working backwards, don't forget you have to use the inverse operations. When you have a solution, think about whether or not your answer makes sense.

Problem-Solving Strategy: Working Backwards

Problem A

You were told that the original owner of the car had it serviced regularly the first year he owned it. The car is now 18 months old. The car has been driven 12,000 miles. Your family drove it one-fourth as many miles as the previous owner. According to the Auto Service Schedule, what services would the original owner have had done during that first year?

Answer: ______________________

____

Problem B

After two years the car had the following special services done to it: Change Automatic Transmission Fluid and Replace Brakes. What is the lowest number of miles the car's odometer reads? If the odometer read 12,000 miles at 18 months, how far did you drive it over the past 6 months?

Answer: ______________________

____

Problem C

After three years, the car's odometer showed 48,000 miles. You spent $423.58 with the Service Department. (This did not include your monthly wash and polish.) What services did you have done? (Note: You brought the car in two months earlier for an oil change and new windshield washer fluid.)

Answer: ______________________

____

____

____

____

Class Challenge

Your car has been driven 100,000 miles and is 5 years old. What Special Services has your car needed in this time frame? How much have you paid total for all of these Special Services?

Part A

Real-Life Problem Solving: Making a Difference!

Community service is a great way for people to get involved in the world around them. There are many organizations that provide people with opportunities to volunteer their time and talents to help others. There are different groups at work in your community every day. Some service groups work with an organization that builds houses for people in need. This organization is called Habitat for Humanity International.

Habitat for Humanity International was founded in 1976. Millard and Linda Fuller began the organization in Americus, Georgia. The organization began small. However, today houses are built in all 50 states and in over 70 different countries. Habitat for Humanity International works in partnership with local businesses and service groups.

Families in need purchase the Habitat homes. This is made possible because of Habitat's non-profit, no-interest loans and volunteer labor. The average cost of a Habitat for Humanity home is less than $50,000. Habitat for Humanity describes their houses as simple, decent, and affordable.

Volunteers come from all different backgrounds. Many volunteers have never worked in construction. Working on a Habitat home allows volunteers to help people in their community. Volunteers learn about framing a house, putting up siding, roofing, painting, and plumbing. Imagine what you could learn helping to build a home for a family in need.

Material	Cost
roll of tar paper (4 squares)	$ 15
asphalt shingles (per square)	$ 25
wood shingles (per square)	$135
clay tile (per square)	$300
steel (per square)	$260

What Is a Habitat Home Like?

- Homes average about 1,000 sq. ft.
- Houses have one bathroom.
- Wide doors and hallways allow wheelchairs to pass.
- In the United States, houses have vinyl siding and shingles.
- In Africa, houses are built with clay bricks.
- In Latin America, houses have adobe walls and metal roofs.

Could You Roof a House?

- Roofing felt or tar paper is laid under shingles on a roof.
- One roll of roofing felt covers about four squares.
- A "square" in roofing terms is 100 sq. ft.

Real-Life Problem Solving: Making a Difference! *(cont.)*

Part B

Directions: Use the information on page 62 and in the problems below to answer the questions. Before you begin solving the problems, be sure to locate the key information you will need.

What Is the Problem?

You have been studying about community service in school. You and some classmates decide to help in your community by volunteering for Habitat for Humanity. The project manager has put you on the roofing crew.

Hint: Think about what operations are needed to find the answers to the problems. When working backwards, don't forget to use inverse operations. When you have a solution, think about whether or not your answer makes sense.

Problem-Solving Strategy: Working Backwards

Problem A

Half of the roof was completed by someone else. One-half of what's left already has tar paper laid down. There is 400 sq. ft. on which you need to lay tar paper and shingles. What is the area (in sq. ft.) of the whole roof?

Answer: ______________________

____

____

____

Problem B

You spend a total of $660. You spend one-tenth as much on the tar paper as you do on the shingles. You have to buy asphalt shingles and 4 rolls of tar paper. How many squares of shingles did you purchase? How much square footage of roof can be covered using the materials you bought?

Answer: ______________________

____

Problem C

The area of a roof is 1,200 sq. ft. The project manager gave you $500 to purchase the roofing supplies. You need to pick up asphalt shingles and tar paper at the local hardware store. Is this enough money to purchase all the shingles and tar paper that are needed to cover the entire roof? If so, will you have any money left over? If not, how much more money do you need to complete the job?

Answer: ______________________

____

Class Challenge

After a hurricane, there are a lot of families who need new homes. After two months, 6 families had new homes. About four weeks later, 4 families moved into their new homes. Finally, eight weeks later, the last 7 families moved in. How many total homes were built?

Name ______________________________

Real-Life Problem Solving: Working Backwards

Directions: Use the strategy to solve each problem. Then, explain each answer.

The Problem

Janice is trying to figure out how many red gumballs are in the gumball machine. There are 371 gumballs in all. A total of 177 of them are yellow and 51 are blue. The rest are red. How many red gumballs are in the machine?

Using the Strategy—Show Your Work

Explain Your Answer

Real-Life Problem Solving:
Working Backwards *(cont.)*

The Problem

Rebecca had some golf tees. She gave half of the tees to Robert. He gave half of his tees to Annie. She gave half of her tees to Neil. He gave half of his tees to Gretchen. Gretchen has 5 tees. How many tees each do Rebecca, Robert, Annie, Neil, and Gretchen now have?

Using the Strategy—Show Your Work

Explain Your Answer

Names ______________________________

Cups and Chips 1

Directions: Solve the following equations using cups and chips.

1. $2x - 3 = 5x - 1$

2. $4x + 2 = -2x - 3$

3. $3x - 2 = -5x + 2$

4. $4x + 2 = 2x - 1$

5. $6x - 3 = 4x + 1$

6. $-2x + 3 = x - 2$

Names ______________________________

Cups and Chips 2

Directions: Solve the following equations using cups and chips.

1. $2x + 3 = x + 1$

2. $-3x + 5 = 2x - 1$

3. $x - 2 = 3x + 1$

4. $3x - 3 = 4 + 2x - 6$

5. $-1x + 5 = 2x - 2$

6. $-2x + 1x - 5 = 3x + 2$

Names ______________________________

Cups and Chips 3

Directions: Solve the following equations using cups and chips.

1. $2x - 3 = 1x + 4$

2. $3x - 2 = 2x - 4$

3. $3x - 6x - 2 = 2x - x + 3$

4. $-2x = -3x + 5x - 3$

5. $4x - 2 = 2x + 5$

6. $-4x - 2x - 3 = 2x - 5$

Name ______________________________

Solving Equations 1

Directions: Solve. Show all work.

1. $2x + 3 = 6x - 5$
2. $8x + 4 = 6x - 1$
3. $4x - 2 = 6x + 3$
4. $8m - 4 = 3m + 8$
5. $4p - 3 = 8p + 5$
6. $8k + 4 = 2k - 3$
7. $3x - 5x + 4 = 6x - 2 - 3x$
8. $2p + 3 - 5 = 6p - 8 - 10p$
9. $8 - 4m - 6m = 3m - 4m + 2$
10. $3k + 1 - 6k = 4k + 8 - 9k$
11. $6x - 5 = 3x + 1$
12. $4x - 7 = 2x$

Name ________________________________

Solving Equations 2

Directions: Solve. Show all work.

1. $3x - 4 = 7x + 2$
2. $6p + 2 = -3p + 1$
3. $4m - 7 = 8m + 2$
4. $5x + 1 = 7x - 3$
5. $2m - 3 = 6m - 4$
6. $8a + 3 = 6a + 2$
7. $3x + 2x - 1 = 7x - 5 - 5$
8. $3a - 5a - 2 = 6a + a - 7$
9. $2x - 3 = 7x + 3 - 4x$
10. $4x + 5 = 10x - 6$

Solving Equations 2 *(cont.)*

11. $5f + 2 - 4 = 2f - 4f - 8$

12. $-8x - 6 = -9x - 4$

13. $7a + 9 - a = 3a + 4$

14. $10x + 6 = 7x + 5 + 1$

15. $-x - 2 = 4x + 6$

16. $3z + 12 = 6z + 10$

17. $6y - 8 - y = 19 + 9y$

18. $8x + 1 = 2x + 3$

19. $-9u - 17 = -5u - 7$

20. $11n - (-6) = 13n - 3$

Name ____________________________________

Adding and Subtracting Fractions 2

Directions: Solve.

1. $-3 - 1\frac{1}{3}$

2. $6 + 2\frac{1}{2}$

3. $-4 - 2\frac{3}{5}$

4. $8 - 3\frac{2}{3}$

5. $-6\frac{1}{2} - 3\frac{1}{4}$

6. $5\frac{1}{4} - 3\frac{2}{5}$

7. $-4\frac{3}{4} + 6\frac{1}{3}$

8. $-7\frac{1}{8} - 4\frac{1}{2}$

9. $6\frac{2}{5} - 3\frac{1}{3}$

10. $-6 - 4\frac{2}{3}$

11. $-8 + 2\frac{1}{2}$

12. $-10 + 4\frac{1}{5}$

Name ______________________________

Multiplying and Dividing Fractions 2

Directions: Solve.

1. $-3 \cdot 2\frac{1}{3}$

2. $6 \div -1\frac{1}{2}$

3. $-4 \cdot -5\frac{2}{5}$

4. $-3\frac{3}{4} \div 2$

5. $-5\frac{1}{2} \div -3$

6. $-4\frac{3}{4} \cdot 7$

7. $-6\frac{2}{3} \div -3$

8. $-4 \cdot -2\frac{3}{4}$

9. $-6 \div 2\frac{1}{3}$

10. $8\frac{1}{2} \div -2$

11. $-10\frac{2}{3} \div -3$

12. $-4 \cdot -6\frac{1}{4}$

Name ______________________________

Algebra Applications with Angles

Directions: Solve for the variable and find the measure of each angle.

1.

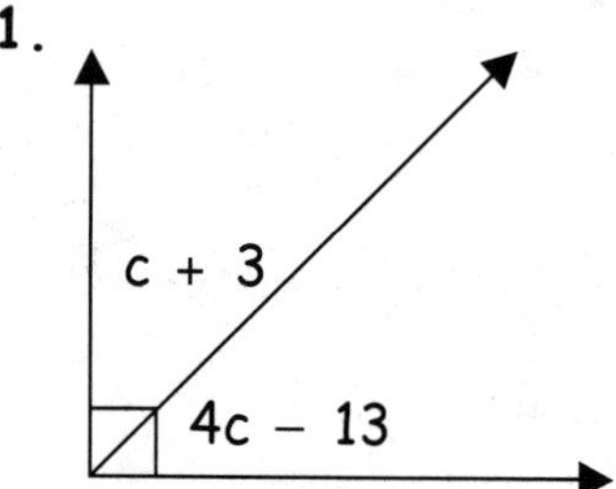

2.

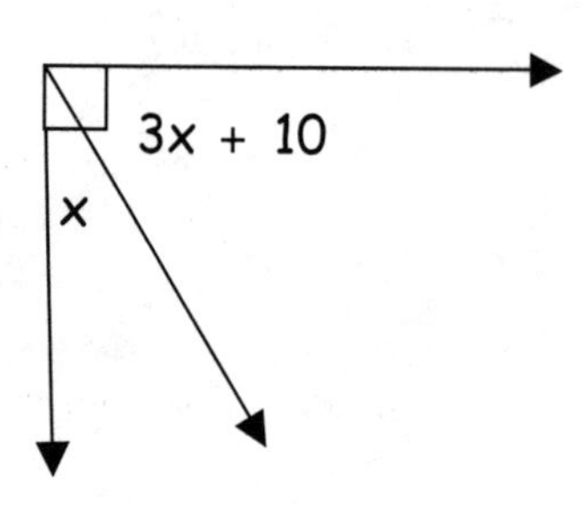

3.

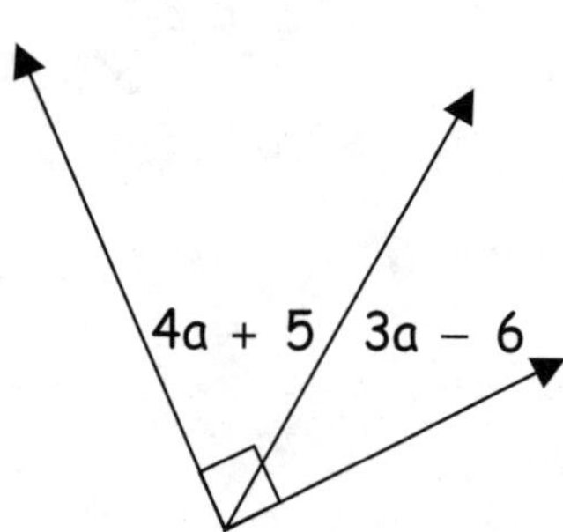

4.

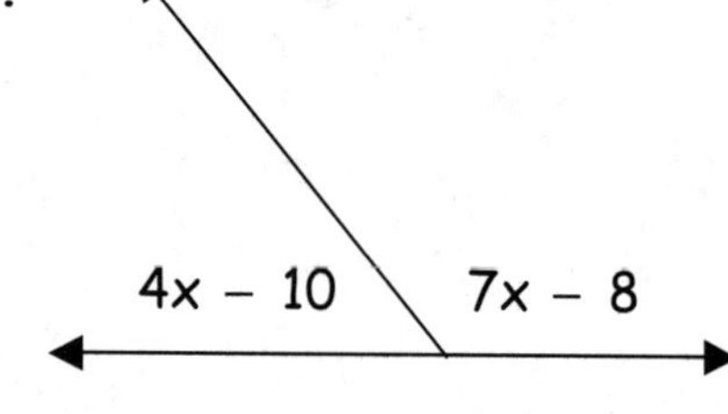

5.

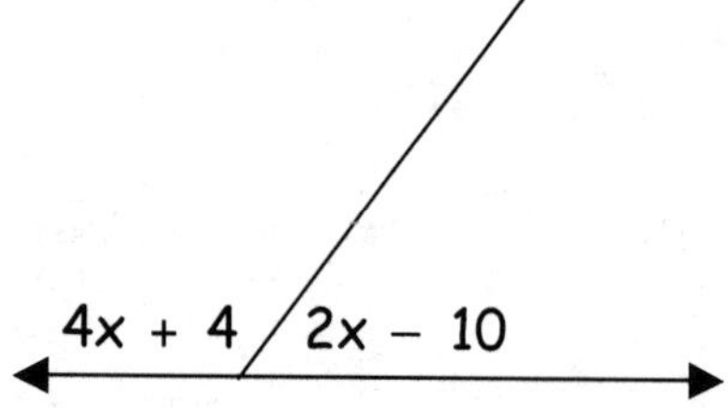

6.

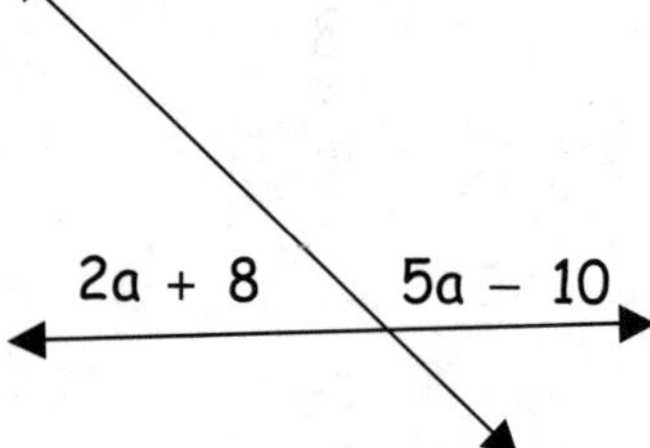

Algebra Applications with Angles *(cont.)*

7.

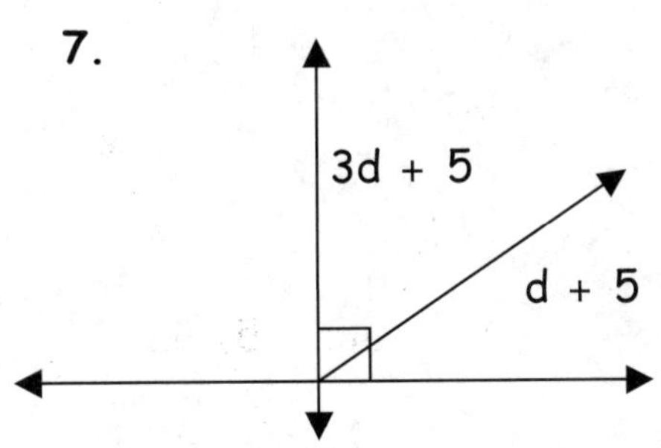

8.

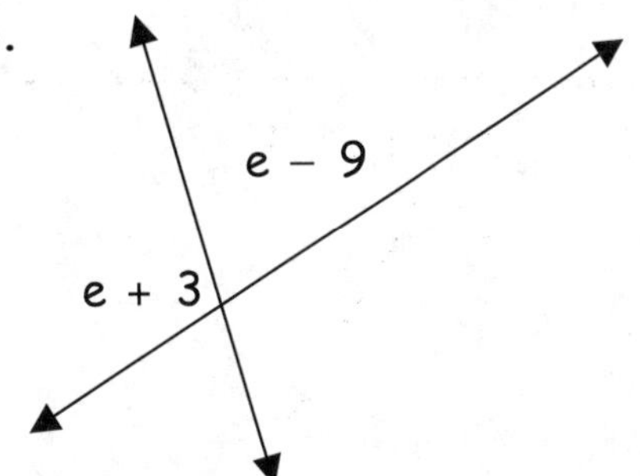

9.

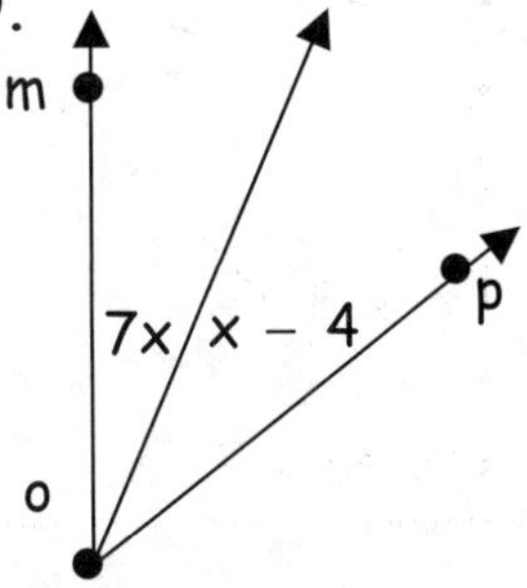

m

7x

x − 4

p

o

∠mop = 60°

10.

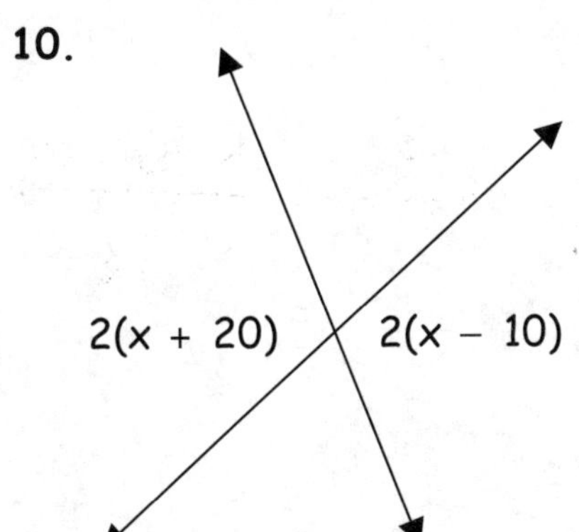

11.

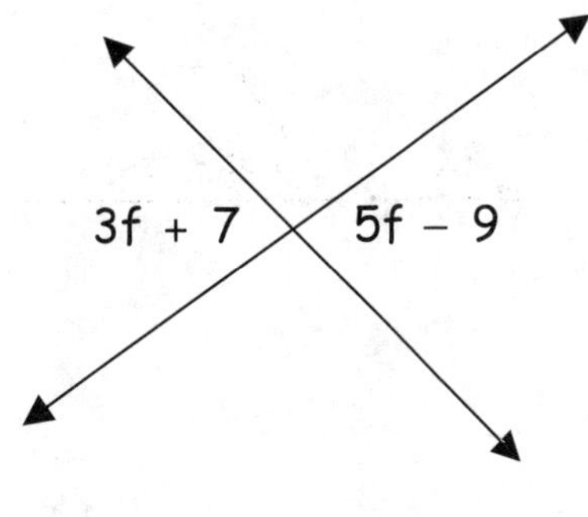

12.

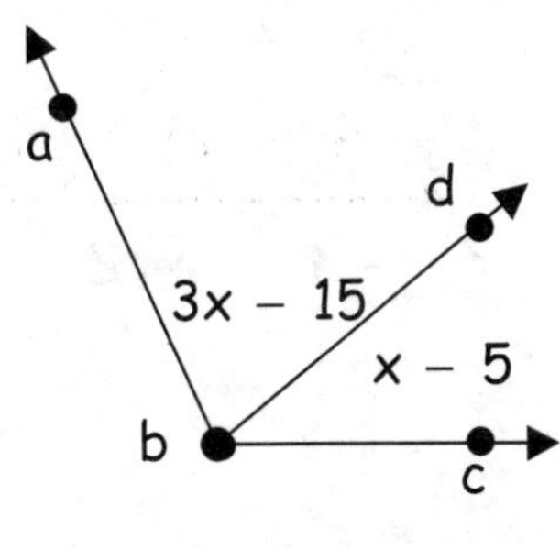

∠abc = 100°

Name ______________________________

Mixed Fractions

Directions: Solve.

1. $-3 \cdot 2\frac{1}{2}$

2. $-3 - 1\frac{1}{3}$

3. $-6 \div 1\frac{1}{2}$

4. $6 + 2\frac{1}{2}$

5. $-4 \cdot 5\frac{2}{5}$

6. $-4 - 2\frac{3}{5}$

7. $-3\frac{3}{4} \div 2$

8. $-8 + 3\frac{2}{3}$

9. $5\frac{1}{2} \div -3$

Mixed Fractions *(cont.)*

10. $6\frac{1}{2} - 3\frac{1}{4}$

11. $-4\frac{3}{4} \cdot 7$

12. $-5\frac{1}{4} - 3\frac{2}{5}$

13. $-6\frac{2}{3} \div 3$

14. $-4\frac{3}{4} + 6\frac{1}{3}$

15. $-4 \cdot 2\frac{3}{4}$

16. $-8\frac{1}{2} \div 2$

17. $-7\frac{1}{8} - 4\frac{1}{2}$

18. $-10\frac{2}{3} \div -3$

Part A

Problem Solving Strategy Notes: Using Logical Reasoning

Logical reasoning is different from the other strategies, where sometimes guesses are made and then checked. When logical reasoning is used, you begin with the knowledge that each piece of information is a piece of the puzzle. By putting the pieces together, you will find a solution.

You will work step-by-step to solve logical reasoning problems. Using the process of elimination is very common in solving logical reasoning problems.

Read Each Clue Thoroughly

Reading each clue carefully is a vital step in solving problems using logical reasoning. It is very important that you take the time to read the clues and understand each one before reading the next clue. Once you understand each clue, you can decide where to begin solving the problem.

Decide Where to Begin

Often the clues need to be considered in a different order than they are presented.

Check It Out!

Julie, Yoshiko, and Saul are each about to eat a sandwich for lunch. There is a ham sandwich, a peanut butter sandwich, and a grape jelly sandwich. Use the following clues to find out which sandwich belongs to each person.

- Julie's sandwich has cheese on it.
- Saul is allergic to peanuts.
- Yoshiko does not like sweet things on her sandwiches.

It is probably easiest to begin with the fact that Saul is allergic to peanuts, which means the peanut butter sandwich cannot be his. Julie's sandwich has cheese on it, so it is not likely to be the peanut butter sandwich or the grape jelly sandwich. She must have the ham sandwich. This leaves Saul with the grape jelly sandwich (which Yoshiko would not have had since she does not like sweet sandwiches). So, Yoshiko has the peanut butter sandwich.

Draw Up a Grid Listing the Names and Choices

Drawing up a grid can be a convenient way of visualizing the information in the problem.

For the previous example, the grid would look like this:

	Ham	Peanut Butter	Grape Jelly
Julie	✔	X	X
Yoshiko	X	✔	X
Saul	X	X	✔

You can mark off each option on the grid to solve the problem. An **X** means "no," and a ✔ means "yes."

Problem Solving Strategy Notes: Using Logical Reasoning *(cont.)* Part B

Sample Problem

Godrell, Paul, Brione, and Frita own four dogs named Bubba, Penny, Ginger, and Foxy. Use the clues to find out which dog belongs to which owner:

- ❏ Nobody owns a dog whose name starts with the same letter as their own name.
- ❏ Brione and Penny's owner are friends.
- ❏ Paul's sister owns Foxy.
- ❏ Frita gives Ginger's owner a bone.
- ❏ Godrell wished he had a dog like Bubba.

Understanding the Problem

What do we know?

- There are four people, and each owns a dog.
- Each dog's name starts with a different letter than its owner's name.

What do we need to find out?

- Which dog belongs to which person?
- What clue will be a good starting point?

Planning and Communicating a Solution

Draw a 5 x 5 grid. Use the symbols **X** (no) and ✔ (yes) to record the information you know from the clues. Your completed grid would look like this:

	Bubba	Penny	Ginger	Foxy
Godrell	X	✔	X	X
Paul	X	X	✔	X
Brione	X	X	X	✔
Frita	✔	X	X	X

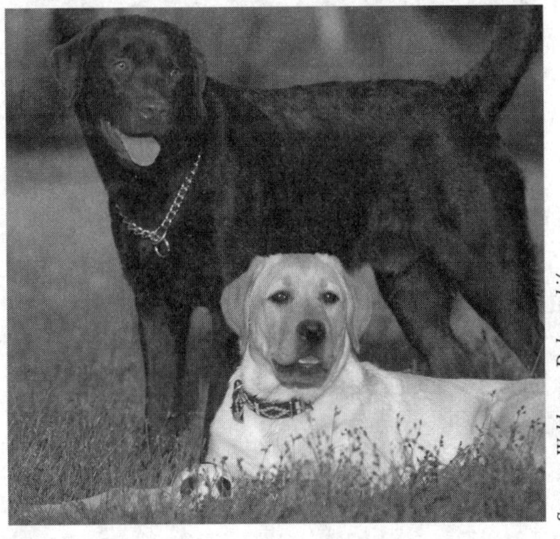

Source: Waldemar Dabrowski/ Shutterstock, Inc.

Reflecting and Generalizing

Think about the strategy of creating a grid and using check marks to represent the information in the grid. Is this a logical approach to use when several statements are made? Is there another way to solve the problem?

Extension

Write your own logic problem like this one using five people and five objects. Make sure you have included enough clues to allow the problem to be solved.

Part A

Real-Life Problem Solving: Red Lights Are Flashing

Imagine you are stopped at a railroad crossing. The red lights are flashing, and the gates are down. Train car after train car zooms by. You try to count how many, but soon you lose track. "Will this train ever end?" you wonder.

Trains that transport cargo from one place to another are called freight trains. Some freight trains have as many as 200 cars, depending on their weight. A locomotive, the power source for pushing or pulling the cars, can handle up to about 100,000 pounds.

There are different types of freight cars to carry various types of cargo. A boxcar is like a big rectangular box. It's enclosed on all sides, so it keeps cargo clean and dry. It can transport electronic equipment and food, for example. A hopper car is open on the top and can carry things like sand, gravel, or coal. A flatcar looks like a big tabletop on wheels since it has no roof or sides. It can carry cars, boats, truck trailers, and very large, bulky equipment. A tank car looks like a big round cylinder lying on its side. It is designed to carry liquids such as milk, gasoline, oil, or dangerous chemicals that shouldn't be exposed to the air. A freight train is usually made up of a mixture of these types of cars.

It takes a crew of workers to run a freight train. The driver, who sits in the locomotive, is called the engineer. The engineer uses levers to make the train stop and go. Other crew members are brakemen, switchmen, and yard foremen. They work with the engineers to assemble various cars into a train. Then, the freight train takes off down the tracks to deliver its cargo to its destinations. It may make many stops to drop off or pick up freight. Crew members help at every stop.

So, the next time a long freight train is holding you up, see if you can tell what kinds of cars are being pulled by the locomotive.

Real-Life Problem Solving: Red Lights Are Flashing *(cont.)*

Part B

Directions: Use the information on page 80 and in the problems below to answer the questions. Before you begin, be sure to locate the key information you will need.

What Is the Problem?

You are in charge of putting the trains together. The train crew has given you some guidelines on how to connect the cars. Using the guidelines given, connect the cars correctly.

Problem-Solving Strategy: Using Logical Reasoning

Problem A

Connect the six cars in the correct order. In what place is the heaviest car?

The locomotive must be first.
The caboose must be last.
The boxcar must be next to the caboose.
The hopper car cannot connect to the boxcar.
The flatcar and tank car must connect.
The hopper car is connected to the tank car.

Answer: ______________________________

____

____

Problem B

Connect the seven cars in the correct order. In what place is the second lightest car?

The locomotive must be first.
The caboose must be last.
The boxcar must be next to the caboose.
The hopper car or the flatcar cannot connect to the boxcar or the locomotive.
The hopper car comes before the flatcar.
There are two tank cars.

Answer: ______________________________

____

____

Problem C

Use the information given below to connect the eight cars correctly. What is the total weight of the train?

The locomotive must be first.
The caboose must be last.
The boxcar must touch the caboose.
The tank car must connect to the hopper car.
The flatcar cannot connect to the hopper car, the locomotive, or the boxcar.
There are two hopper cars and two tank cars.

Answer: ______________________________

____

____

Class Challenge

Connect the nine cars correctly.

Every car type must be used at least once.
A locomotive must be first.
A caboose must be last.
A boxcar must connect to each locomotive and caboose.
A hopper car must connect to each boxcar.
A flatcar cannot connect to a hopper car.
The total weight is 16,000 lbs.

Part A

Real-Life Problem Solving: Football Playoffs

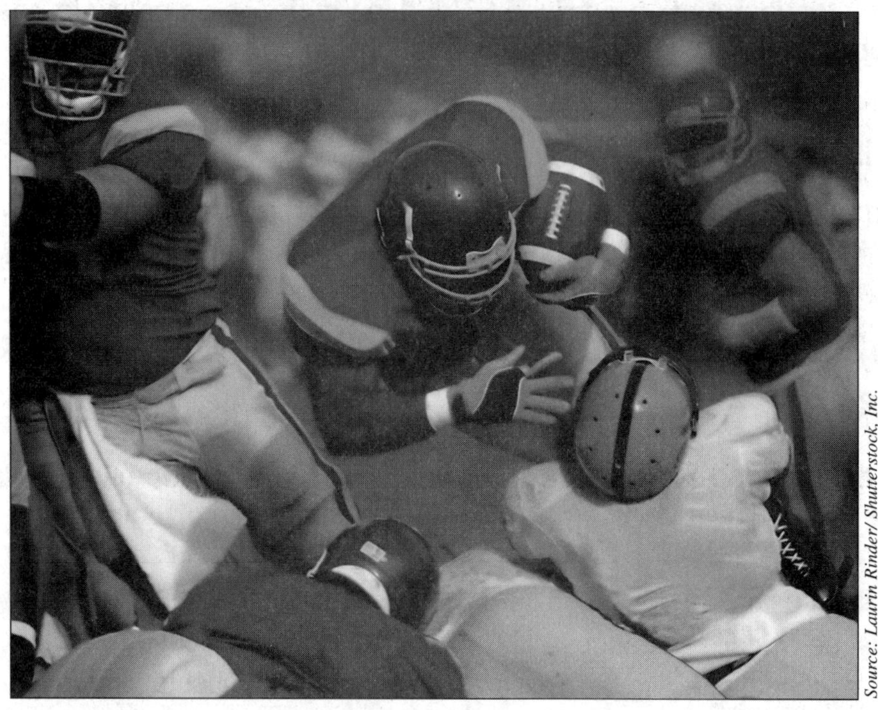
Source: Laurin Rinder/ Shutterstock, Inc.

At the start of every football season, professional football teams want to accomplish one goal. The goal is to win the Super Bowl. To win the Super Bowl, the team must first make the playoffs. There are times when it comes down to the last week of the regular season to find out which teams will make it to the playoffs. This season both the NFC and AFC have two more playoff spots to fill. Which teams will make it?

NATIONAL FOOTBALL CONFERENCE (NFC)

Team	Scenario
Minnesota Vikings	in with win and Rams loss
Carolina Panthers	in with win and Vikings loss
New Orleans Saints	in with win and Falcons loss
St. Louis Rams	in with win and Vikings loss

Note
For These Problems
A Touchdown = 7 points
(assuming 1pt. kick)
A Field Goal = 3 points

AMERICAN FOOTBALL CONFERENCE (AFC)

Team	Scenario
New York Jets	in with win and Bills loss or Broncos loss
Denver Broncos	in with win
Buffalo Bills	in with win and Jets loss or Broncos loss
Jacksonville Jaguars	in with win and losses by Broncos and Bills
Baltimore Ravens	in with win and losses by Broncos, Bills, and Jaguars

Real-Life Problem Solving: Football Playoffs *(cont.)* — Part B

Directions: Use the information on page 82 and in the problems below to answer the questions. Before you begin, be sure to locate the key information you will need.

What Is the Problem?

You are the sportswriter for your school's newspaper. It is your job to report which two teams from the NFC made the playoffs. Use the outcomes from the games played on Sunday to determine the winners and losers. For each problem, write a number sentence to calculate the score of each game. Show your work and write your number sentences on another sheet of paper. Below, use the outcomes to determine and list which two teams will make the playoffs. Each problem below has different results for the Sunday games. So, different teams will make the playoffs.

Problem-Solving Strategy: Using Logical Reasoning

Problem A

Game 1—Vikings and Redskins—Total of 44 points. Redskins scored 24 points.

Game 2—Saints and Panthers—Total of 41 points. Panthers scored 20 points.

Game 3—Rams and Jets—Total of 73 points. Rams scored 38 points.

Game 4—Seahawks and Falcons—Total of 38 points. Falcons scored 17 points.

Answer: ______________________

____

Problem B

Game 1—Seahawks scored 3 touchdowns. Falcons scored 2 touchdowns and 2 field goals.

Game 2—Redskins scored 3 touchdowns and one field goal. Vikings scored 4 touchdowns.

Game 3—Rams scored 5 touchdowns and one field goal. Jets scored 6 touchdowns.

Game 4—The Saints scored 3 touchdowns. The Panthers scored 2 touchdowns and a field goal.

Answer: ______________________

____

Problem C

Game 1—The Redskins scored 3 touchdowns and 1 field goal. The Redskins and Vikings scored a total of 44 points.

Game 2—The Saints scored 2 touchdowns and 3 field goals. The Saints and Panthers scored a total of 63 points.

Game 3—The Jets scored 5 touchdowns. The Jets and Rams scored a total of 73 points.

Game 4—The Seahawks scored 3 touchdowns and 1 field goal. The Falcons and Seahawks scored a total of 41 points.

Answer: ______________________

____

Class Challenge

Determine the two teams that will make it to the playoffs from the AFC.

Game 1—Steelers and Bills—Total of 53 points. Bills scored 3 touchdowns and 1 field goal.

Game 2—Jets and Ravens—Total of 53 points. Jets scored 3 touchdowns and 3 field goals.

Game 3—Jaguars and Raiders—Total of 19 points. Raiders scored 2 field goals.

Game 4—Colts and Broncos—Total of 47 points. Broncos scored 3 touchdowns and 4 field goals.

Name ________________________________

Real-Life Problem Solving:
Using Logical Reasoning

Directions: Use the strategy to solve each problem. Then, explain each answer.

The Problem

Every Friday night, the kids in Anchorage, Alaska, like to go out and have fun.

- 20 kids enjoy playing laser tag.
- Two times as many kids go to the movies instead of playing laser tag.
- Half as many kids like to go skating instead of playing laser tag.

At the end of the evening, everyone gets together to play hockey. How many kids enjoy participating in each activity?

Using the Strategy—Show Your Work

Explain Your Answer

Real-Life Problem Solving: Using Logical Reasoning *(cont.)*

The Problem

The juggler has five balls with different shapes on them: square, trapezoid, parallelogram, rhombus, and rectangle. Find the order in which the balls were dropped.

- The first ball dropped has a shape with only 90° angles.
- The last ball dropped has a shape where each pair of opposite sides are parallel and no angles are 90°.
- The ball dropped third has a shape with four sides of equal lengths but no right angles.
- The ball dropped second is not the ball with the trapezoid.
- The first ball dropped is not the ball with the rectangle.

Using the Strategy—Show Your Work

	1	2	3	4	5
square					
trapezoid					
parallelogram					
rhombus					
rectangle					

Explain Your Answer

Brain Break

Directions: Have you ever seen a political cartoon in a newspaper or news magazine? Political cartoons have been around for hundreds of years. They are usually funny and sometimes sarcastic. Political cartoons use symbols to represent real-life items. For example, a cartoon might use a pencil to represent school or a gavel to represent the government. Now, it's your turn to draw a political cartoon. Your topic is mathematics. Use any symbols you can think of to represent everything you feel about mathematics. Your cartoon can be funny or serious. Just go for it! Have fun sharing what you feel about math. Don't forget to give your cartoon a title and caption.

Name ______________________________

Percent of Region Packet

Directions: Shade the given percent of each region.

1. 50%

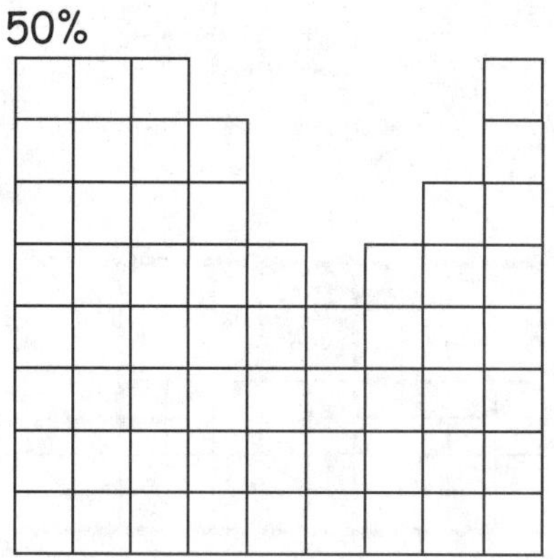

Number of blocks shaded:__________

2. 25%

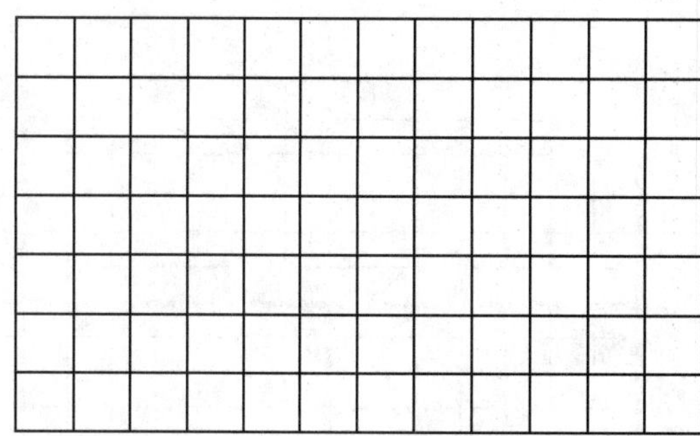

Number of blocks shaded:__________

3. 60%

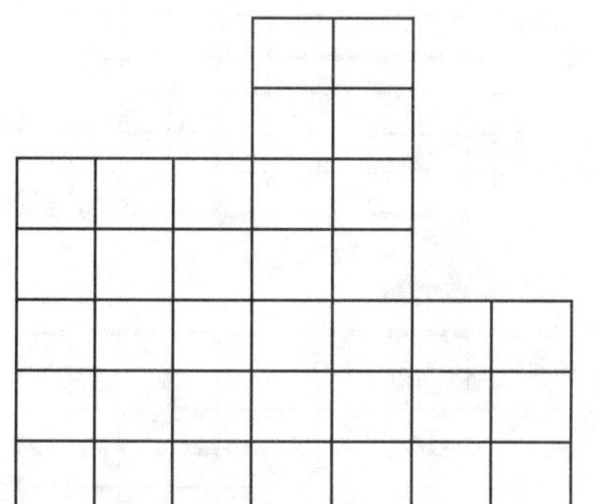

Number of blocks shaded:__________

4. 12.5%

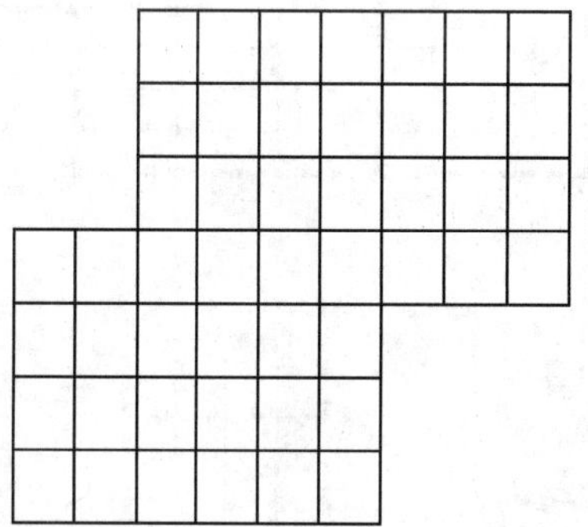

Number of blocks shaded:__________

5. 87.5%

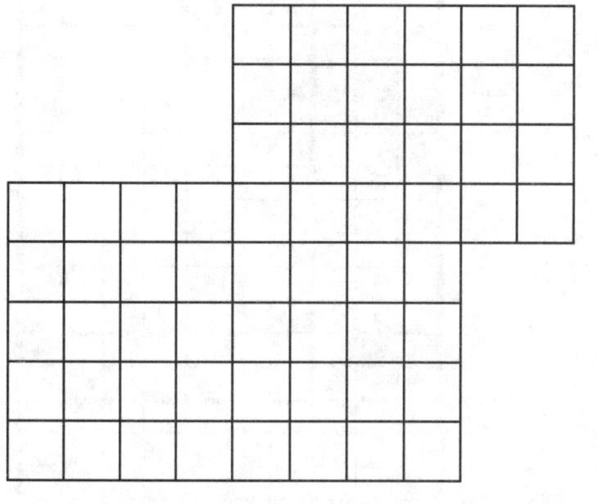

Number of blocks shaded:__________

6. 30%

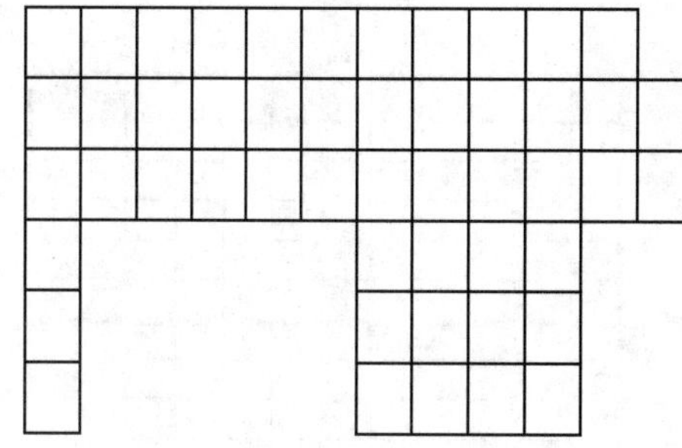

Number of blocks shaded:__________

Percent of Region Packet *(cont.)*

Directions: Count the number of squares in each region and complete the answer sheet.

7.
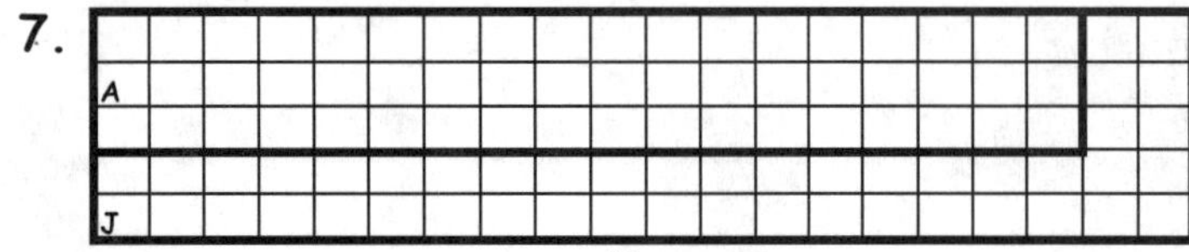

8.
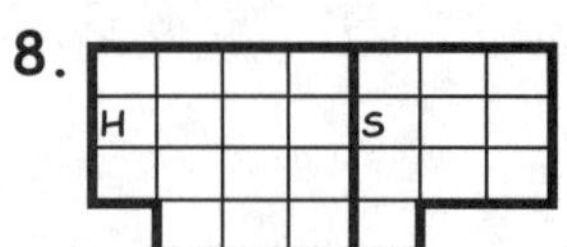

9.
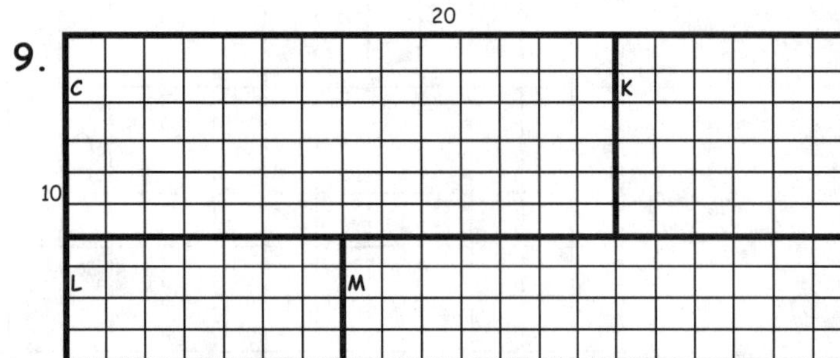

10.
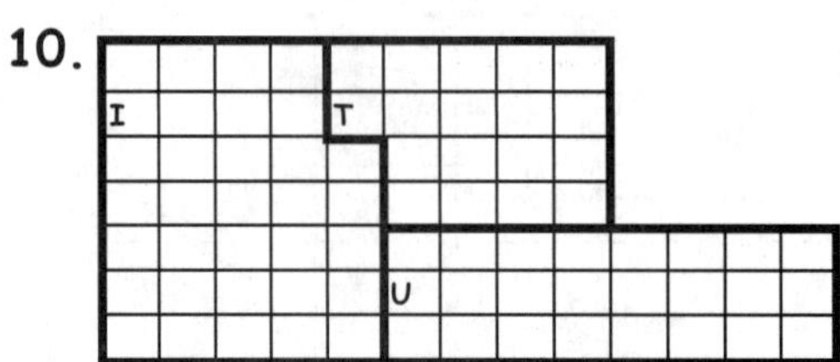

11.
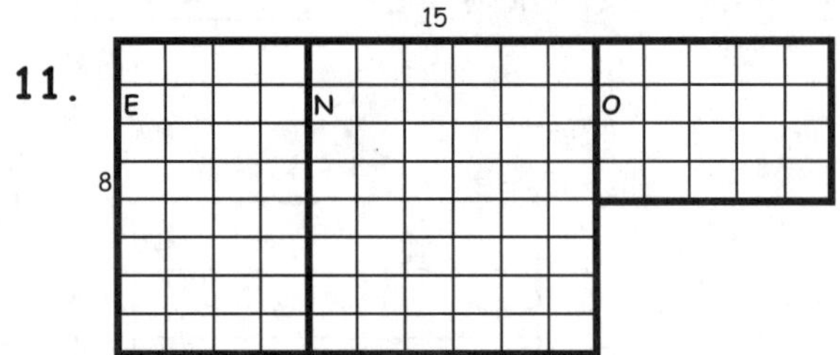

12.
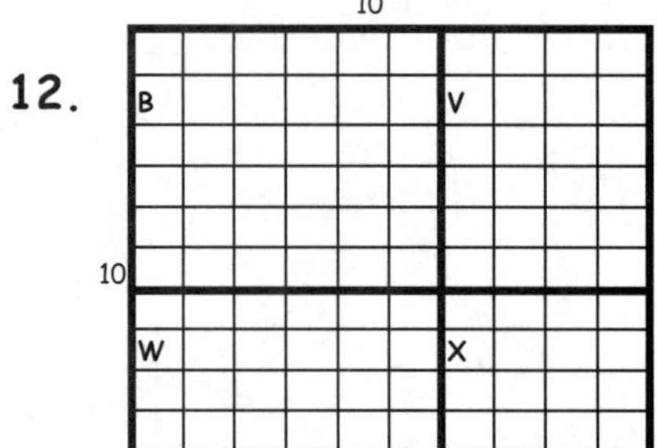

13.
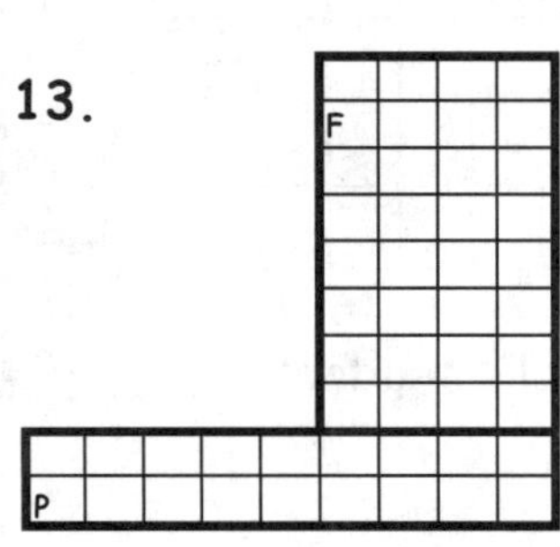

14.
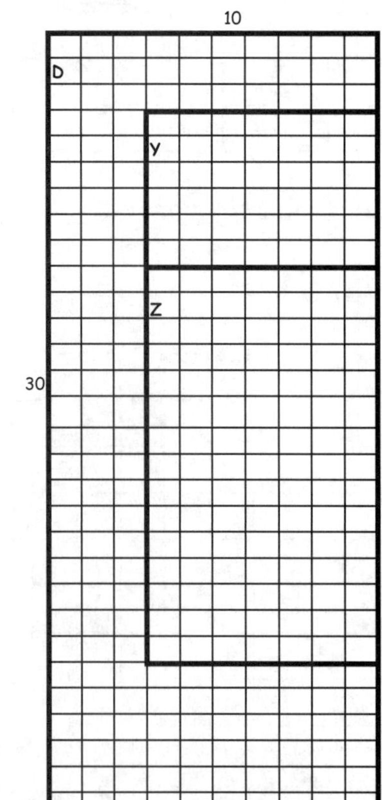

15.
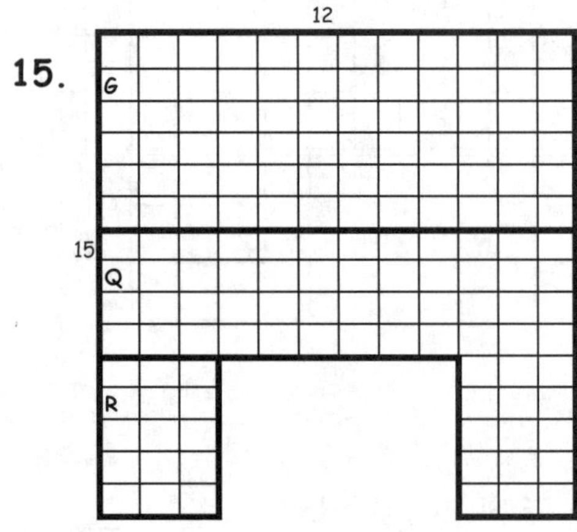

Percent of Region Packet *(cont.)*

Directions: Record your answers on this chart.

		# of Boxes	Fraction	Decimal	Percent
7.	A				%
	J				%
	Total				%
8.	H				%
	S				%
	Total				%
9.	C				%
	K				%
	L				%
	M				%
	Total				%
10.	I				%
	T				%
	U				%
	Total				%
11.	E				%
	N				%
	O				%
	Total				%

Percent of Region Packet *(cont.)*

Directions: Record your answers on this chart.

		# of Boxes	Fraction	Decimal	Percent
12.	B				%
	V				%
	W				%
	X				%
	Total				%
13.	F				%
	P				%
	Total				%
14.	D				%
	Y				%
	Z				%
	Total				%
15.	G				%
	Q				%
	R				%
	Total				%

Name ______________________________

Percent of Region Notes

Directions: Shade the given percent of each region.

1. 87.5%

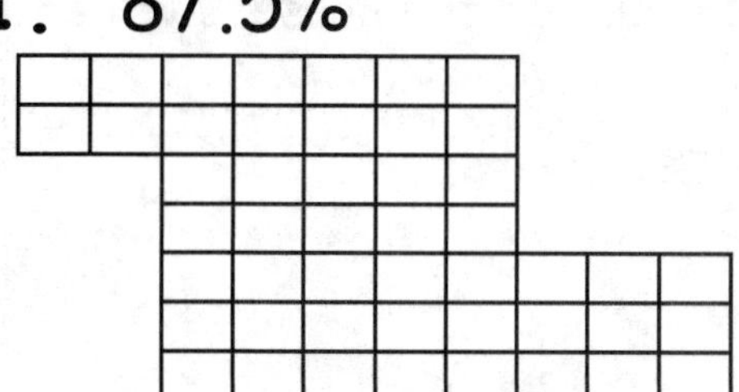

Number of boxes shaded:________

2. 20%

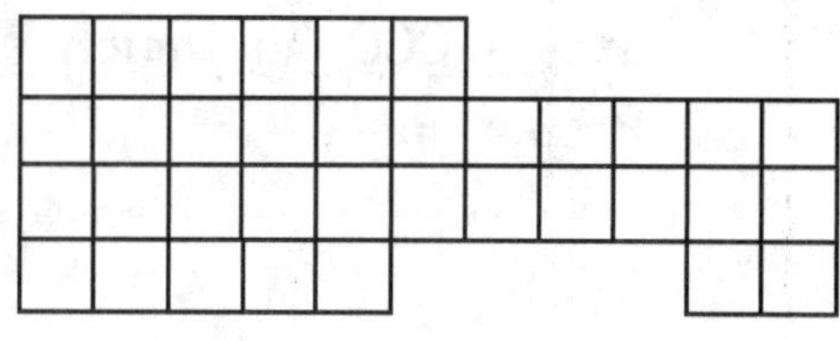

Number of boxes shaded:________

Directions: Count the number of squares in each region and complete the answer sheet.

3.

H I

4.

I T U

		# of Boxes	Fraction	Decimal	Percent
3.	H				%
	I				%
	Total				%
4.	I				%
	T				%
	U				%
	Total				%

Name ______________________________

Percent 1

Directions: Set up each proportion and solve. Write a "therefore statement" for each solution.

1. The Riddicks insured their house for 80% of its value. If the house is valued at $74,000, how much is it insured for?

   Proportion　　　　　　　　　　Solve

2. The Maddings insured their house for $70,000, which is 70% of its value. What is the value of their house?

   Proportion　　　　　　　　　　Solve

3. The Lees insured their house for 85% of its value. If the house is valued at $115,200, how much is it insured for?

   Proportion　　　　　　　　　　Solve

4. Jamar scored 80% on a test and got 20 problems correct. How many problems were on the test?

   Proportion　　　　　　　　　　Solve

5. Brittany scored 84% on a test and got 8 problems wrong. How many problems were on the test?

   Proportion　　　　　　　　　　Solve

6. Raul scored 72% on a test and got 7 problems wrong. How many problems were on the test?

   Proportion　　　　　　　　　　Solve

Percent 1 *(cont.)*

7. Rose received a commission of 5% on the sale of a new house. If the selling price of the house was $61,000, what was Rose's commission?

Proportion Solve

8. Nicholas sold a new truck for $18,500 and made $1,295 in commission. What was his rate of commission?

Proportion Solve

9. On Wednesday, Just Deals received a shipment of 40 cases of cereal. This was 80% of the cases of cereal ordered. How many cases of cereal were ordered?

Proportion Solve

10. On Tuesday, Joshua Tree Nursery received a shipment of 80 peach trees. The manager had ordered 100 peach trees. What percent of trees were delivered?

Proportion Solve

11. Brandy made 60 out of 80 free throws that she attempted. What percent were successful throws?

Proportion Solve

12. Shantel made 80% of her shots during the basketball season. If she made 140 shots, how many shots did she attempt?

Proportion Solve

Name ______________________________

Probability

Directions: Solve these problems, and choose the best answer for each.

1. If 3 nickels are flipped at the same time, what is the probability that all 3 nickels will show tails?

   A. $\frac{3}{8}$ B. $\frac{1}{2}$ C. $\frac{1}{8}$ D. $\frac{1}{6}$

2. How many possible outcomes exist if a 6-sided die is rolled and then a spinner with 3 sections is spun?

   A. 9 B. 6 C. 3 D. 18

3. What is the probability of tossing a coin and getting tails, and then rolling a die and getting an odd number?

   A. $\frac{1}{3}$ B. $\frac{3}{4}$ C. $\frac{3}{8}$ D. $\frac{1}{4}$

4. A drawer contains 3 white pairs of socks, 2 black pairs of socks, and 4 brown pairs of socks. Without replacing the socks, what is the probability of choosing a black pair, a white pair, and then a brown pair?

   A. $\frac{1}{21}$ B. $\frac{8}{243}$ C. $\frac{1}{8}$ D. $\frac{1}{7}$

5. The Snack Shack has 4 different soda pops, 6 different types of chips, and 10 different types of candy. How many possible combinations exist?

   A. 20 B. 240 C. 180 D. 54

6. Jaron has 3 red shirts, 4 blue shirts, and 5 white shirts in his closet. If he picks 1 shirt without looking, what is the probability that it will be blue?

   A. $\frac{1}{3}$ B. $\frac{1}{4}$ C. $\frac{5}{12}$ D. $\frac{2}{5}$

7. In how many different ways can all 3 of the pictures be arranged in a row?

   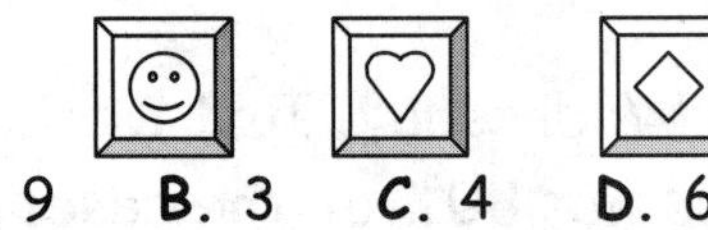

   A. 9 B. 3 C. 4 D. 6

8. A purse contains 2 silver dollars, 4 pennies, 2 nickels, 4 dimes, and 6 quarters. Without looking, what is the probability of picking a quarter, not putting it back, and then picking another quarter?

   A. $\frac{5}{51}$ B. $\frac{30}{256}$ C. $\frac{5}{31}$ D. $\frac{5}{8}$

9. Over a four-week period, Chang earned $52.25, $48.25, $51.25, and $50.25. What is his mean pay?

   A. $51 C. $50.50
   B. $49.50 D. $51.50

10. Jaden's grades in Algebra are 85, 92, 83, 85, 98, and 74. What is the mode?

    A. 86 B. 85 C. 87 D. 88

11. How many ways can 4 people stand in a line?

    A. 6 B. 8 C. 12 D. 24

Probability *(cont.)*

12. If each spinner is spun once, how many possible outcomes exist?

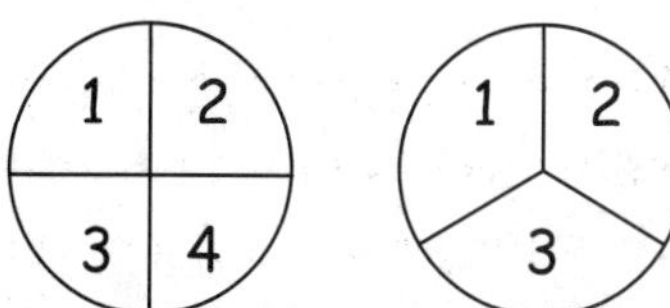

A. 7 **B.** 12 **C.** 8 **D.** 10

13. What is the probability of spinning a 4 on the first spinner and then spinning a 2 on the second spinner?

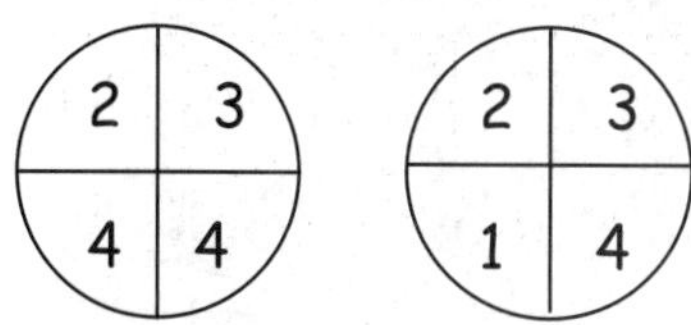

A. $\frac{1}{2}$ **B.** $\frac{3}{8}$ **C.** $\frac{1}{8}$ **D.** $\frac{1}{4}$

14. There are 10 girls and 14 boys in Mrs. Robin's Algebra I class. All of the students' names are in a bag. Without looking, what is the probability of choosing a girl's name?

A. $\frac{7}{12}$ **B.** $\frac{5}{12}$ **C.** $\frac{3}{5}$ **D.** $\frac{4}{7}$

15. If the digits cannot be repeated, how many 4-digit numbers can be formed by using the digits 4, 8, 1, 6, and 3?

A. 125 **B.** 40 **C.** 120 **D.** 625

16. If digits cannot be repeated, how many 3-digit numbers can be formed by using the digits 8, 4, 2, and 5?

A. 24 **B.** 64 **C.** 256 **D.** 625

17. How many different ways can all 5 of the cards be arranged in a row?

A. 3,125 **B.** 64 **C.** 120 **D.** 15

18. A police officer wrote speeding tickets to 5 different drivers. Their speeds were 72, 77, 75, 82, and 80. What was their mean speed?

A. 76.2 **B.** 78.2 **C.** 77.0 **D.** 77.2

19. Joaquin keeps all of his markers in a bag. He has 4 red markers, 6 blue markers, and 4 black markers. Without replacing the markers, what is the probability of drawing a black marker, a red marker, and then a blue marker?

A. $\frac{4}{9}$ **B.** $\frac{4}{91}$ **C.** $\frac{3}{51}$ **D.** $\frac{5}{51}$

20. Jafar listed his grades in history on a sheet of paper. His grades are 68, 75, 82, 92, 87, 82, and 88. What is his mean grade?

A. 65 **B.** 92 **C.** 75 **D.** 82

Name ______________________________________

Percent 2

Directions: Set up each proportion and solve. Write a "therefore statement" for each solution.

1. The Jacksons insured their house for 85% of its value. If the house is valued at $88,000 how much is it insured for?

   Proportion — Solve

2. Bridgette scored 90% on a test and got 4 problems wrong. How many problems were on the test?

   Proportion — Solve

3. A baseball glove was purchased at a discount of 30% for $84. What was the price of the glove before the discount?

   Proportion — Solve

4. The Houston Texans won 12 out of 16 football games. What percent did they lose?

   Proportion — Solve

5. Tayshawn bought a car stereo for $250. He had to make a down payment of $75. What percent did he pay as a down payment?

   Proportion — Solve

6. Gus received a commission of 6% on the sale of a pair of shoes. If the shoes cost $60, how much did he receive as a commission?

   Proportion — Solve

Percent 2 *(cont.)*

7. A logging company cut 72 trees on a piece of property. This was 90% of the trees on the property. How many trees were originally on the property?

   Proportion Solve

8. Antwan got 84 hits out of 400 trips to the plate during the baseball season. What percent of his attempts were hits?

   Proportion Solve

9. The Bulldogs won 24 out of 30 games this season. What percent of their games did they win?

   Proportion Solve

10. Juri bought a truck for $8,000 and paid 20% as a down payment. How much money did she give as a down payment?

    Proportion Solve

11. The manager of Regal Shoes put a pair of shoes on sale for $48. The original cost of the shoes was $60. What percent was saved?

    Proportion Solve

12. On Thursday, Jonas spent 6 hours studying for his algebra exam. What percent of his day did he spend studying for the exam?

    Proportion Solve

Name ______________________________

Percents Review

Directions: Solve.

1. There are 85 members of the Key Club at Kennard High School. For a fundraiser, $\frac{7}{8}$ of them sold candy. To find the number of students who sold candy, multiply the number of students by _______.
decimal

2. Exactly 50% of the freshman class went on a field trip. To find out how many of the 48 students went, multiply the number of students by _______.
decimal

3. What is 60% as a decimal? _______ as a fraction? _______

4. What is $\frac{1}{8}$ as a decimal? _______ as a percent? _______

5. A shirt is on sale for $\frac{3}{5}$ off of the regular price of \$10.

   A. Multiply the regular price by _______ to find the amount saved.
   decimal

   B. How much money was saved? _______

   C. How much money was spent? _______

   D. What percent is saved? _______

   E. What percent was spent? _______

6. Namiko scored 4 out of the 5 runs in the game. What percent did she score?
   Proportion Solve

   What percent did she not score? _______

Percents Review *(cont.)*

7. Sal is going to spend 30% of his savings on new shoes. He has $150 saved. How much is he going to spend on the shoes?

   Proportion — Solve

8. If you shade 12 out of 16 blocks, what percent did you shade?

   Proportion — Solve

   What percent was not shaded? ________

9. If there are 40 problems on a test, how many need to be correct to make at least an 80%?

   Proportion — Solve

Name ______________________________

Quick Percents

Directions: Solve.

1. What is the correct way to express $\frac{2}{5}$ as a percent? _____.

2. A pair of shoes that originally cost $24 is on a sale table marked "25% off." To find the amount of savings, multiply $24 by _____.
decimal

3. A motorcycle is discounted 12.5% off of the original retail price of $8,495.25. To find the discounted amount, multiply the original price by ____.
decimal

4. What is .3 expressed as a percent?
_____%

5. The correct way to express $\frac{8}{20}$ as a decimal is _____.

6. What fraction of a dollar is $0.48?
_____

7. Exactly 60% of the students at Central High School attended the school play. What fraction of the students attended the play?
_____

8. The correct way to express 0.75 as a fraction is _____.

9. The correct way to express 0.7% as a decimal is ______.

10. In all, 80% of the 240 students passed the test. To find out how many students passed, multiply 240 by _____.
fraction

11. A school survey indicates that $\frac{1}{5}$ of the people surveyed prefer orange juice to milk. 400 people took the survey. To find out how many people prefer orange juice, multiply the number of participants by _____.
decimal

12. Which is the correct way to write 6% as a fraction?
_____

13. Which is the correct way to write 0.685 as a percent?
_____%

14. Amy entered a dance marathon. Of the 200 dancers who entered the contest, only $\frac{7}{8}$ of the dancers finished. To find how many of the dancers finished the contest, multiply 200 by _____.
decimal

15. The correct way to write $\frac{4}{5}$ as a percent is _____%.

16. Altogether, $\frac{3}{8}$ of all shoppers bought the batteries that were on sale. What percent of shoppers bought batteries that were on sale?
______%

17. The correct way to write 0.25 as a percent is _____%.

Name ______________________________

Proportions 1

Directions: Set up each proportion and solve. Show your work.

1. Japa gets 3 hits every 8 times at bat. At this same rate, how many hits will he get after 200 times at bat?

Record and bubble your answer below.

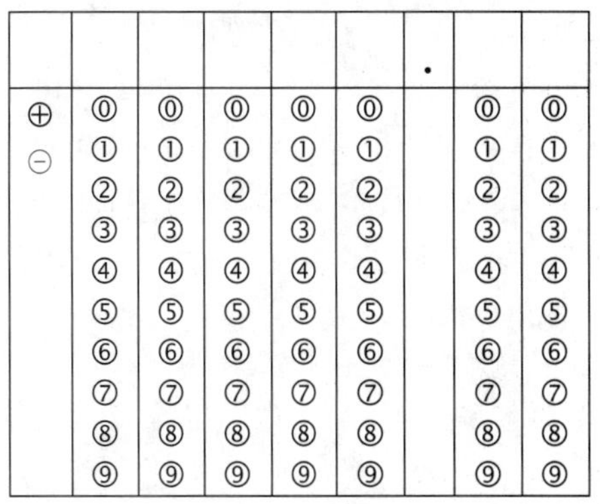

2. Serena bought Christmas presents over the Internet last year. Before Christmas, 14 out of 16 items arrived. What percent of her order arrived before Christmas?

Record and bubble your answer below.

						.		
⊕	⓪	⓪	⓪	⓪	⓪		⓪	⓪
⊖	①	①	①	①	①		①	①
	②	②	②	②	②		②	②
	③	③	③	③	③		③	③
	④	④	④	④	④		④	④
	⑤	⑤	⑤	⑤	⑤		⑤	⑤
	⑥	⑥	⑥	⑥	⑥		⑥	⑥
	⑦	⑦	⑦	⑦	⑦		⑦	⑦
	⑧	⑧	⑧	⑧	⑧		⑧	⑧
	⑨	⑨	⑨	⑨	⑨		⑨	⑨

3. A box of cake mix that makes one cake calls for $\frac{1}{4}$ cup of oil. Mia has $3\frac{1}{2}$ cups of oil.

How many cakes can she make?

Record and bubble your answer below.

						.		
⊕	⓪	⓪	⓪	⓪	⓪		⓪	⓪
⊖	①	①	①	①	①		①	①
	②	②	②	②	②		②	②
	③	③	③	③	③		③	③
	④	④	④	④	④		④	④
	⑤	⑤	⑤	⑤	⑤		⑤	⑤
	⑥	⑥	⑥	⑥	⑥		⑥	⑥
	⑦	⑦	⑦	⑦	⑦		⑦	⑦
	⑧	⑧	⑧	⑧	⑧		⑧	⑧
	⑨	⑨	⑨	⑨	⑨		⑨	⑨

Proportions 1 *(cont.)*

4. Montel's Snack Store stocks 3 candy bars for every 7 bags of chips. If the manager counts an inventory of 45 candy bars, what is the total number of snacks in the store?

Record and bubble your answer below.

						.		
⊕	⓪	⓪	⓪	⓪	⓪		⓪	⓪
⊖	①	①	①	①	①		①	①
	②	②	②	②	②		②	②
	③	③	③	③	③		③	③
	④	④	④	④	④		④	④
	⑤	⑤	⑤	⑤	⑤		⑤	⑤
	⑥	⑥	⑥	⑥	⑥		⑥	⑥
	⑦	⑦	⑦	⑦	⑦		⑦	⑦
	⑧	⑧	⑧	⑧	⑧		⑧	⑧
	⑨	⑨	⑨	⑨	⑨		⑨	⑨

5. Lucita types 5 documents every 4 hours. At this rate, how many hours will it take her to type 300 documents?

   A. 200 hours
   B. 240 hours
   C. 375 hours
   D. 420 hours

6. Joy's salary is $24,000 per year. How much money will Joy earn in 9 months?

   A. $4,500
   B. $10,000
   C. $18,000
   D. $216,000

7. A map key shows that every 3 centimeters represents 50 miles. How many miles is represented by 12 centimeters?

   A. .72 miles
   B. 6.25 miles
   C. 100 miles
   D. 200 miles

Proportions 1 *(cont.)*

8. Over the last three seasons, the PSJA North Raiders basketball team won 3 out of every 5 games. If they played 70 games, how many games did they lose?

   A. 28 games
   B. 42 games
   C. 175 games
   D. 200 games

9. Last Friday, 7 out of every 8 students enrolled in Algebra I at Mabank High School passed the unit test. If 200 students took the test, how many students failed?

   A. 40 students
   B. 200 students
   C. 175 students
   D. 25 students

10. The semester ratio of quizzes to test is 6:1. If there are 77 grades taken during the semester, how many are tests?

    A. 5 tests
    B. 7 tests
    C. 11 tests
    D. 14 tests

11. This year, 231 boys signed up to play baseball. Altogether, 6 out of every 7 boys sold candy for the league. How many boys chose not to sell candy?

    A. 27 boys
    B. 33 boys
    C. 35 boys
    D. 42 boys

Name ______________________________

Measurement Review

Directions: Find the formula(s) for each of the following.

1. Circle

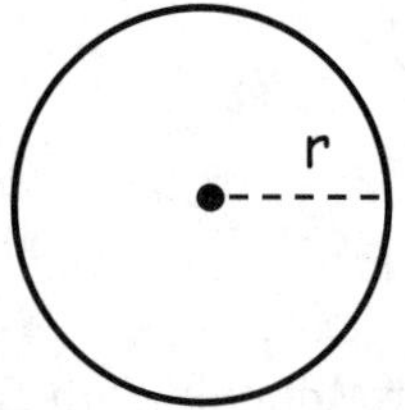

Area = ______________________

Circumference = ______________

2. Rectangular pyramid

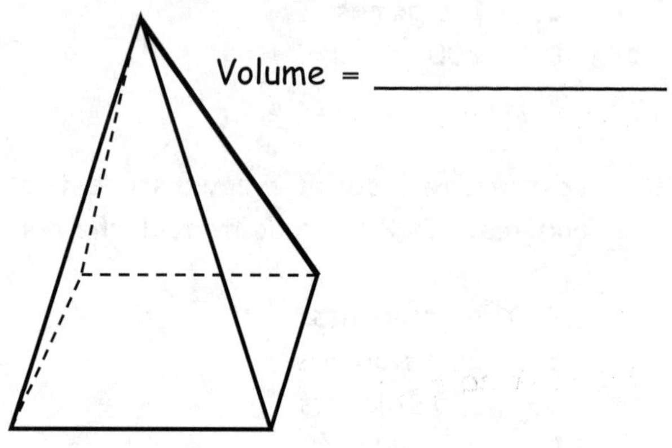

Volume = ______________

3. Cone

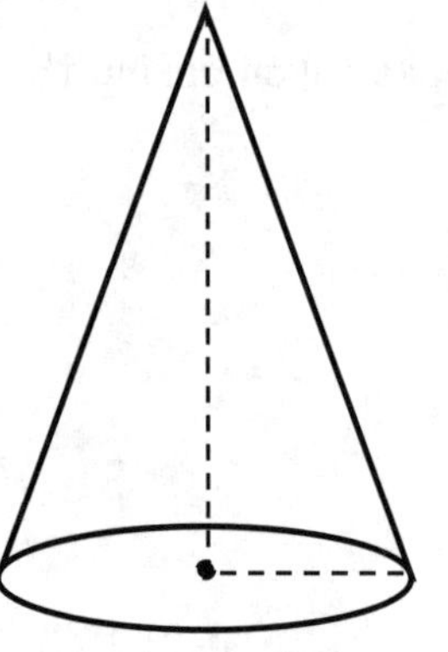

Volume = ___________

4. Trapezoid

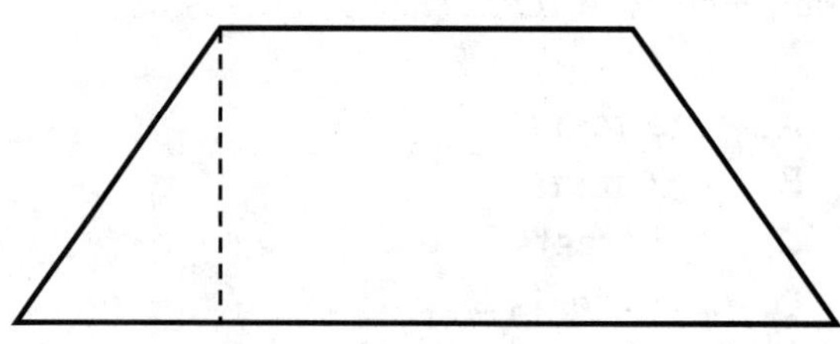

Area = ________________

5. Rectangular prism

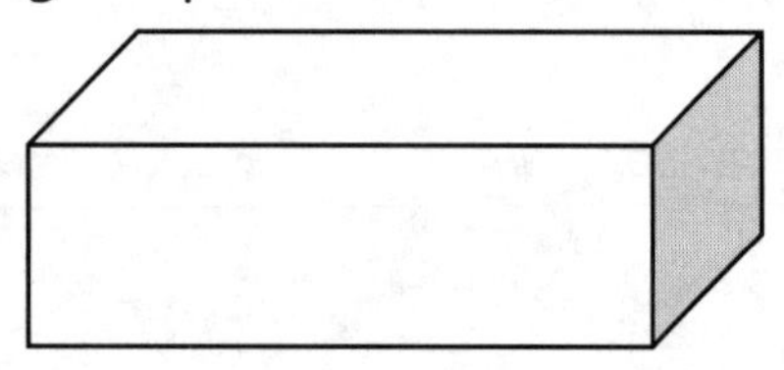

Volume = ____________________

6. Cube

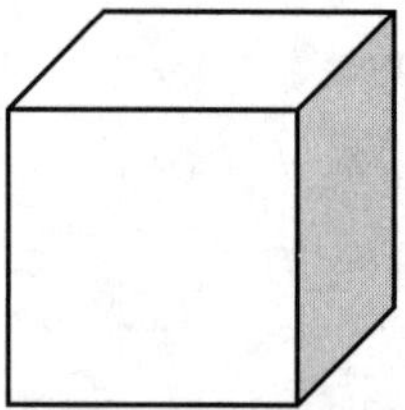

Volume = __________________

Surface Area = _____________

Measurement Review *(cont.)*

7. Find the area or volume of the following shapes with the given dimensions.

A. Circle

Radius is 6 cm.

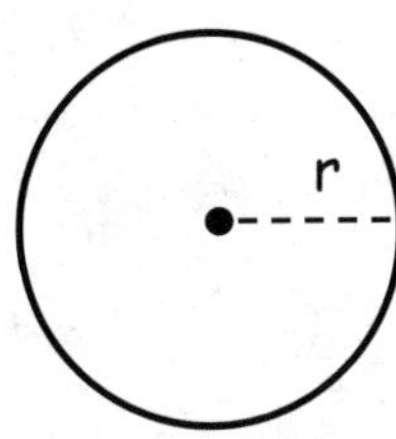

Area = ____________________

B. Square pyramid

Side is 10 cm.
Height is 15 cm.

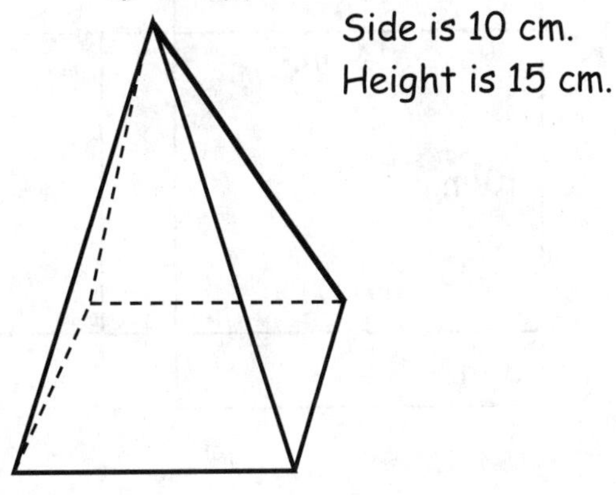

Volume = ______________

8. Find the area of the following figure:

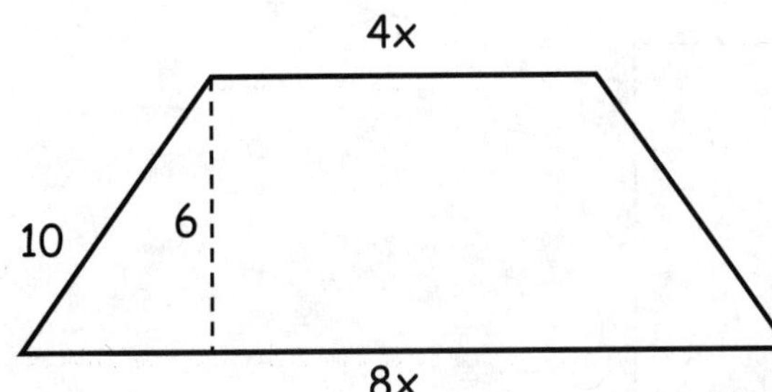

Area = ______________

9. Which formula can be used to find the volume of the following composite solid?

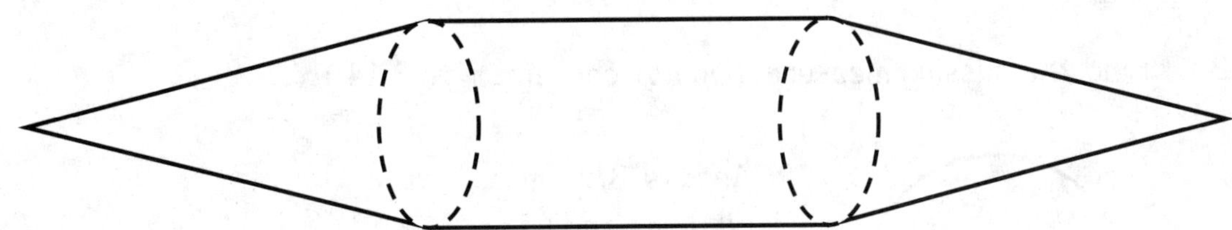

A. $V = \pi r^2 h + \frac{1}{3}\pi r^2 h$

B. $V = \pi r^2 h - \frac{1}{3}\pi r^2 h - \frac{1}{3}\pi r^2 h$

C. $V = \pi r^2 h - \frac{1}{3}\pi r^2 h$

D. $V = \pi r^2 h + \frac{1}{3}\pi r^2 h + \frac{1}{3}\pi r^2 h$

Measurement Review *(cont.)*

10. Find the surface area of the following net.

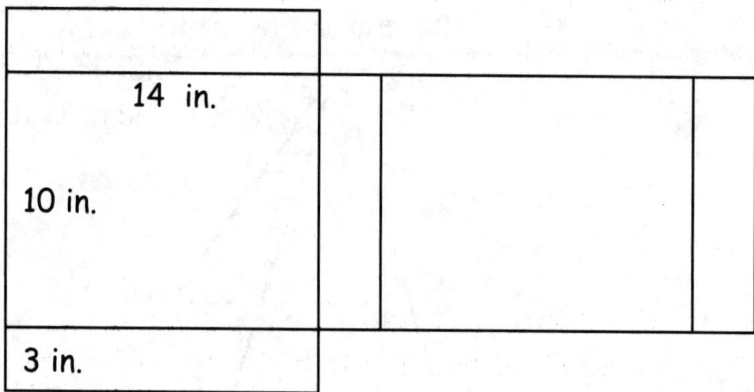

Surface Area = ____________________

11. Find the area of the given figure.

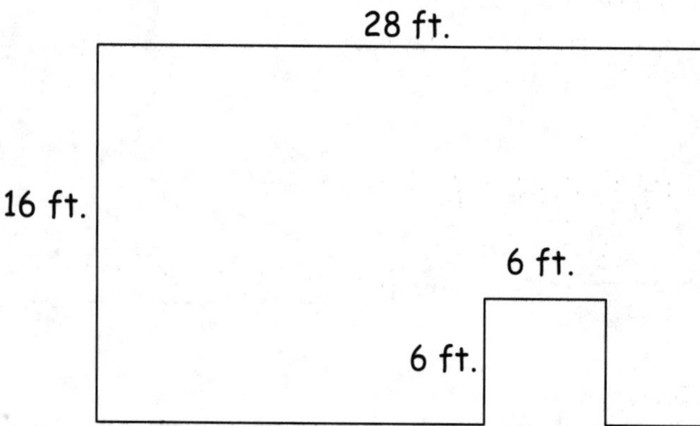

Area = ____________________

12. Find the missing measure. (Do not convert π to 3.14.)

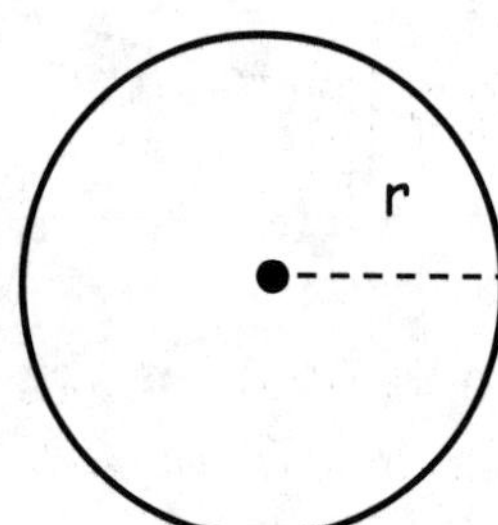

Area is 81π cm^2.
Find the radius.

Radius = __________

Measurement Review *(cont.)*

13. A rectangle with the dimensions of 6.3 cm and 5.8 cm is reduced by a scale factor of $\frac{1}{3}$. What are the dimensions of the new image? (Round to the nearest hundredth.)

14. A cylindrical can of punch has a volume of 120 fluid ounces. A second cylindrical can has dimensions that are $\frac{3}{5}$ the size of the larger can. Which is the closest volume of the smaller can?

A. 26 fl. oz.

B. 43 fl. oz.

C. 72 fl. oz.

D. 100 fl. oz.

15. Find the missing measure. (Do not convert π to 3.14.)

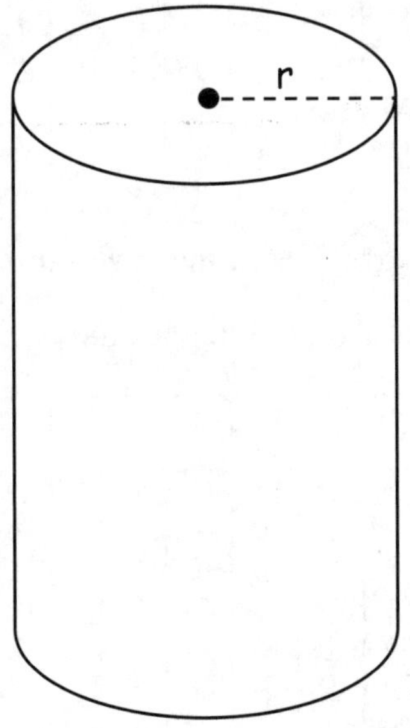

Radius is 6 cm.
Volume is 180π cm^3.
Find the height.

Height = ___________

Name ______________________________

Proportions 2

Directions: Write proportions for the following and solve.

1. The freshman football team won 6 out of the 8 games they played last year. At this same rate, how many games will they win if they play 12 games this year?

Record and bubble your answer below.

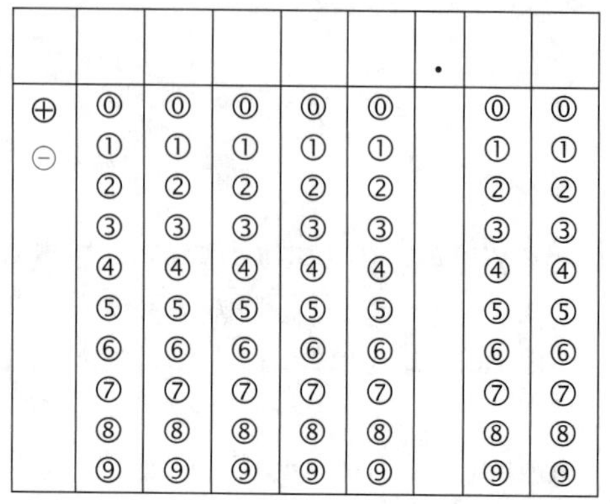

2. Mrs. Jamael ordered kitchen supplies from a mail order catalog. She received 9 out of 12 items ordered in one shipment. What percent of her order arrived?

Record and bubble your answer below.

3. A box of cake mix that makes one cake calls for $\frac{3}{4}$ cup of water. How much water would be needed to make 54 cakes?

Record and bubble your answer below.

Proportions 2 *(cont.)*

4. To paint the first wing at Edinburg High School, you would need 5 gallons of blue paint and 3 gallons of red paint. If it would take 120 gallons of paint to paint all the hallways in the school, how many gallons of blue paint would it take?

Record and bubble your answer below.

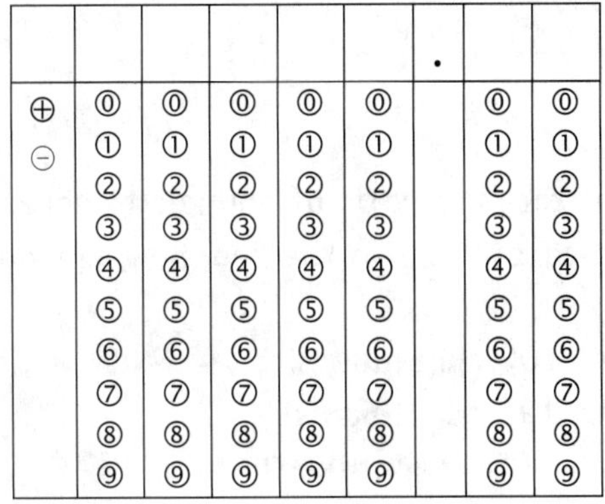

5. In a jewelry store, the ratio of rubies to opals is 3 to 2. If there are 150 rubies in the store, how many opals are there?

   A. 75 opals
   B. 100 opals
   C. 200 opals
   D. 225 opals

6. Tricia received an 8% commission on the sale of a digital phone package. The amount of the package was $50.00. How much commission did she earn?

   A. $1.00
   B. $2.00
   C. $3.00
   D. $4.00

7. On Wednesday, 9 out of 11 students attended tutorials. If 55 students were assigned tutorials, how many students did not attend tutorials?

   A. 10 students
   B. 12 students
   C. 30 students
   D. 40 students

Proportions 2 *(cont.)*

8. Cassandra bought a stereo with 80% of the money she received on her birthday. The stereo cost $219. How much money did Cassandra receive on her birthday?

   A. $36.53
   B. $250
   C. $273.75
   D. $17,520

9. In a zoo, the ratio of animals to caretakers is 6 to 1. If there is a total of 1,372 animals and caretakers in the zoo, how many are caretakers?

   A. 100 caretakers
   B. 196 caretakers
   C. 1,000 caretakers
   D. 1,176 caretakers

10. The average person has 32 teeth. If you have 32 teeth and 6 of them have fillings, what percent of your teeth do not have fillings?

    A. 18.75%
    B. 50.25%
    C. 75.50%
    D. 81.25%

11. Manny makes $405 every 9 days. At this rate, how much will he make in two weeks?

    A. $260.36
    B. $630
    C. $31
    D. $790

Name ______________________________

Probability, Percent, and Proportion Review

1. Give the decimal value for each fraction.

$\frac{3}{4}$ = ______ $\frac{2}{3}$ = ______ $\frac{4}{5}$ = ______ $\frac{2}{5}$ = ______

$\frac{3}{8}$ = ______ $\frac{5}{8}$ = ______ $\frac{1}{2}$ = ______ $\frac{1}{3}$ = ______

$\frac{3}{5}$ = ______ $\frac{1}{5}$ = ______ $\frac{7}{8}$ = ______ $\frac{1}{4}$ = ______

$\frac{1}{8}$ = ______

Directions: Solve.

2. $3\frac{2}{5} \cdot 4$

3. $10 - 5\frac{1}{4}$

4. $3\frac{2}{3} + 4\frac{1}{4}$

5. The Rhodes insured their house for $78,400, which is 80% of the total value of the house. What is the value of their house?

Proportion

Solve

6. A walking cane was purchased at a discount of 25% for $187.50. What was the price of the cane before the discount?

Proportion

Solve

Probability, Percent, and Proportion Review *(cont.)*

7. Shameka scored 85% on a test, and 6 problems were wrong. How many problems were on the test?

   Proportion — Solve

8. Sean received a commission of 6% on the sale of a new house. If the amount of his commission was $6,300.00, what was the selling price of the house?

   Proportion — Solve

9. On Tuesday, Only Deals received a shipment of 240 Christmas trees. The manager had ordered 300 trees. What percent of her order arrived Tuesday?

   Proportion — Solve

10. Badu has 4 different baseball gloves, 3 different baseball bats, and 4 different baseballs. How many different combinations are there if he chooses 1 glove, 1 bat, and 1 ball?

    A. 11 C. 48
    B. 30 D. 36

11. If the digits can be repeated, how many 4-digit numbers can be formed using the digits 8, 3, 5, and 2?

    A. 64 C. 32
    B. 24 D. 256

Probability, Percent, and Proportion Review *(cont.)*

12. How many ways can four people be arranged in a row?

    A. 256 C. 64
    B. 32 D. 24

13. If the digits cannot be repeated, how many 3-digit numbers can be formed using only the digits 3, 8, 4, and 2?

    A. 64 C. 256
    B. 24 D. 32

14. A die and a coin are tossed. What is the probability of tossing a 5 and heads?

    A. $\frac{1}{4}$ C. $\frac{1}{12}$
    B. $\frac{1}{8}$ D. $\frac{1}{6}$

15. If 4 coins are tossed, what is the probability of tossing all heads?

    A. $\frac{1}{2}$ C. $\frac{1}{4}$
    B. $\frac{1}{16}$ D. $\frac{1}{8}$

16. Yuri can make 12 bows every hour. Which proportion will give the amount of bows Yuri can make in 20 hours?

    A. $\frac{12}{1} = \frac{x}{20}$ C. $\frac{12}{20} = \frac{1}{x}$
    B. $\frac{12}{1} = \frac{20}{x}$ D. $\frac{20}{12} = \frac{x}{1}$

Probability, Percent, and Proportion Review *(cont.)*

17. The Bruins scored 420 points after 5 games. If the team continues to score at this same rate, how many points will the team have scored after 30 games?

Proportion | Solve

18. Tomicka can solve 18 out of every 20 equations correctly. At this rate, how many equations can she solve correctly if she solves 300 equations?

Proportion | Solve

19. On the legend of a map, 3 inches represent 20 miles. How many inches are needed to represent 260 miles?

Proportion | Solve

20. Keisha's dog, Buddy, eats 4 cups of dog food every day. At this rate, how many cups of food will Buddy eat in 3 weeks?

Proportion | Solve

Problem Solving Strategy Notes: Part A

Creating a Table

When a problem has lots of information, placing the information in a table is a good idea. A table helps you organize the information so that it can be easily understood.

A table makes it easy to see what information is there and what information is missing. When a table is drawn, the information often shows a pattern, or part of a solution, which can then be completed.

You will usually have to create some of the information in order to complete the table and then solve the problem.

Using a table can help reduce the chance of making mistakes or repeating something.

It is not always easy to decide how to divide up the information in the problem or make a table that works with the information. With practice, you will learn how to use a table to solve problems.

Before you begin using tables, read the following information to learn more about how and when to use tables to solve problems.

Deciding on the Number of Columns and Rows

- First, decide how many pieces of information are included in the problem.
- Next, think about whether the information needs to be in a row or a column. Be sure you understand what the table is going to tell you.
- Headings are also important because they show the exact contents of the table.

Example problem: Research shows that three out of every 10 people have blonde hair. How many blondes can be found among 1,000 people?

For this problem, you need to make a table with two columns: *Number of Blondes* and *Number of People*.

Number of Blondes	Number of People
3	10
30	100
300	1,000

A quick look at the table shows that 300 blondes can be found among 1,000 people.

Hint: In this problem, you worked with multiples of 10. When working with multiples, a table can help you find patterns.

Part B

Problem Solving Strategy Notes: Creating a Table *(cont.)*

Sample Problem

A group of students is learning a long poem for a school assembly. Each week they are taught a certain number of verses.

The first week they learn one verse, and by the end of the second week, the students know three verses.

At the end of the third week, the students can recite six verses. At the end of the fourth week, they know 10.

How many verses would they be able to recite after eight weeks?

Understanding the Problem

What do we know?

- In the first week, students learn 1 verse.
- At the end of the second week, they know 3 verses.
- At the end of the third week, they know 6 verses.
- By the end of the fourth week, they know 10 verses.

What do we need to find out?

- How many verses do they know after 8 weeks?

Planning and Communicating a Solution

To solve this problem, draw a table with 2 rows and 9 columns (or 2 columns and 9 rows).

The first row should list the week numbers (1–8).

The second row should list the number of verses.

Place the numbers in the table. Do you see a pattern?

Week	1	2	3	4	5	6	7	8
Number of Verses	1	3	6	10	15	21	28	36

The pattern for the number of verses is +1, +2, +3 . . .

The students would be able to recite 36 verses by the end of week 8.

Reflecting and Generalizing

The table makes it easy to see a pattern. If you discover the pattern right away, you can simply complete the pattern mentally to solve the problem.

Extension

What if the students were not able to practice for one or two weeks?

How would this change the results?

Real-Life Problem Solving: Part A
French Fries

Source: Hemera Technologies, Inc.

On average, each American eats over 16 pounds of french fries each year. The consumption of french fries makes for sales of $6 billion each year.

French fries are made by boiling potatoes in fat. The Incas first discovered potatoes as early as 200 B.C., they were cultivating them. In the sixteenth century, Spanish explorers brought the potato back to Europe. The potato spread to countries such as Germany, Ireland, and France and became a popular staple. Both the French and the Belgians take credit for the idea of frying potatoes in order to make the french fries with which we are familiar. By the mid-1830s, fried potatoes were a popular dish in France and Belgium. At that time, the fried potatoes were sold by vendors on the streets of Paris and Brussels.

President Thomas Jefferson sampled fried potatoes while in Paris, France. When he returned to the United States, he served fried potatoes at a White House dinner. He called the dish "potatoes served in a French manner."

It has been said that it was American soldiers stationed in France during World War I who gave fried potatoes the name french fries. However, the word "french" also refers to a way of cutting things into thin strips. So, this is probably how french fries got their name.

In England, french fries are called "chips" and are most often served with fried fish. In the United States, french fries are often served with hamburgers.

Part B

Real-Life Problem Solving: French Fries *(cont.)*

Directions: Use the information on page 117 and in the problems below to answer the questions. Before you begin, be sure to locate the key information you will need.

What Is the Problem?

You are hungry for lunch. You have a coupon for your favorite hamburger restaurant. The restaurant is offering 20% off french fries and soft drinks when you order a hamburger. Your job is to determine how much your lunch will cost if you use the coupon. The total cost will vary depending on what you order.

Jo's Hamburgers Menu

Small french fries	$2.00
Large french fries	$3.00
Small soft drink	$1.00
Large soft drink	$2.00
Hamburger	$3.00

Jo's Hamburgers Coupon
20% OFF
French fries and a soft drink with the purchase of a hamburger
No limit on number of orders

Problem-Solving Strategy: Creating a Table

Problem A

What is the cost of each small and large order of french fries and soft drinks if you use the coupon? Create a table to show your answers.

Answer: ____________________

____

Problem B

How many different combinations of sizes of french fries and soft drinks can be made? What is the total amount of money you would spend on each combination of french fries and soft drinks if you use the coupon? Create a table to show your answers.

Answer: ____________________

____

Problem C

During the special, the restaurant decides to add a "jumbo" size of french fries for the price of $4.00. How many different combinations of sizes of french fries and soft drinks can be made? What is the total amount of money you would spend on each combination if you use the coupon? Create a table to show your answers.

Answer: ____________________

____

Class Challenge

A family of four goes to the same restaurant for lunch. How much would lunch cost if each orders a hamburger, small french fries, and small drink? What would the total bill be without the coupon? What would the total bill be with the 20% off coupon?

Real-Life Problem Solving: Back to School

Part A

At the end of the summer, kids and their parents start thinking about going back to school. Kids are sad to see the summer coming to an end. Parents begin thinking about back-to-school shopping. This is a great time to get bargains on summer and fall clothes. Some states even have tax-free weekends in August or September before school starts. Parents like the extra discount on school clothes, but they do not like the lines.

Look at the advertisement above. Think about all the things that are needed when school starts in the fall.

Part B

Real-Life Problem Solving: Back to School *(cont.)*

Directions: Use the information on page 119 and in the problems below to answer the questions. Before you begin, be sure to locate the key information you will need.

What Is the Problem?

You and your friends want to go shopping on your own this year. Your parents have agreed to let you make your own selections on school clothes. They want you to make responsible decisions. Before your parents will let you go shopping on your own, they want you to make a list of the clothing items you want to buy. They also want you to show how much you are going to spend on each item. Since many items are on sale, you will have to figure the cost of the item after the discount. Discounts are subtracted from the original price. Sales tax is added to the final price of an item. Create your charts on another sheet of paper.

Problem-Solving Strategy: Creating a Table

Problem A

Create a chart of the items you want to buy at the back-to-school sale. Your chart should include the cost of each item. How much money would you spend? Your parents decide to give you $100. Revise your chart so that you don't spend more than $100.

Answer: ______________________

____

____

Problem B

Create a chart of the items you want to buy at the back-to-school sale. Your chart should include the cost of each item. How much money would you spend? Your parents decide to give you $200. Revise your chart so that you don't spend more than $200. If you have to pay sales tax at 7%, can you still buy everything on your revised list?

Answer: ______________________

____

____

Problem C

Create a chart of the items you want to buy at the back-to-school sale. Your chart should include the cost of each item. How much money would you spend? Your parents decide to give you $275. Revise your chart so that you don't spend more than $275. If you have to pay sales tax at 7%, can you still buy everything on your revised list? If not, revise your list again.

Answer: ______________________

____

____

Class Challenge

Find a sale advertisement. Make a list of the things you want to buy. Figure the cost including sales tax. How much would it cost to buy everything on your list?

Name ______________________________

Real-Life Problem Solving:
Creating a Table

Directions: Use the strategy to solve each problem. Then, explain each answer.

The Problem

For every $1.00 Carla earns, 25¢ goes into the piggy bank for a "rainy day" and the rest goes into her coin purse. When Carla has saved $3.00 in her coin purse, she likes to spend the money at the local store. How much money will Carla have to earn before she has $3.00 in her coin purse?

Using the Strategy—Show Your Work

Explain Your Answer

Real-Life Problem Solving:
Creating a Table *(cont.)*

The Problem

The Grabber is a machine that picks up items and places some of them into a bag. For every two items it picks up, it puts one in the bag. How many items would it put in the bag if it picked up 22 items?

Using the Strategy—Show Your Work

The Grabber Picks Up	The Grabber Places into a Bag
2	1
4	2
6	3
8	4

Explain Your Answer

Name ________________________________

Functions, Domains, and Ranges

Directions: State the relation as a set of ordered pairs. Determine the domain and range of the relation.

1.

x	y
−3	2
−1	6
1	−2
3	5

Relation ____________________

D = ____________________

R = ____________________

2.

x	y
3	−2
6	4
8	−2
10	−8

Relation ____________________

D = ____________________

R = ____________________

Directions: State whether the following relations are functions.

3.

Domain Range

5 → 3

7 → 3

9 → 3

____

4.

Domain Range

5 → 6

6 → 6

8 → 8

9 → 8

____

5.

Domain Range

Taco → $2

Burrito → $4

Taco Salad → $6

Taco Salad → $4

____

6.

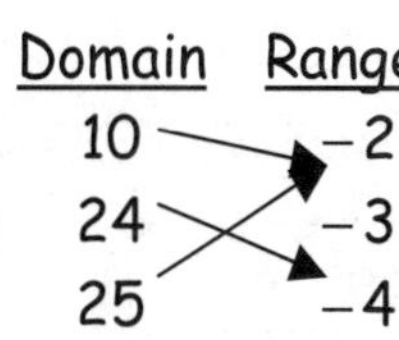

____

7.

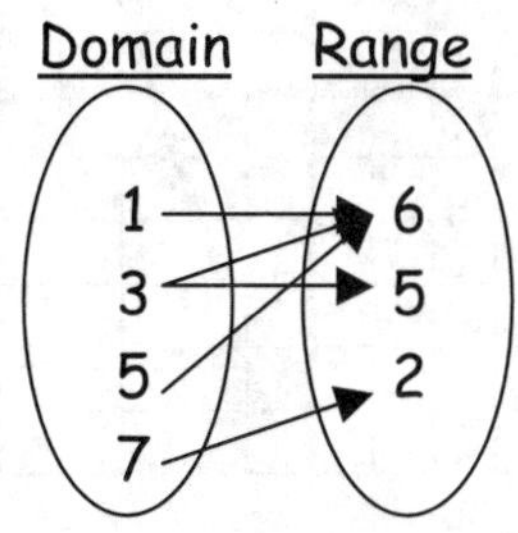

____

8.

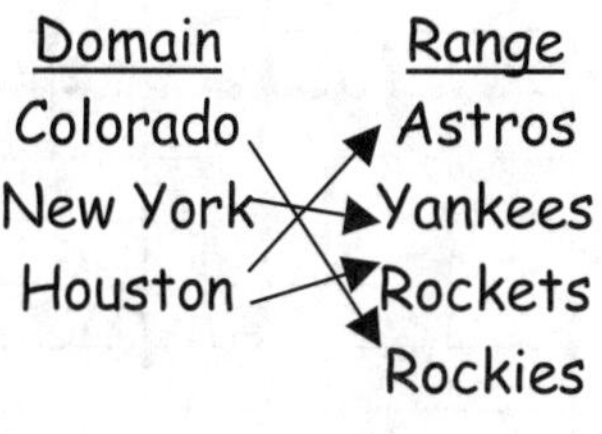

____

Functions, Domains, and Ranges *(cont.)*

Directions: Use the vertical line test to determine which of the following graphs are functions. Write "yes" if the graph is a function and "no" if the graph is not a function.

9.

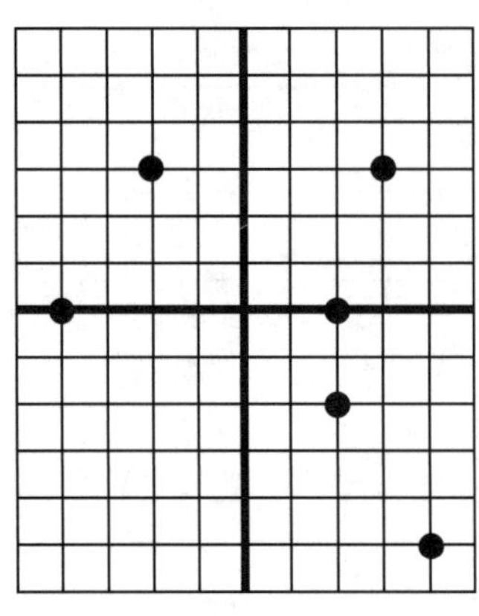

____

10.

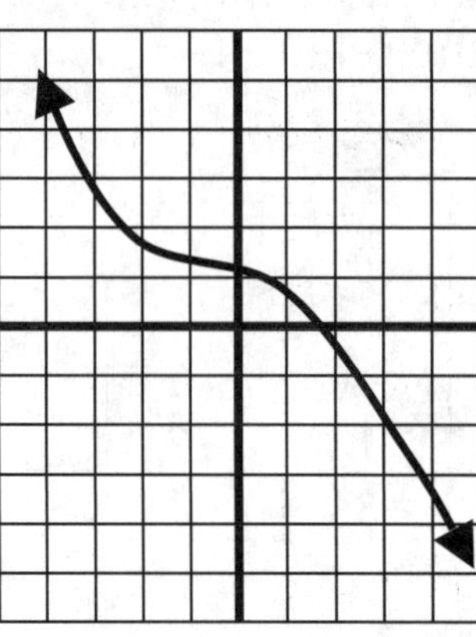

____

11.

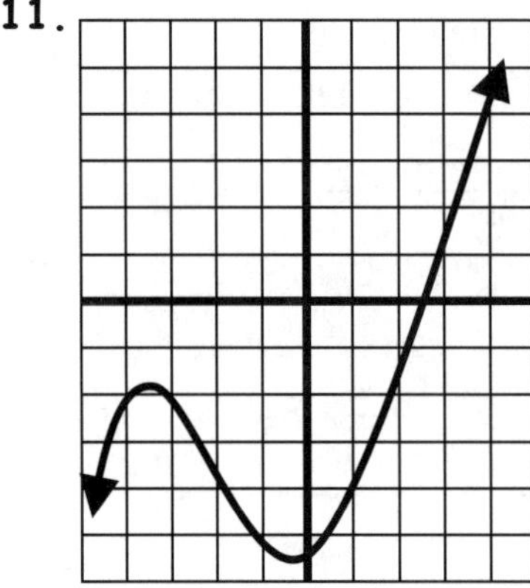

____

12.

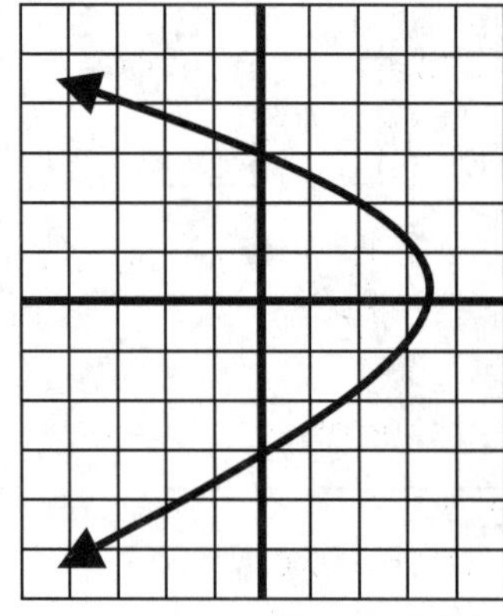

____

13.

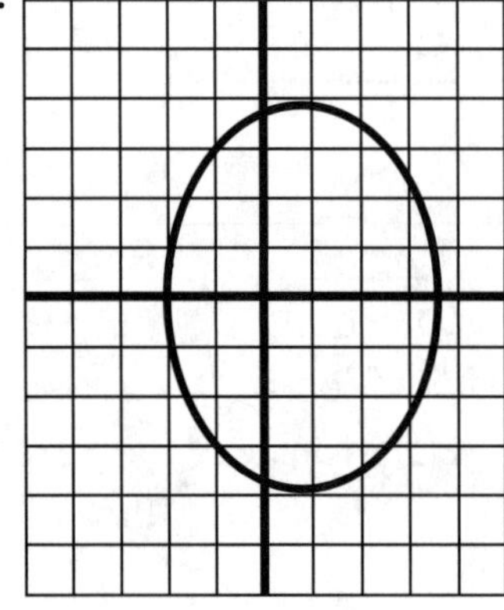

____

14.

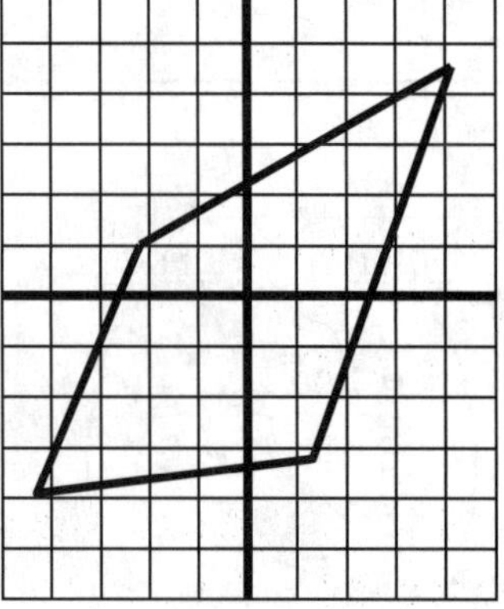

____

Name ______________________________

Graphing Mid-Unit Review

Directions: Solve. Show your work neatly on another sheet of paper.

1. Name the quadrant in which the point (−1, −3) is located.

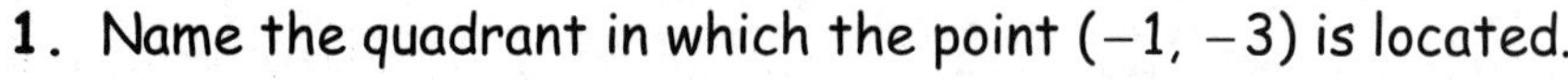

Directions: Use the graph to answer questions 2–4.

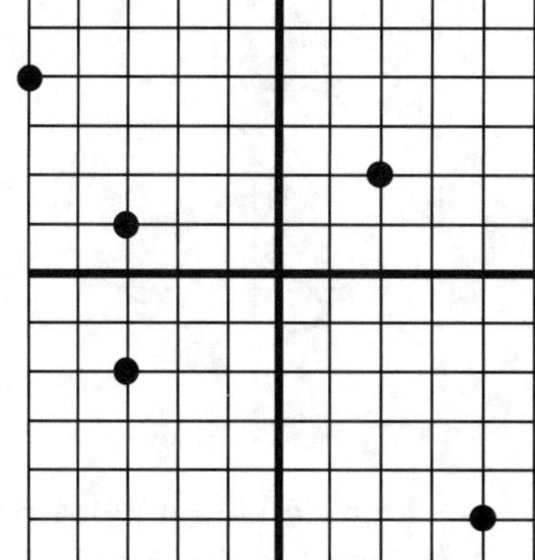

2. State the relation shown in the graph.

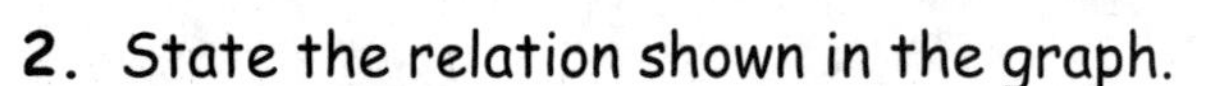

3. What is the domain of the relation shown in the graph?

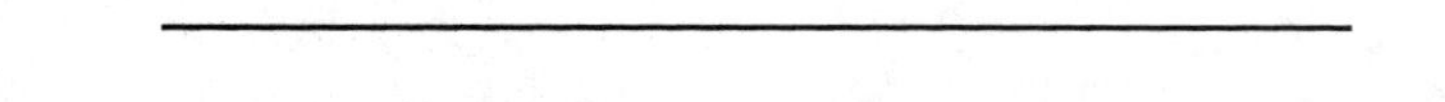

4. What is the range of the relation shown in the graph?

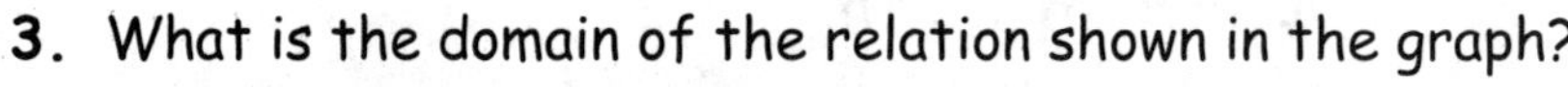

5. What are the domain and range of the relation shown in the table on the right?

x	y
2	3
4	5

A. D = {2, 3} R = {4, 5}   C. D = {2, 5} R = {3, 4}   5.______
B. D = {2, 4} R = {3, 5}   D. D = {3, 2} R = {5, 4}

6. What is the graph of the set of ordered pairs (c, 0), where "c" is any number?

A. the y−axis   C. the origin   6.______
B. the x−axis   D. cannot be determined

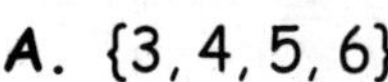

7. What is the domain of the relation shown in the mapping?

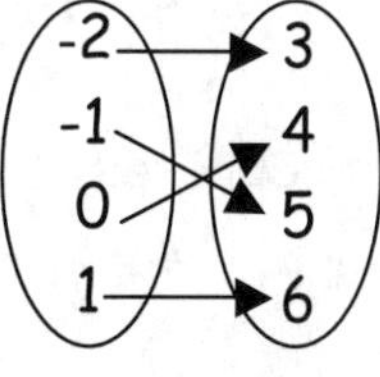

A. {3, 4, 5, 6}   C. {−2, 3, −1, 5}   7.______
B. {−2, −1, 0, 1}   D. {0, 4, 1, 6}

8. What is the range of the solution set of the equation 2c + 4d = 8 if the domain is {−2, 0, 2}?

A. {4, 6, 8}   B. {1, 2, 3}   C. {−1, −2, −3}   D. {0, 4, 8}   8.______

9. What is the domain of the solution set of the equation 3r − 6s = 6 when the range is { −3, 0, 3 }?

A. {−8, −2, 4}   B. $\{-\frac{5}{2}, -1, \frac{1}{2}\}$ C. {−4, 2, 8}   D. {−3, 0, 3}   9.______

Graphing Mid-Unit Review *(cont.)*

10. Which equation is a linear equation? 10.____

A. $y = x^3$ **B.** $y = \frac{1}{x}$ **C.** $y = 2x + 3$ **D.** $x^2 + y^2 = 9$

11. Determine which relation is a function. 11.____

A.

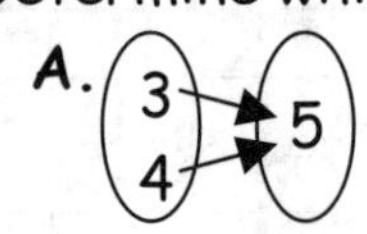

B.

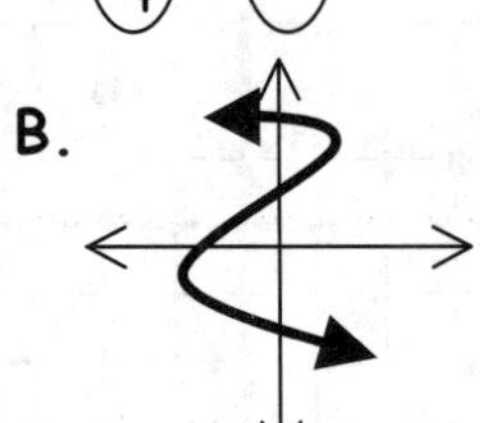

C.

x	y
6	5
7	5
7	6

D. {(2, 3) (2, 6)}

12. Determine which relation is a function.

A. {(2, 5) (3, 5) (6, 5)} **C.** {(1, 7) (2, 8) (1, 9)} 12.____

B. {(2, 3) (2, 6) (2, 8)} **D.**

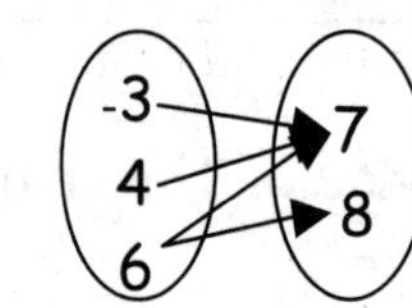

13. If $f(x) = 3x - 2$, what is the value of $f(-2)$?

A. 0 **B.** 4 **C.** –8 **D.** 8 13.____

14. If $g(x) = 2x^2 - 3x$, what is the value of $g(-1)$?

A. 1 **B.** 5 **C.** –7 **D.** 7 14.____

15. Which equation represents the function? 15.____

A. $y = x + 6$ **C.** $y = 2x - 4$

B. $y = 2x + 4$ **D.** $y = 3x + 4$

x	1	3	5	7	9
y	6	10	14	18	22

16. Which equation represents the function? 16.____

A. $y = -5x + 2$ **C.** $y = 4x - 1$

B. $y = 3x - 2$ **D.** $y = -3x + 2$

x	–4	–1	0	2	3
y	14	5	2	–4	–7

17. Which equation represents the function? 17.____

A. $y = \frac{1}{3}x - 2$ **C.** $y = 3x + 2$

B. $y = 3x - 2$ **D.** $y = -\frac{1}{3}x - 2$

x	0	3	6	9	12
y	–2	–3	–4	–5	–6

Name ______________________________

Measurement Review (Mid-Unit Graphing)

Directions: Solve the following problems.

1. Find the volume of the following shape.

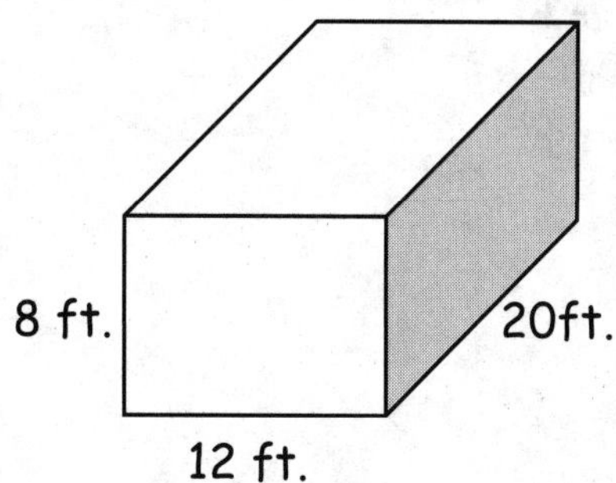

Volume = ____________________

2. Find the volume of the following shape.

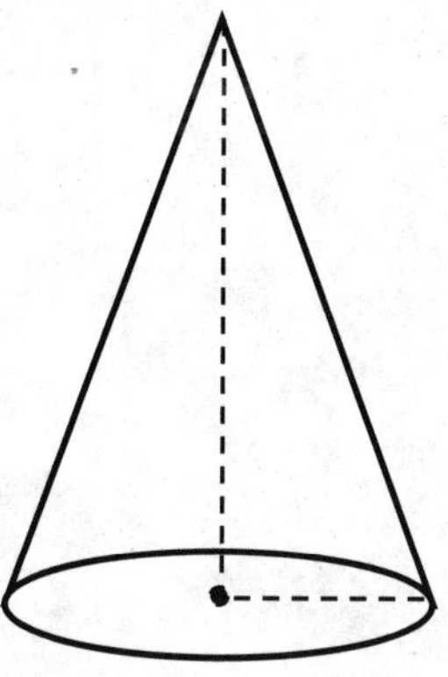

Height is 12 in.
Diameter is 18 in.

Volume = ____________________

3. Find the area of the following shape.

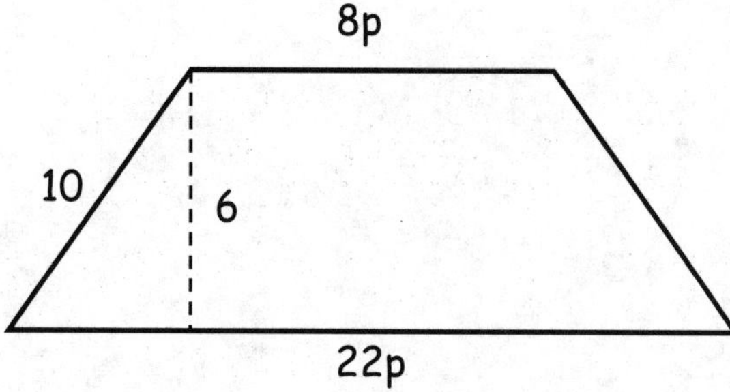

Area = ____________________

Measurement Review (Mid-Unit Graphing) *(cont.)*

4. Which formula can be used to find the volume of the following composite solid?

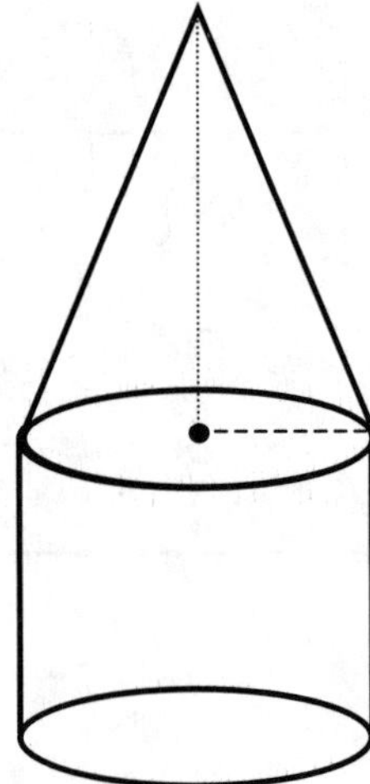

A. $V = \pi r^2 h - \frac{1}{3}\pi r^2 h$

B. $V = \pi r^2 h + \frac{1}{3}\pi r^2 h$

C. $V = \frac{1}{3}\pi r^2 h$

D. $V = \pi r^2 h$

5. Reginald made a stand out of cinder block for his science project, like the one shown below. Find the volume, in cubic inches, of the cinder block. Exclude the volume of the holes.

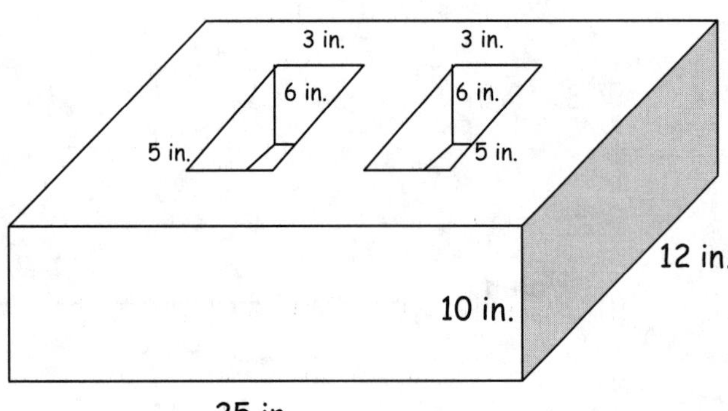

Volume = ______________________

6. Find the surface area of the following net of a rectangular prism.

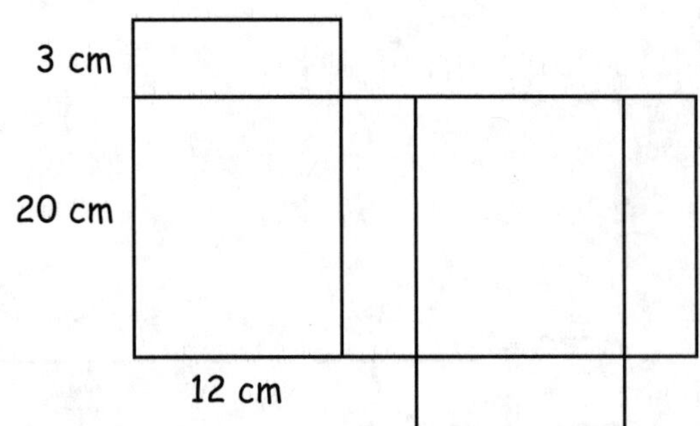

Surface Area = ______________________

Measurement Review (Mid-Unit Graphing) *(cont.)*

7. Find the missing measure. (Do not use 3.14 for π.)

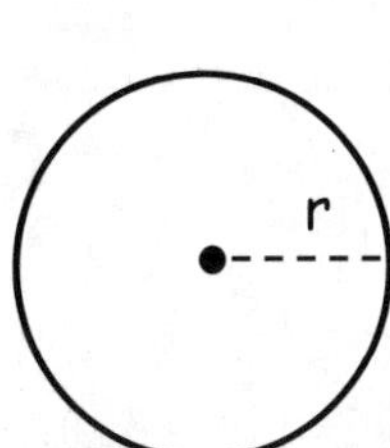

Area is 169π cm^2.
Find the radius.

Radius = ____________________

8. Find the surface area of the following net of a cylinder.

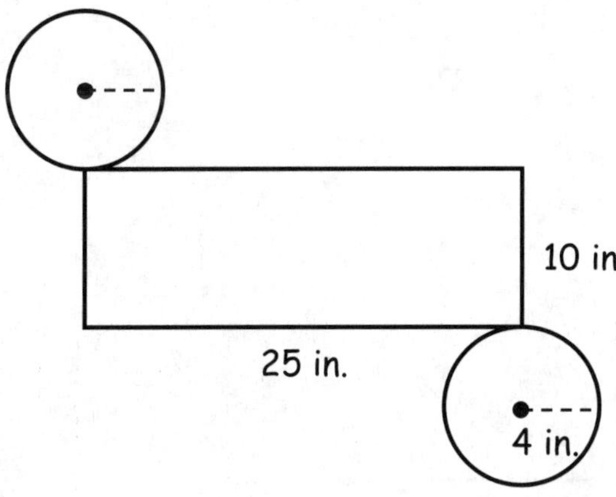

Surface Area = __________________

9. A cylindrical can of cleaner has a volume of 620 fluid ounces. A second cylindrical can has dimensions that are $\frac{2}{3}$ the size of the larger can. Which is the closest to the volume of the smaller can?

A. V = 425 fl. oz.

B. V = 275 fl. oz.

C. V = 300 fl. oz.

D. V = 184 fl. oz.

Measurement Review (Mid-Unit Graphing) *(cont.)*

10. A manufacturing company sells two products that are shipped in cartons shaped like rectangular prisms.

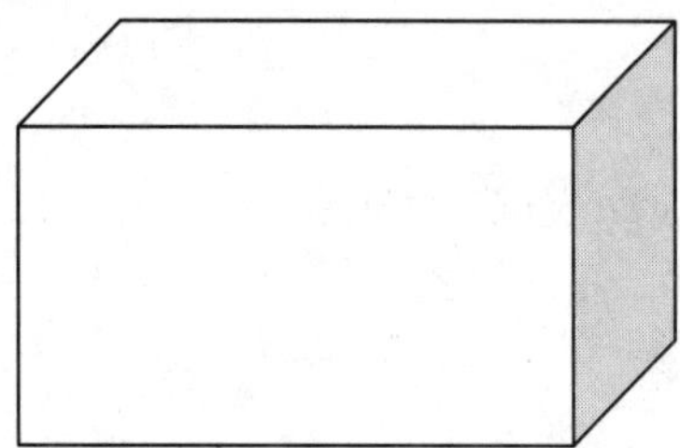

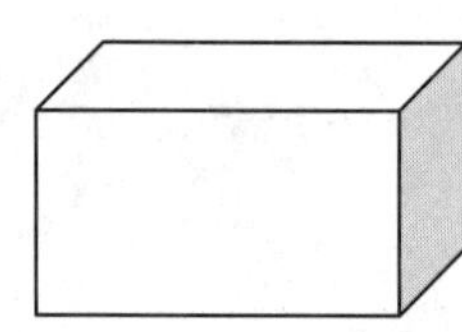

The larger carton has a volume of 1,200 cubic inches. The smaller carton has dimensions that are one-third the size of the large carton. What is the volume, in cubic inches, of the smaller carton? (Round to the nearest cubic inch.)

Volume = ______________________________

Name ______________________________

Adding Integers (for Slope)

Directions: Solve.

1. $-1 + -6 =$ ________
2. $-4 - 1 =$ ________
3. $4 - (-2) =$ ________
4. $4 - 6 =$ ________
5. $2 - (-1) =$ ________
6. $3 + 2 =$ ________
7. $4 - (-1) =$ ________
8. $-3 + -2 =$ ________
9. $-4 - 1 =$ ________
10. $-1 - 1 =$ ________
11. $-2 + 3 =$ ________
12. $-4 - (-2) =$ ________
13. $-2 - 3 =$ ________
14. $6 - 5 =$ ________
15. $3 - 4 =$ ________
16. $-2 - 2 =$ ________
17. $-5 - 1 =$ ________
18. $1 - 3 =$ ________
19. $2 - 2 =$ ________
20. $3 - 1 =$ ________
21. $1 - (-3) =$ ________
22. $-2 - (-4) =$ ________
23. $-3 + 5 =$ ________
24. $6 - (-2) =$ ________
25. $5 - 6 =$ ________
26. $3 - 4 =$ ________
27. $-3 - 4 =$ ________
28. $-1 + -4 =$ ________
29. $-3 - (-5) =$ ________
30. $-3 + 6 =$ ________
31. $-6 - (-9) =$ ________
32. $0 - (-8) =$ ________
33. $3 - (-2) =$ ________
34. $-7 - (-8) =$ ________

Name ______________________________

Slope 1

Directions: Write each ordered pair, and count the slope.

1.

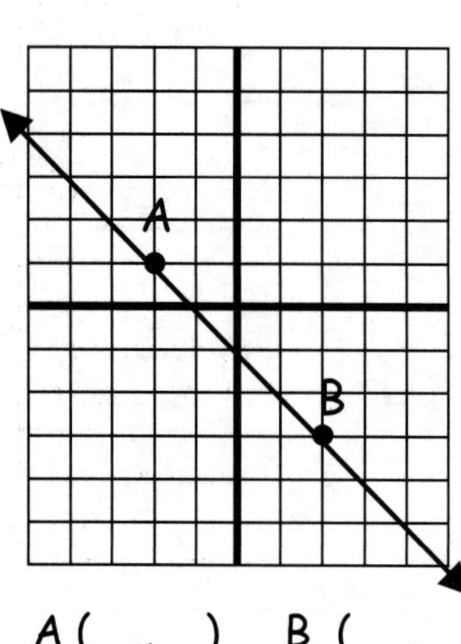

A(,) B (,)

m = ______

2.

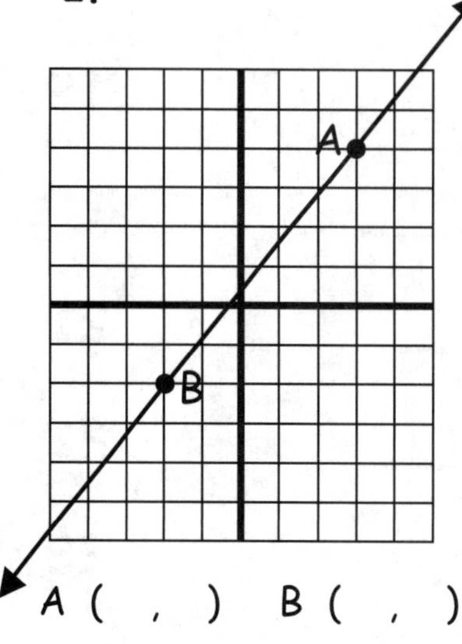

A (,) B (,)

m = ______

3.

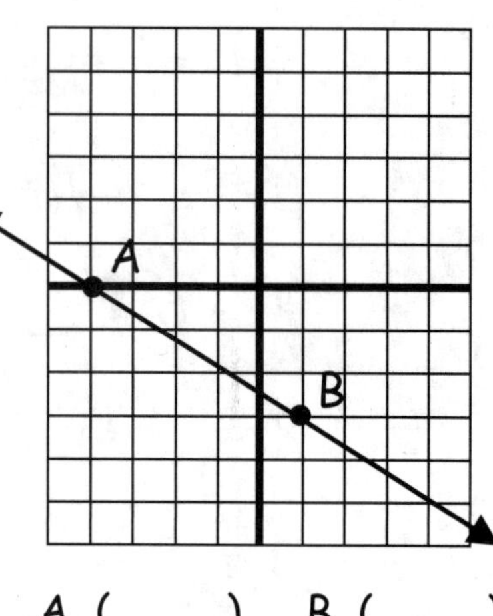

A (,) B (,)

m = ______

Directions: Choose two points, and count each slope.

4.

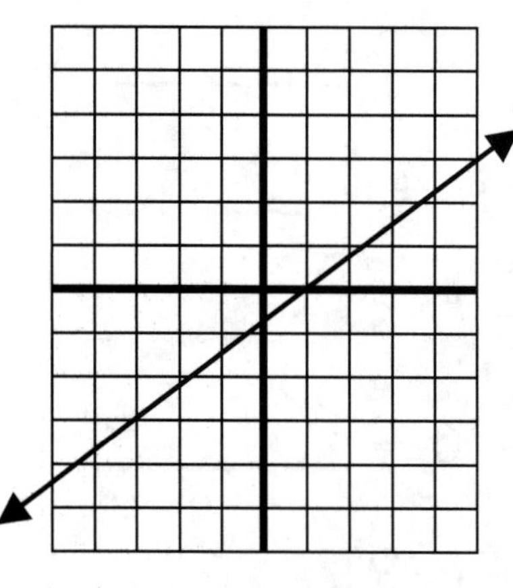

m = ______

5.

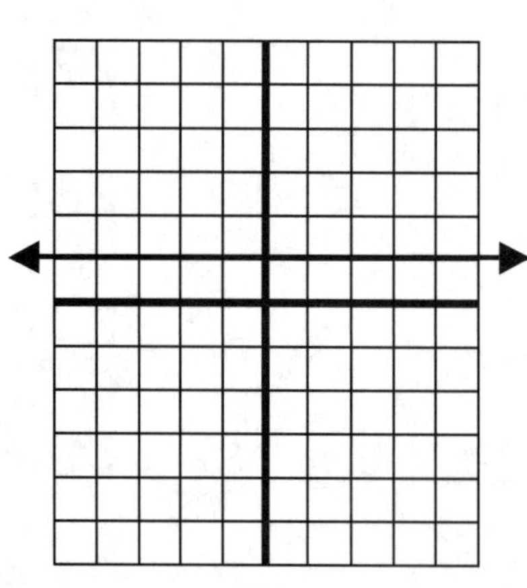

m = ______

6.

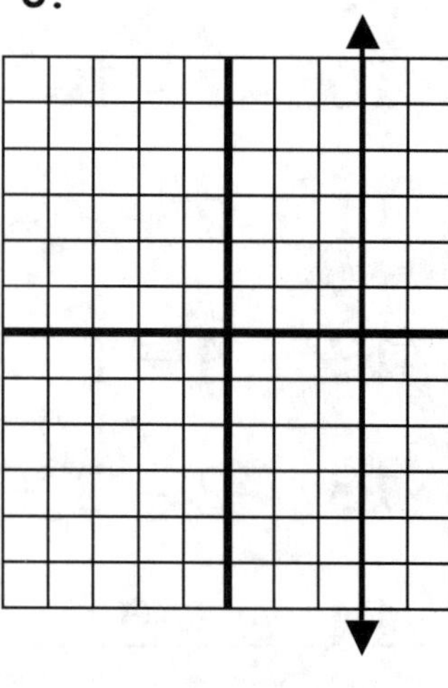

m = ______

Slope 1 *(cont.)*

Directions: Choose two points, and count each slope.

7.

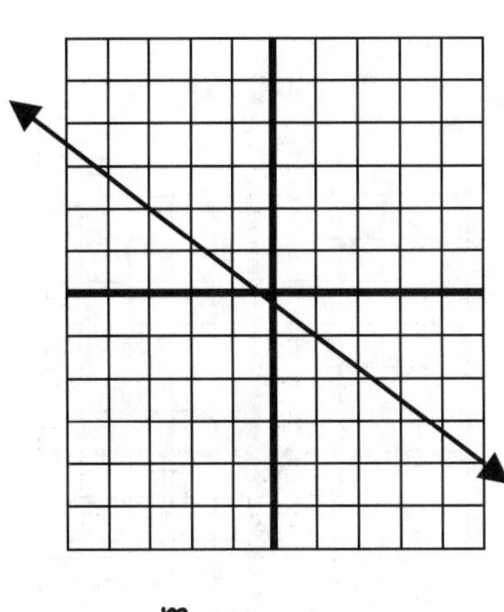

m = _______

8.

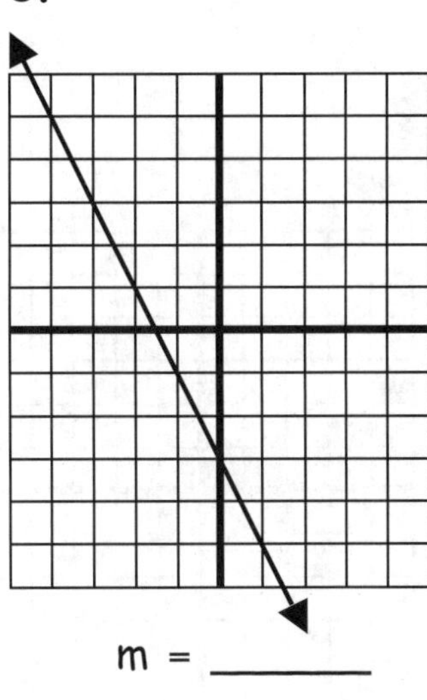

m = _______

9.

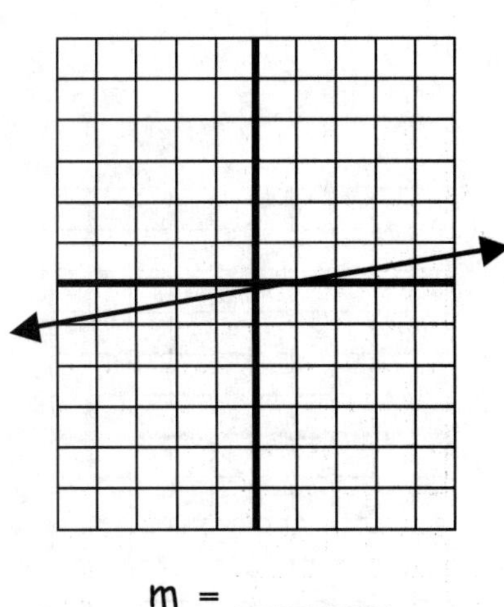

m = _______

Directions: Find each slope using the slope formula. $\left(m = \frac{y_2 - y_1}{x_2 - x_1} \right)$

(x_1, y_1) (x_2, y_2)

10. (3, 5) (0, 1)

11. (4, 5) (1, 3)

12. (4, 2) (0, 3)

Directions: Plot the points, draw each line, and find the slope. $\left(\frac{\text{rise}}{\text{run}} \right)$

13. A(3, 5) B(0, 1)

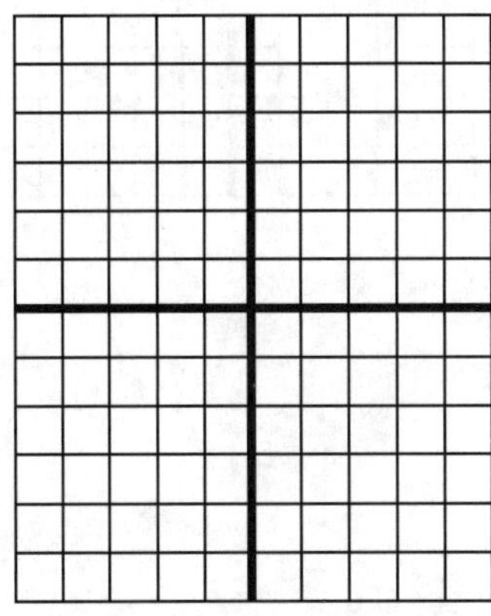

m = _______

14. A(4, 5) B(1, 3)

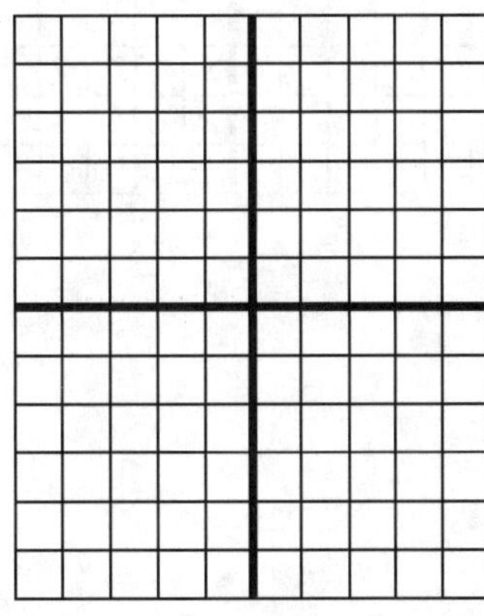

m = _______

15. A(4, 2) B(0, 3)

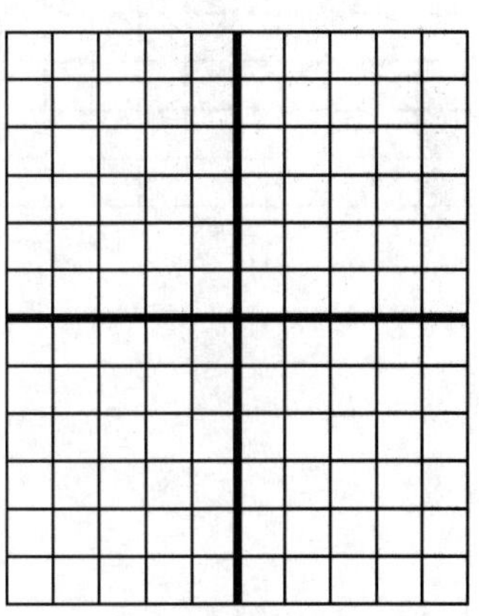

m = _______

Name ________________________________

Slope 2

Directions: Count each slope from the given point.

1. $m = -\frac{2}{3}$

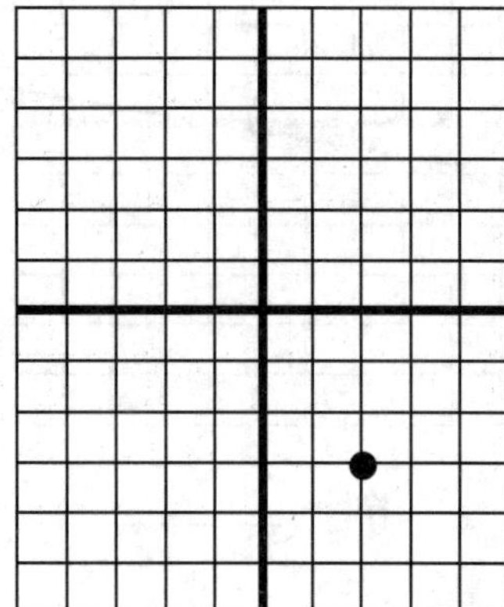

2. $m = -\frac{1}{2}$

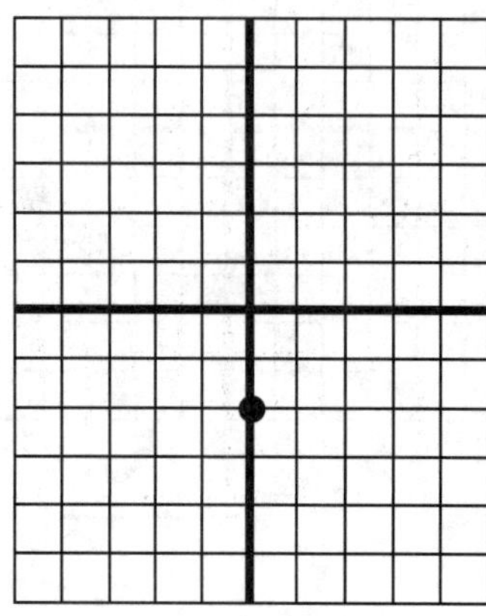

3. $m = 5$

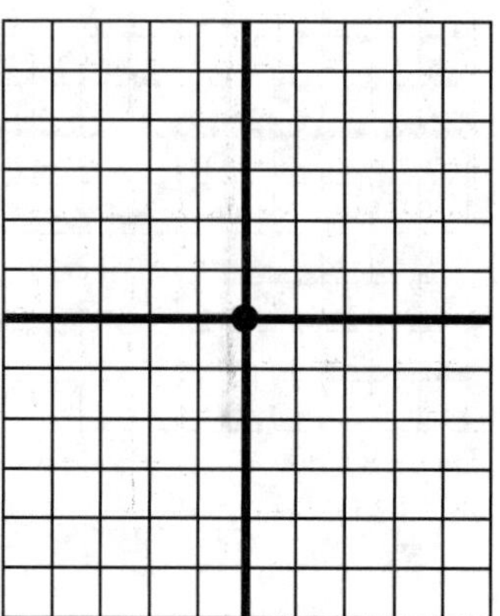

4. $m = -3$

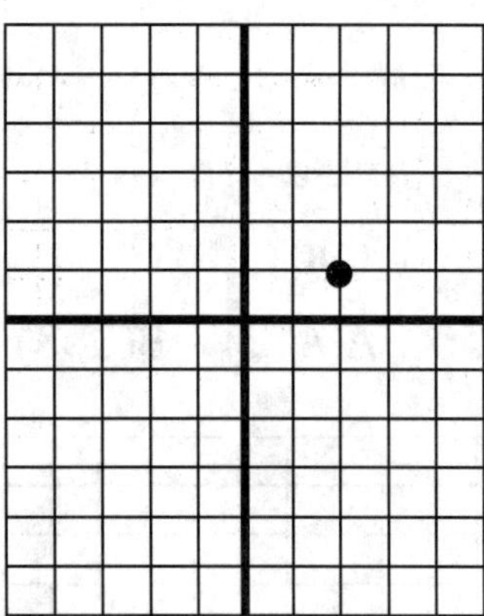

5. $m = \frac{1}{4}$

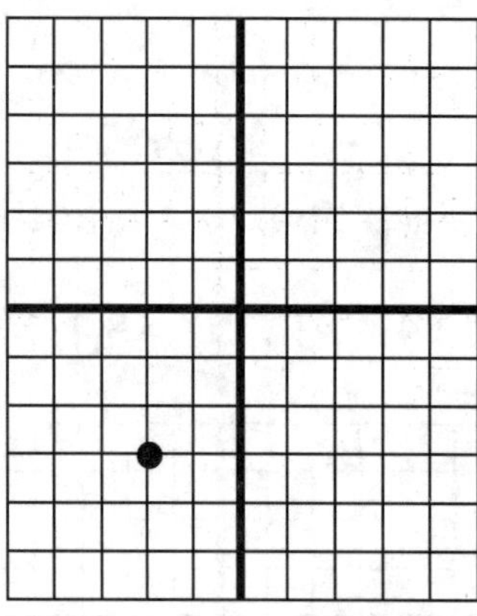

6. $m = -\frac{1}{3}$

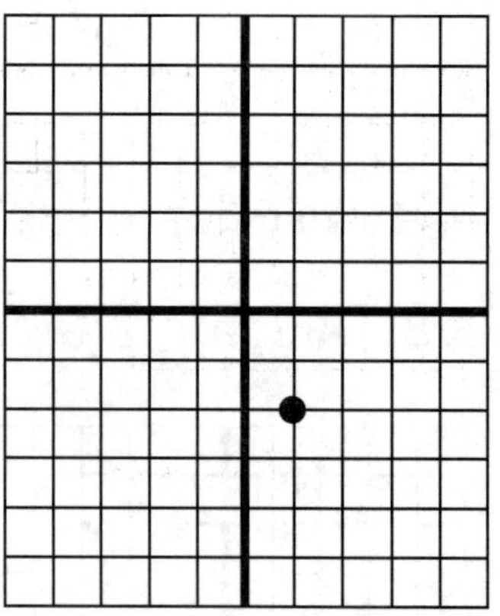

Slope 2 *(cont.)*

Directions: Plot the points, draw each line, and count each slope.

7. (0, 2) m = 3

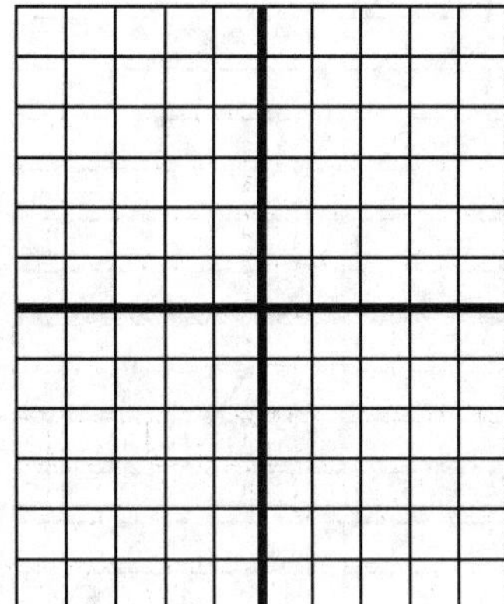

8. (−1, 3) $m = \frac{2}{3}$

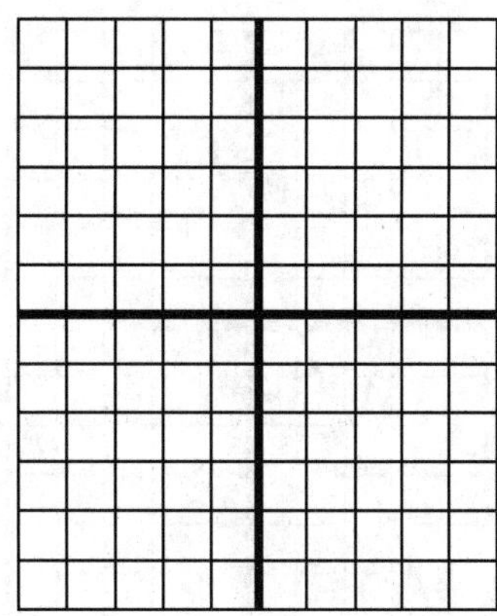

9. (2, 3) m = −2

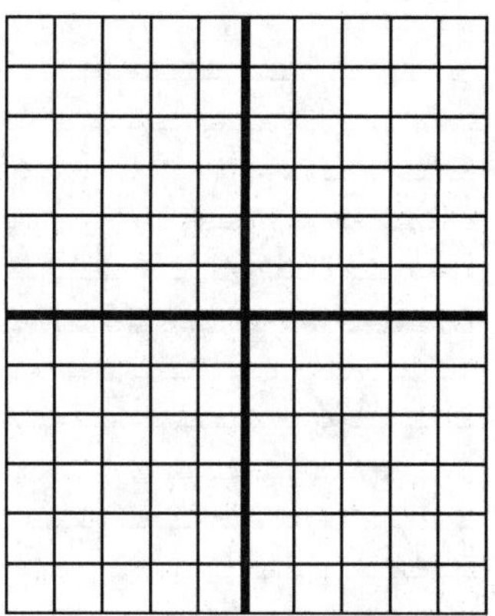

10. (3, 5) (4, 5)

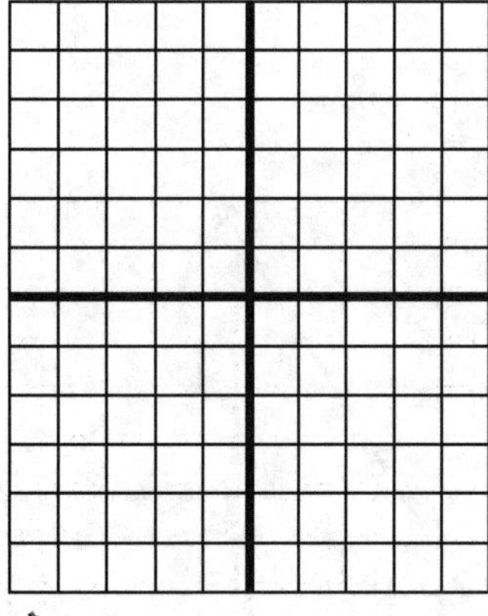

m = ______

11. (3, 1) (3, 2)

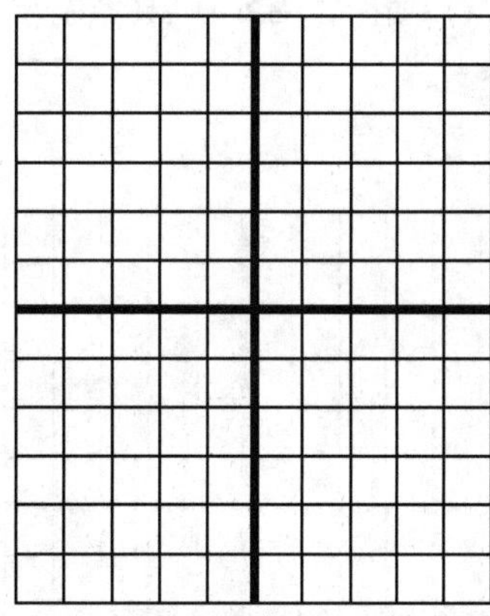

m = ______

12. (2, −1) (−1, −1)

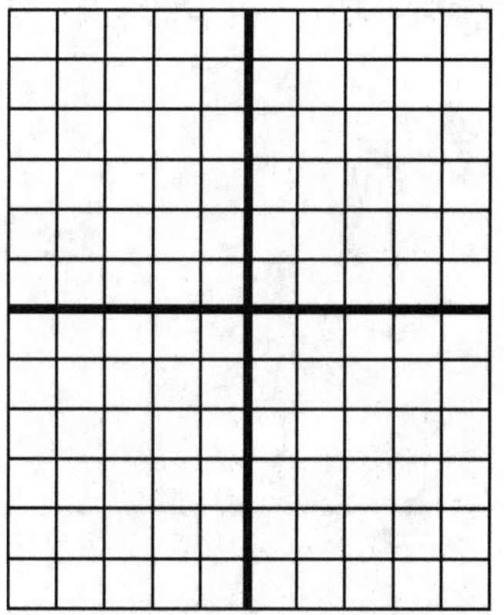

m = ______

Directions: Find each slope using the slope formula. $\left(m = \frac{y_2 - y_1}{x_2 - x_1}\right)$

13. (x_1, y_1) (x_2, y_2)
(−6, 4) (3, −1)

14. (2, 3) (2, 6)

15. (2, 3) (4, −6)

Name ______________________________

Slope 3

Directions: Find each ordered pair, and count the slope.

1.

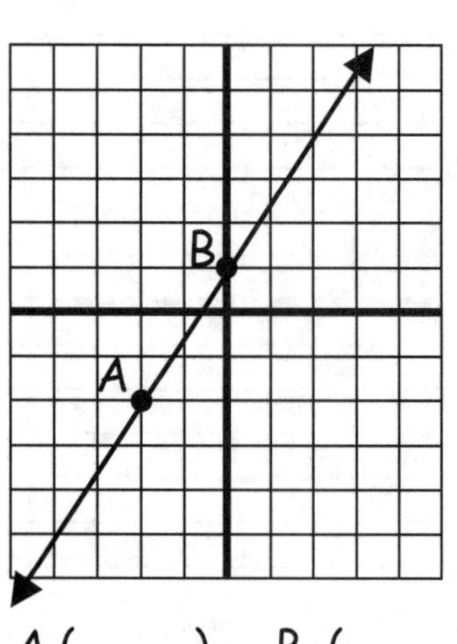

A(,) B(,)

m = ______

2.

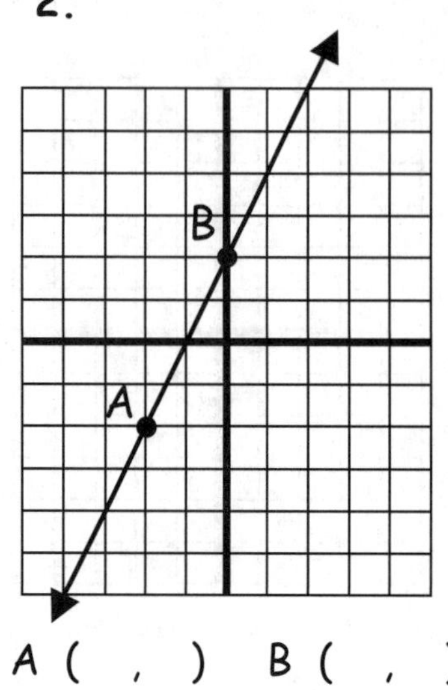

A(,) B(,)

m = ______

3.

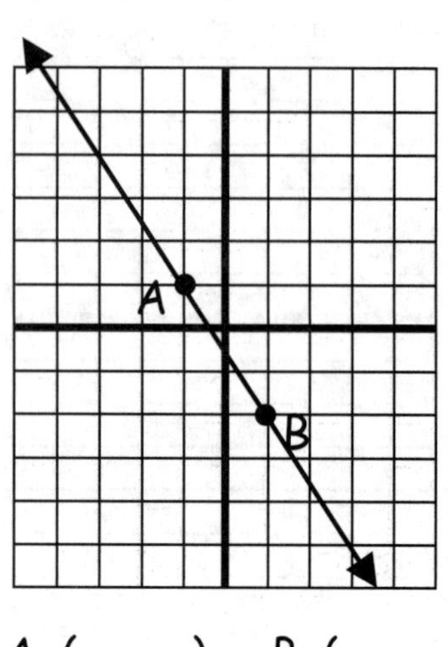

A(,) B(,)

m = ______

Directions: Choose two points, and count each slope.

4.

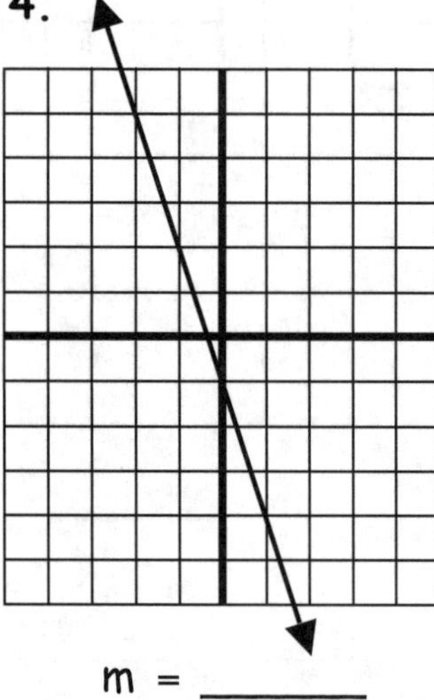

m = ______

5.

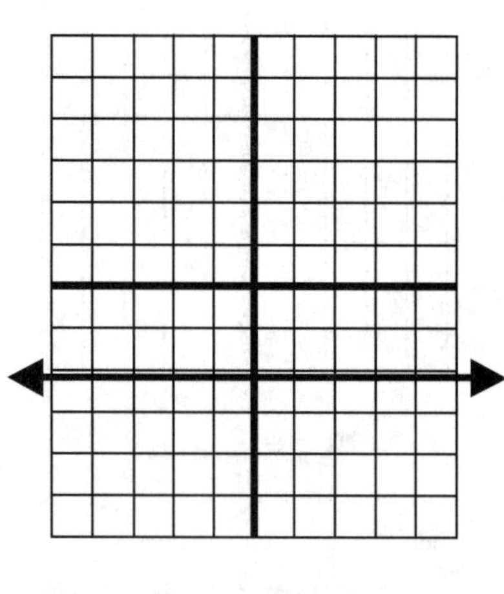

m = ______

6.

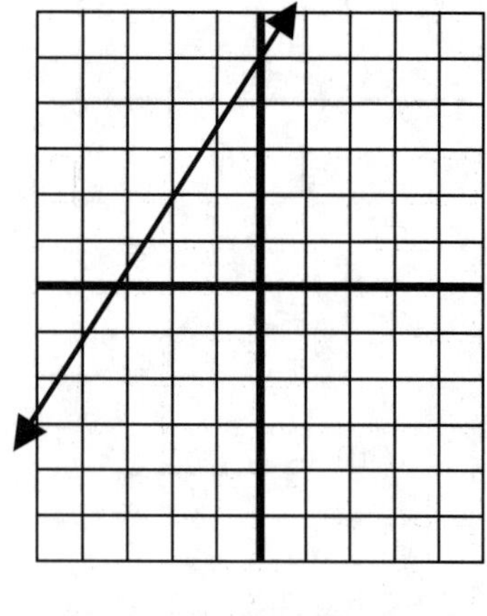

m = ______

Directions: Find each slope using the slope formula. Show your work on another sheet of paper.

$$m = \frac{y_2 - y_1}{x_2 - x_1}$$

(x_1, y_1) (x_2, y_2)

7. (3, 5) (2, 5)

8. (−4, 5) (−3, 2)

9. (4, 2) (4, 6)

Slope 3 *(cont.)*

Directions: Plot the points, draw each line, and find each slope. $\left(\frac{\text{rise}}{\text{run}}\right)$

10. A(3, 4) B(−2, 3)

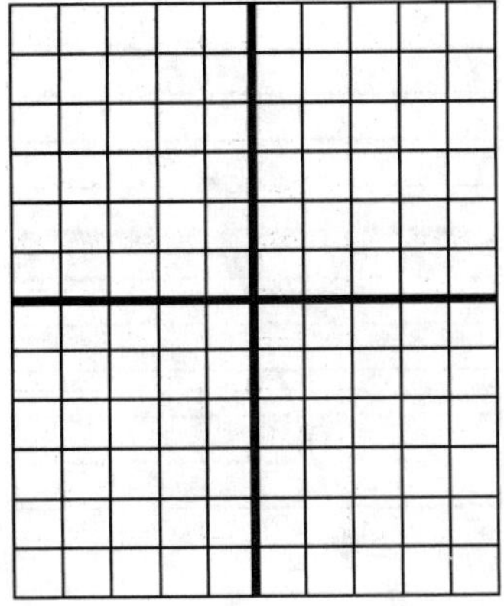

m = ________

11. A(−3, 5) B(0, 2)

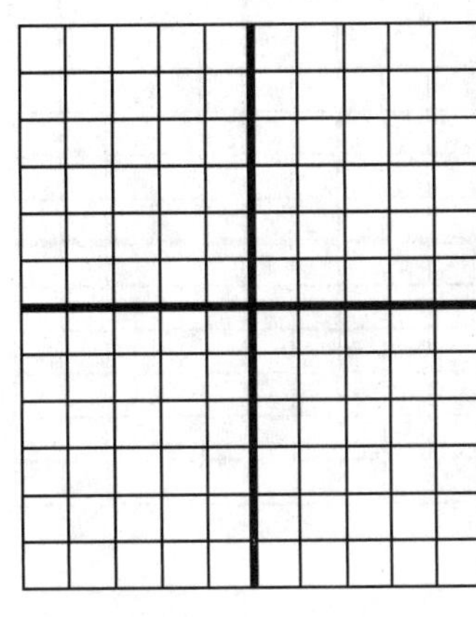

m = ________

12. A(3, 2) B(−1, 5)

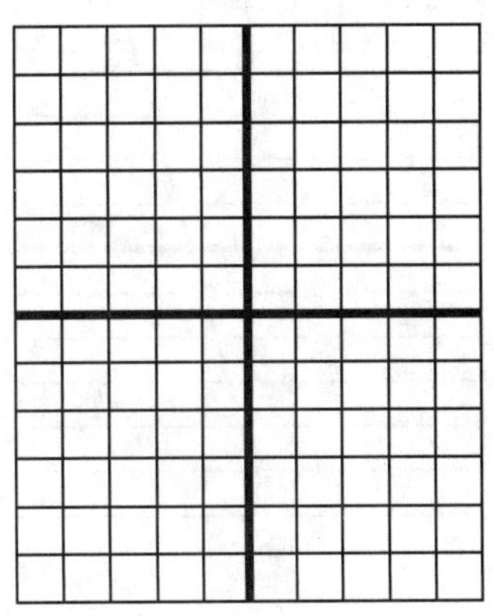

m = ________

13. A(5, 0) B(5, −3)

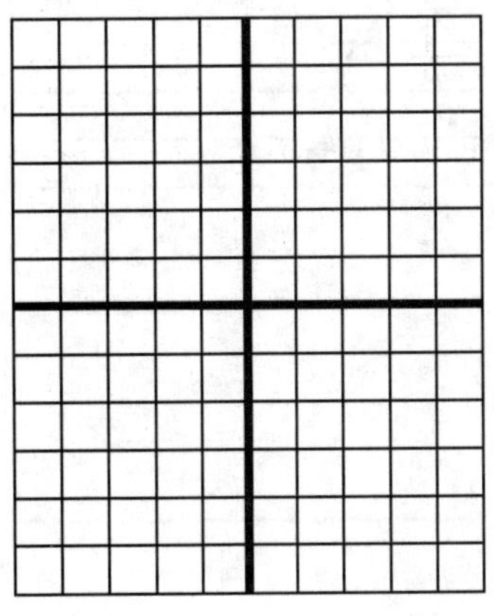

m = ________

14. A(−3, 2) B(−2, 3)

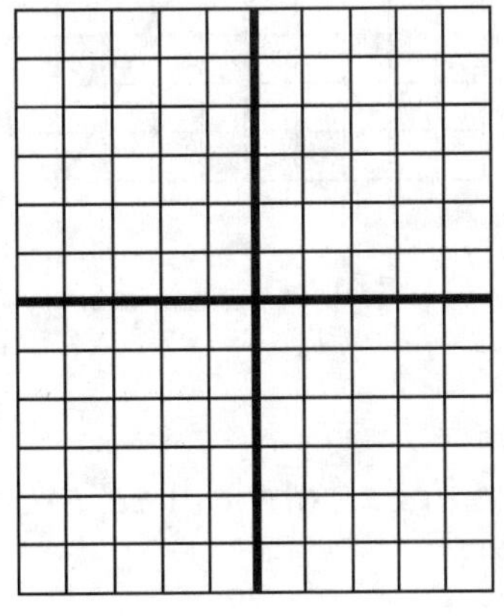

m = ________

15. A(4, 4) B(−2, 4)

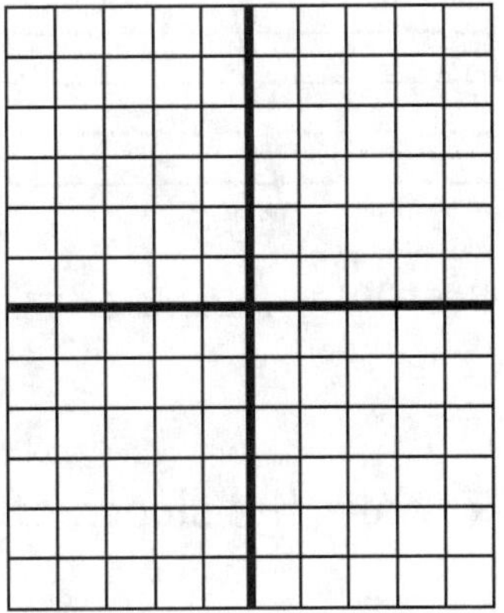

m = ________

Name ______________________________

Slope 4

Directions: Count each slope.

1.

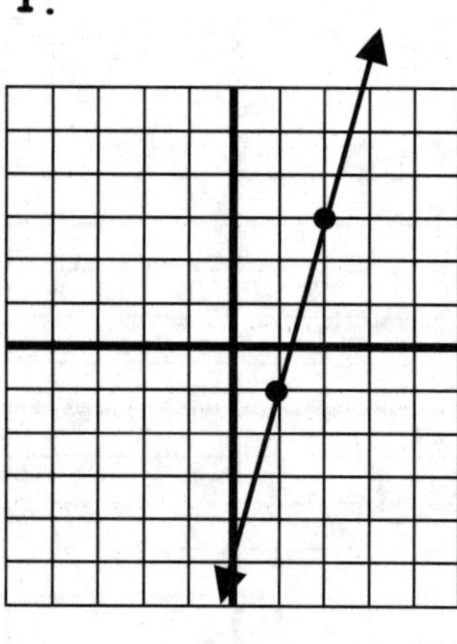

m = ______

2.

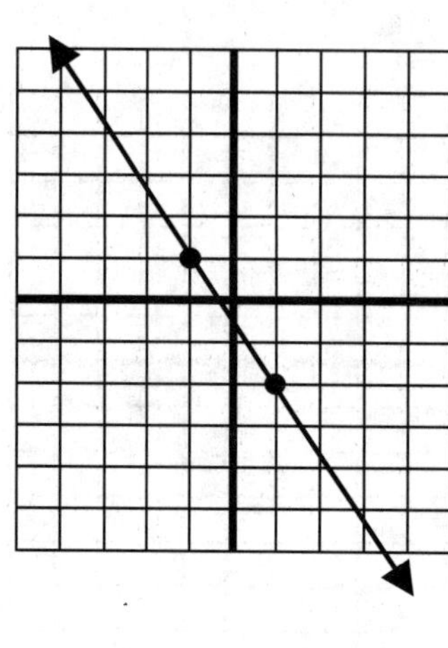

m = ______

3.

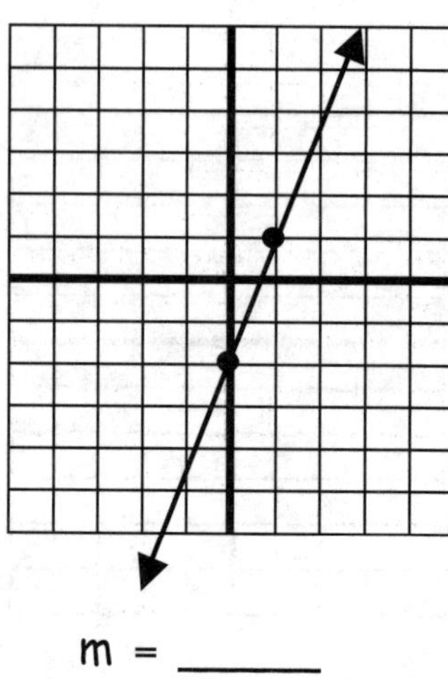

m = ______

4.

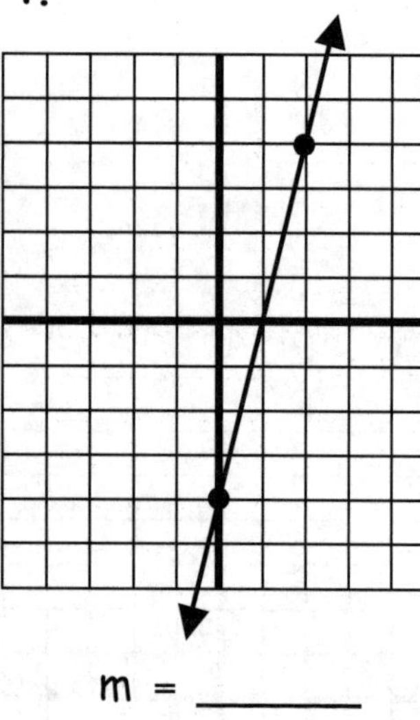

m = ______

5.

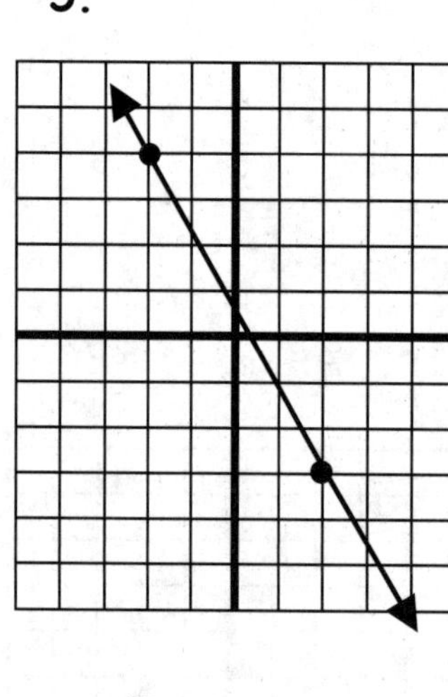

m = ______

6.

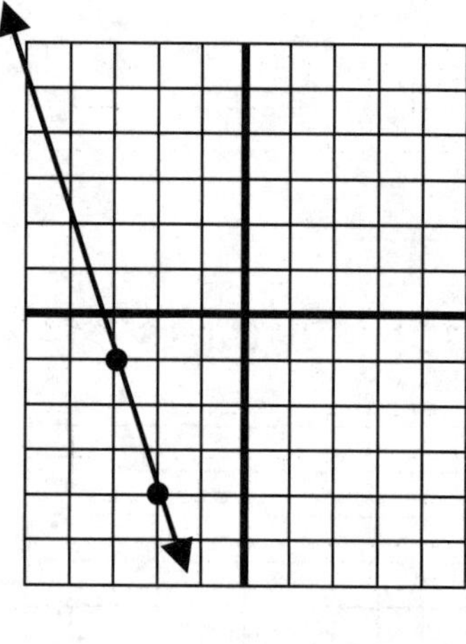

m = ______

7. Are the slopes of the above lines considered steep or flat?______________

8. Why do the lines in #2, #5, and #6 slant to the left?______________

9. Why do the lines in #1, #3, and #4 slant to the right?______________

Slope 4 *(cont.)*

Directions: Count each slope.

10.

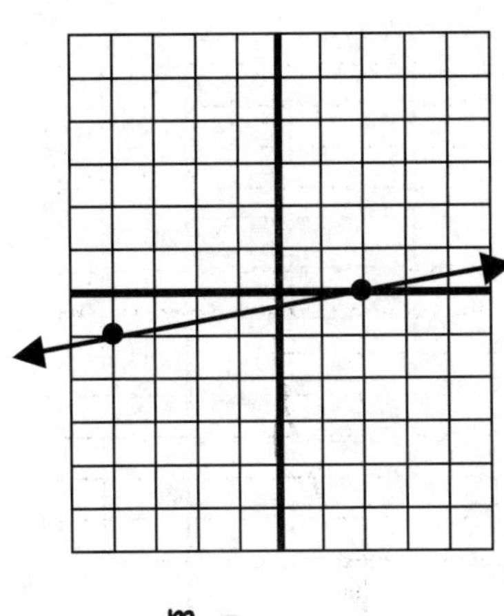

m = ______

11.

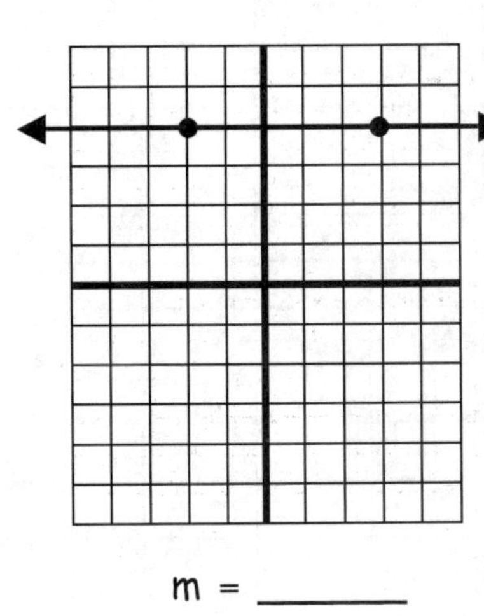

m = ______

12.

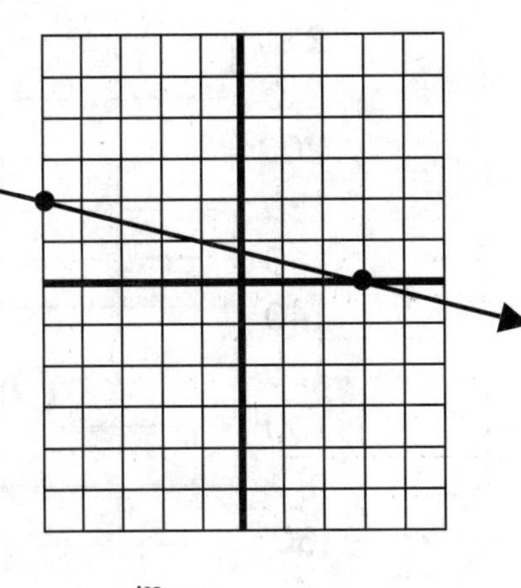

m = ______

13.

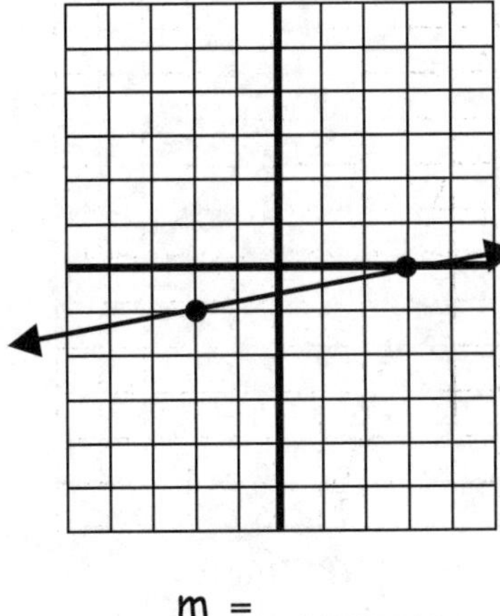

m = ______

14.

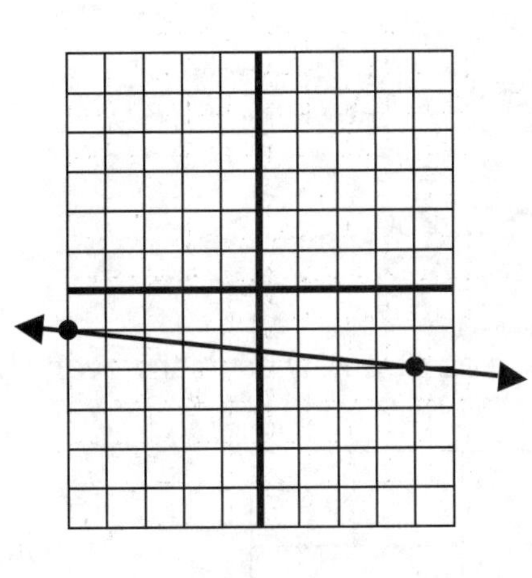

m = ______

15.

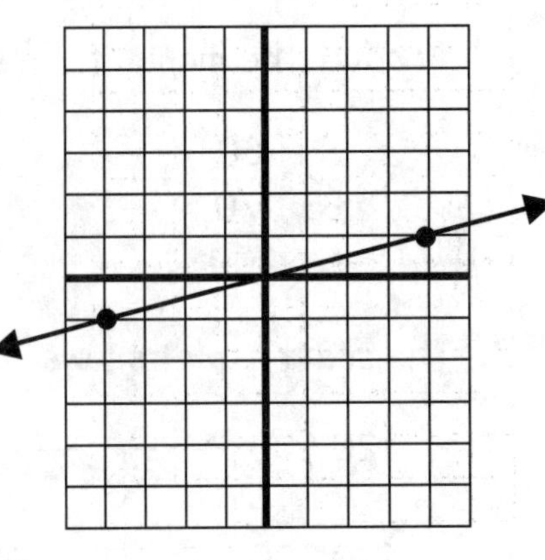

m = ______

16. Are the slopes of the above lines considered steep or flat? ______________

17. What characteristic of the slope makes a line steep or flat?

____

Name ______________________________

Scatter Plots Packet

1. The graph below shows the sale of CDs in millions 1996 – 2005.

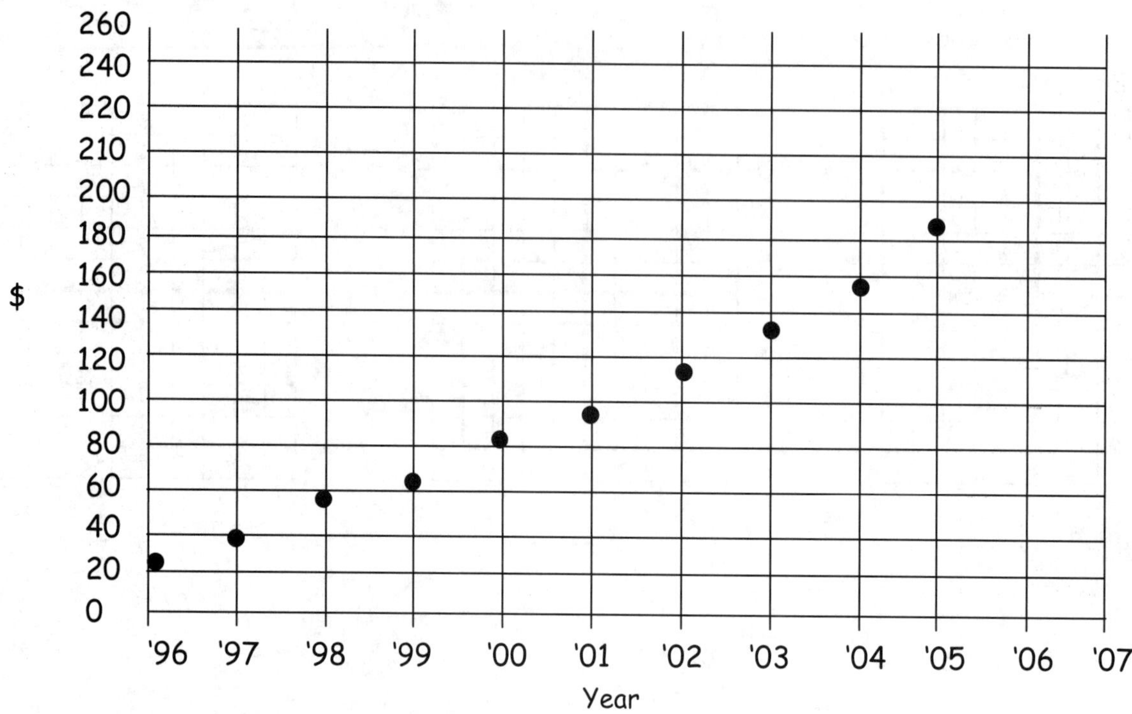

Predict the money from sales of CDs for 2007.

A. 160
B. 170
C. 200
D. 240
E. 260

2. The scatter plot shows the sales at a new company over the last few years.

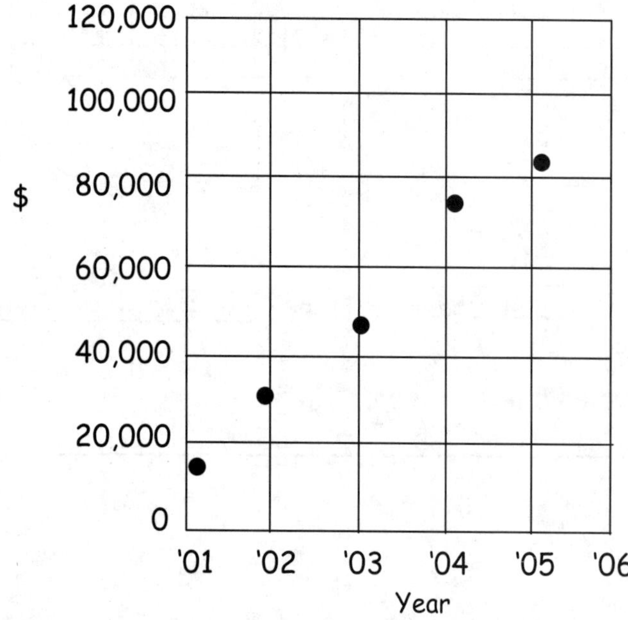

Which is the best estimate for the expected sales for 2006?

A. 120,000
B. 90,000
C. 80,000
D. 125,000
E. 100,000

Scatter Plots Packet *(cont.)*

3. The graph below shows the percentage of female police officers in the United States for 1980–2000.

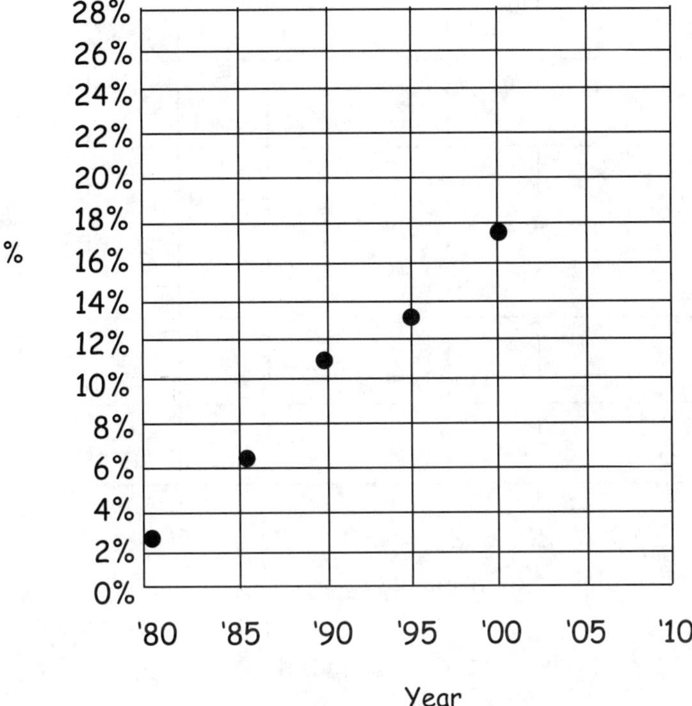

Predict the percentage of female police officers in the year 2010.

A. 18%
B. 25%
C. 29%
D. 20%
E. 30%

4. The scatter plot shows the year-to-date expenditures for teacher supplies at Warren High School.

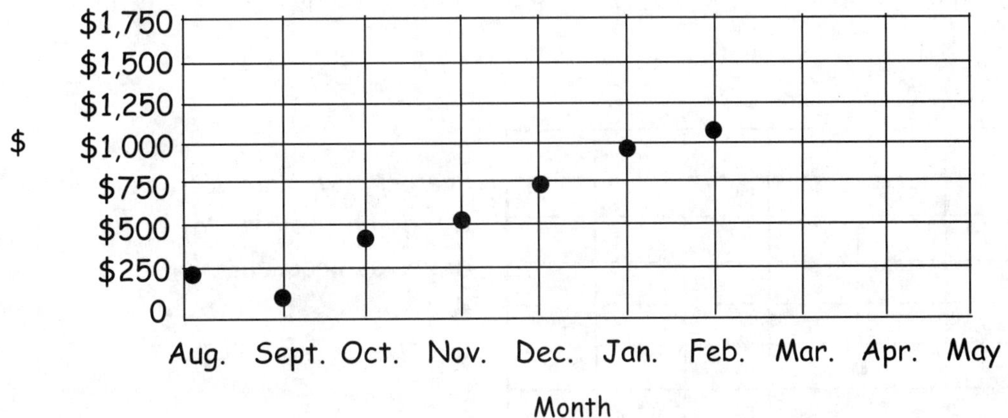

Predict the high school's end-of-year (May) total expenditures.

A. $1,850
B. $1,175
C. $2,000
D. $1,600
E. $1,000

Scatter Plots Packet *(cont.)*

5. LeBron is shooting free throws after school. The graph shows the total number of free throws he has made so far.

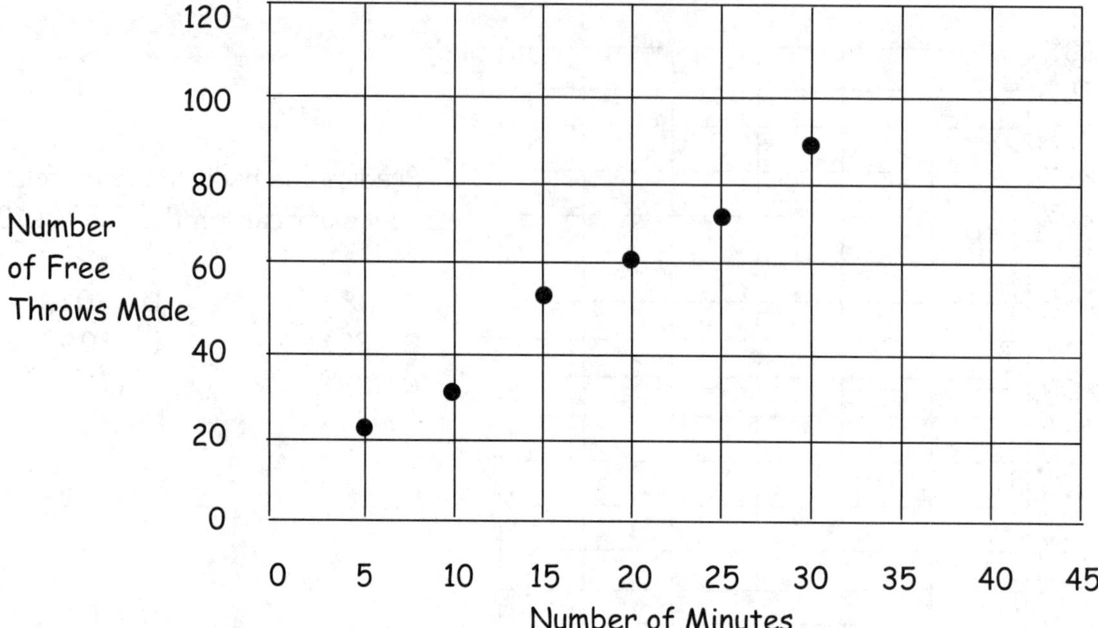

Predict the total number of free throws LeBron will make in 45 minutes.

A. 80
B. 90
C. 100
D. 110
E. 120

6. Carlos started an exercise program in January. He kept a record of how many sit-ups he did each day.

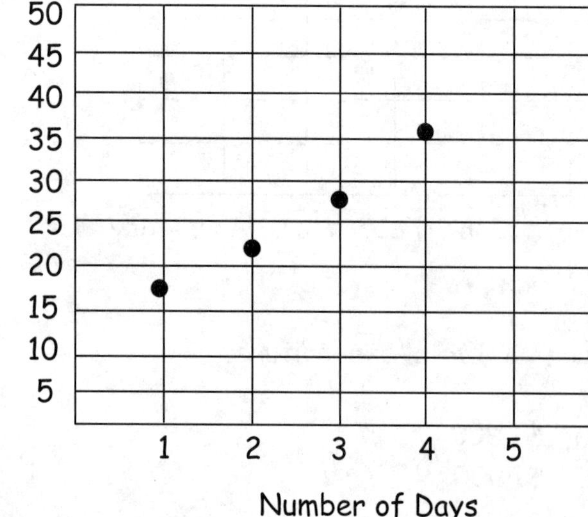

Predict how many sit-ups Carlos will do on the 6th day of his exercise program.

A. 35
B. 40
C. 50
D. 60
E. 70

Scatter Plots Packet *(cont.)*

7. The graph below shows the average selling price of vehicles from 2000 to 2004.

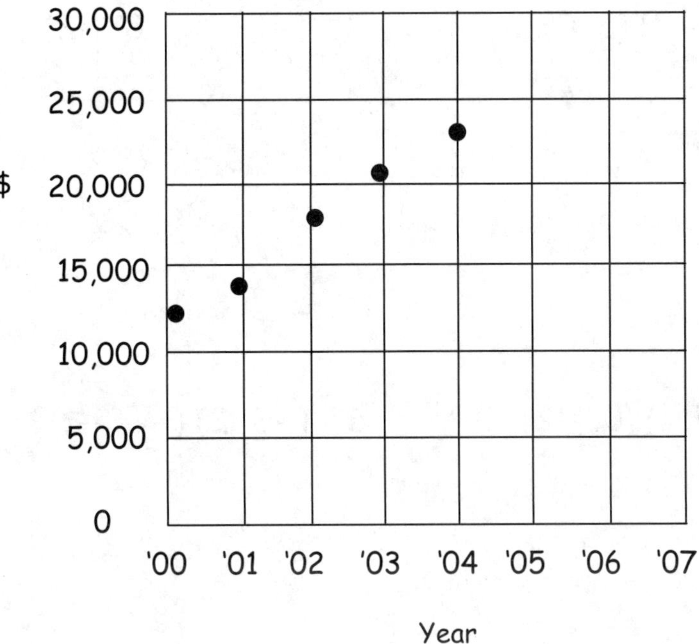

Based on this information, which is the best prediction for the average selling price for vehicles in 2007?

A. 23,000
B. 25,000
C. 32,000
D. 37,000
E. 40,000

8. Dona mows grass during the summer to earn money. The graph below shows the total number of lawns mowed so far.

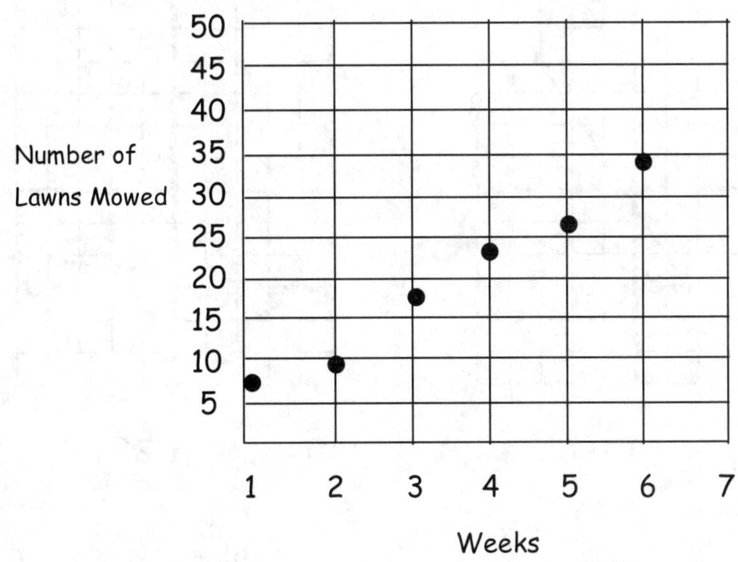

Using the information, predict the total number of lawns mowed by the end of the 7th week.

A. 32
B. 40
C. 47
D. 50
E. 55

Name ______________________________

Slope Review

Directions: Calculate each slope. When applicable, state if the slopes are undefined.

1. (–3, 5) (–2, 6)

2. (3, –2) (3, 0)

3. (–6, 4) (–8, –2)

4. (4, –3) (6, –3)

5. (–5, 1) (0, –2)

6. (–3, 2) (–6, –1)

Directions: Write each ordered pair, and count each slope.

7.

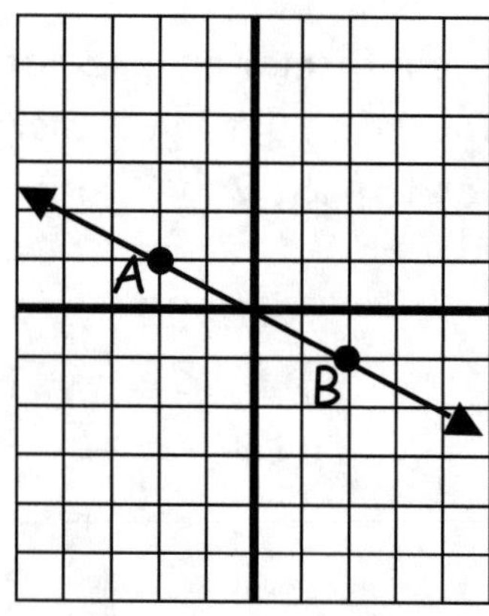

A(,) B(,)

m = ________

8.

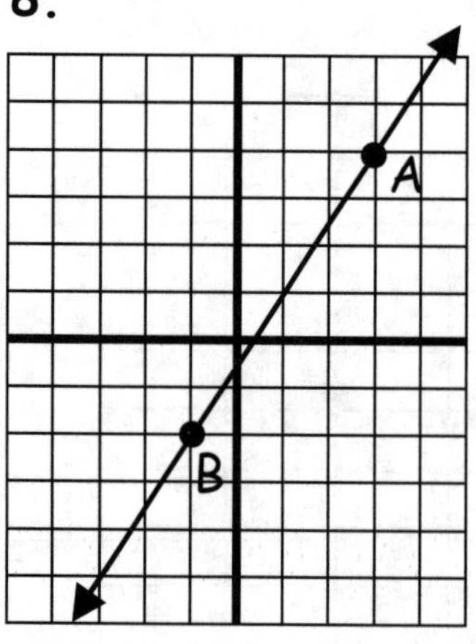

A(,) B(,)

m = ________

9.

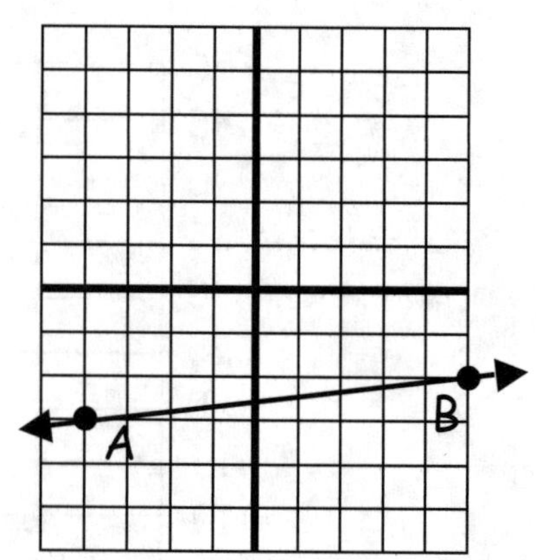

A(,) B(,)

m = ________

Slope Review *(cont.)*

Directions: Choose two points and count each slope.

10.

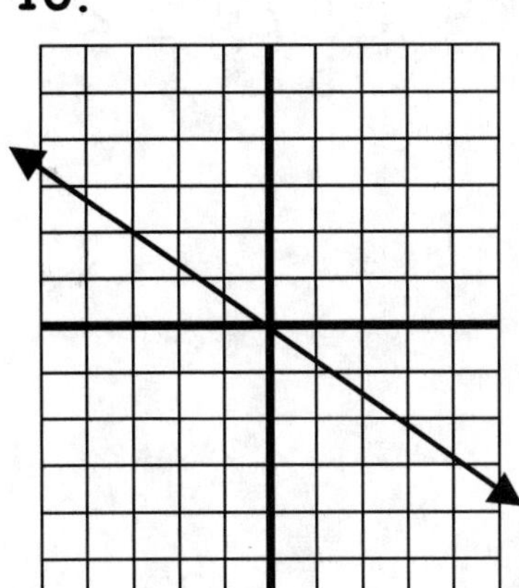

m = ________

11.

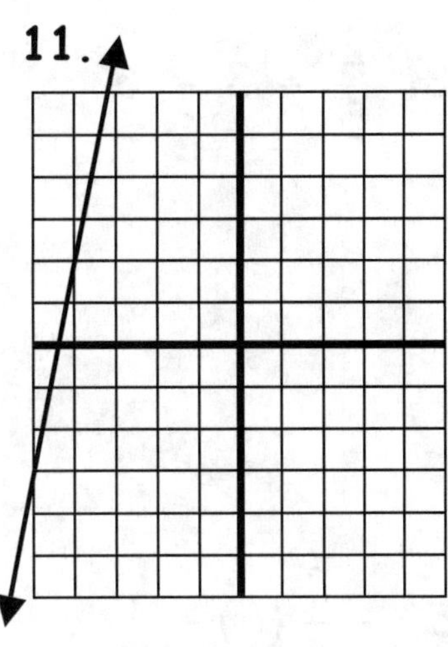

m = ________

12.

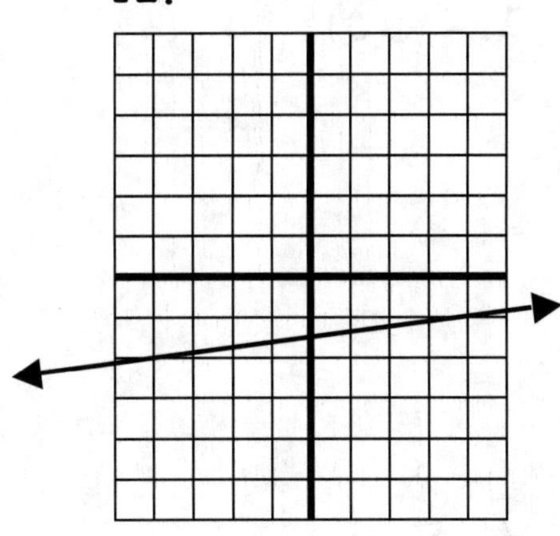

m = ________

Name ______________________________

Fractions Review

Directions: Solve.

1. $\frac{4}{3}(5) - 8$

2. $\frac{2}{5} \div 3 - 6$

3. $-\frac{2}{3}(4) + 6$

4. $5 \div \left(-\frac{1}{2}\right) + 3$

5. $-\frac{3}{2}(6) - 4$

6. $7 \div \left(-\frac{3}{2}\right) + 2$

7. $-\frac{3}{4}\left(\frac{1}{2}\right) - \frac{1}{3}$

8. $-\frac{3}{7}(2) + \frac{2}{7}$

9. $-\frac{1}{6}\left(\frac{4}{5}\right) + 3$

10. $-\frac{1}{5}\left(\frac{4}{3}\right) - 6$

11. $-3 \div \left(-\frac{4}{7}\right) + 2$

12. $\frac{1}{8}\left(-\frac{3}{2}\right) - 3$

Fractions Review *(cont.)*

13. $-6 \div \frac{1}{2} - 3$

14. $2\left(\frac{3}{2}\right) - 5$

15. $\frac{4}{5}\left(\frac{3}{8}\right) - \frac{5}{3}$

16. $-10 \div \frac{2}{3} - 7$

17. $-\frac{8}{9}\left(\frac{3}{4}\right) - 7$

18. $8 - \frac{1}{4}\left(\frac{2}{3}\right)$

19. $-6 - 3 \div \frac{1}{3}$

20. $-4\left(-\frac{1}{2}\right) + \frac{3}{4}$

Bonus: Solve.

$$\frac{\frac{3}{8}\left(\frac{2}{5}\right) - 3}{-\frac{1}{4}\left(\frac{7}{5}\right) - \frac{5}{2}}$$

Name ______________________________

Graphing 1

Directions: Find the *y*-intercept, slope, and equation of each line.

1.

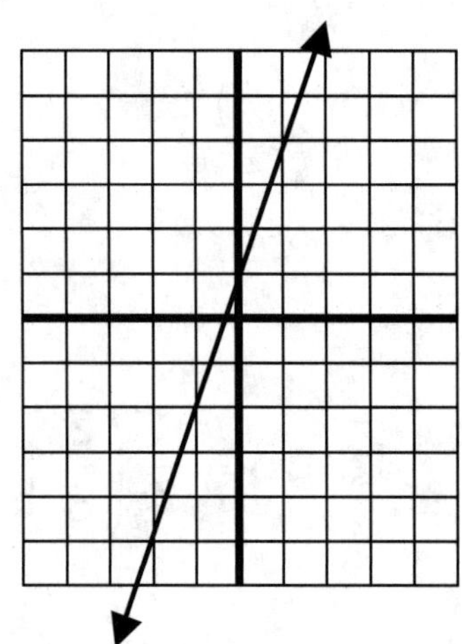

b = _____ m = _____

y = ________________

2.

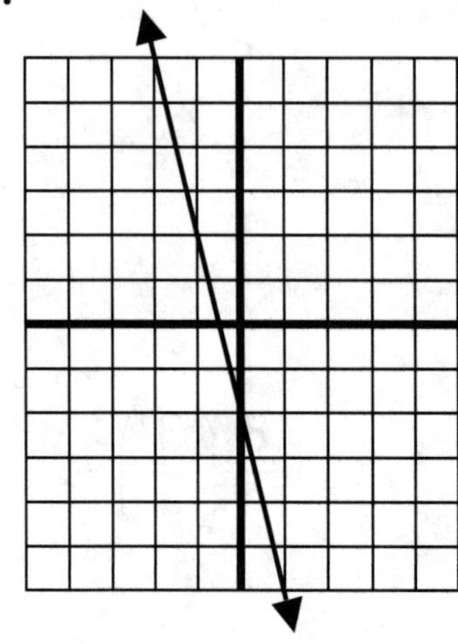

b = _____ m = _____

y = ________________

3.

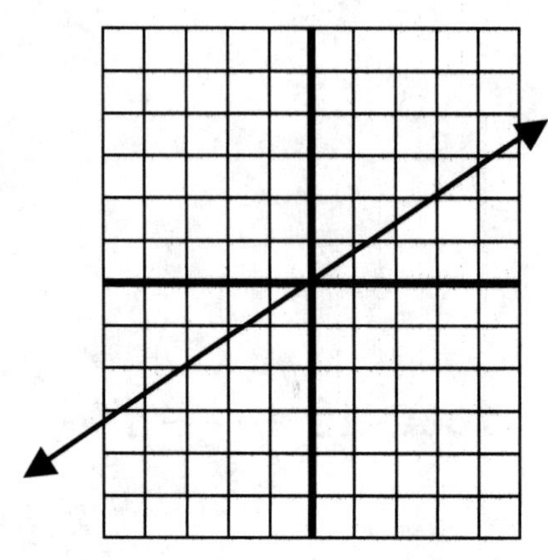

b = _____ m = _____

y = ________________

4.

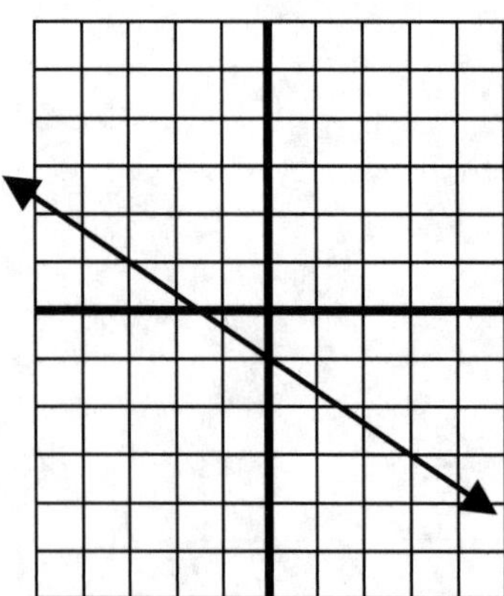

b = _____ m = _____

y= ________________

5.

b = _____ m = _____

y = ________________

6.

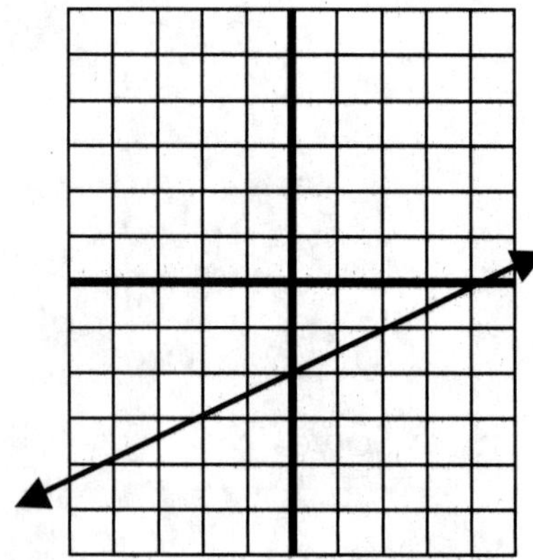

b = _____ m = _____

y = ________________

Graphing 1 *(cont.)*

Directions: Graph each line using the given information, and write an equation.

7.

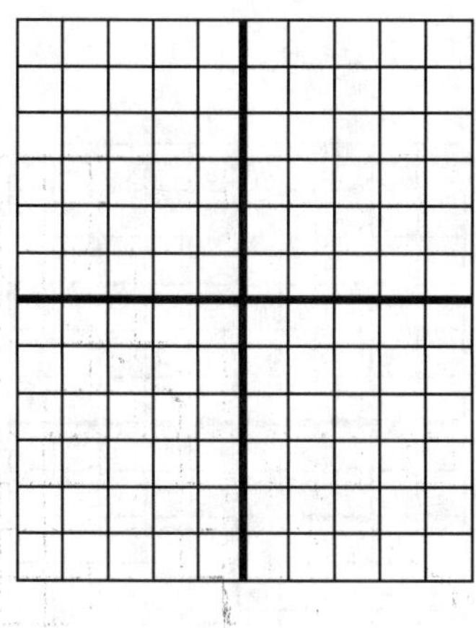

$b = -2 \quad m = -\frac{2}{3}$

y = ______________

8.

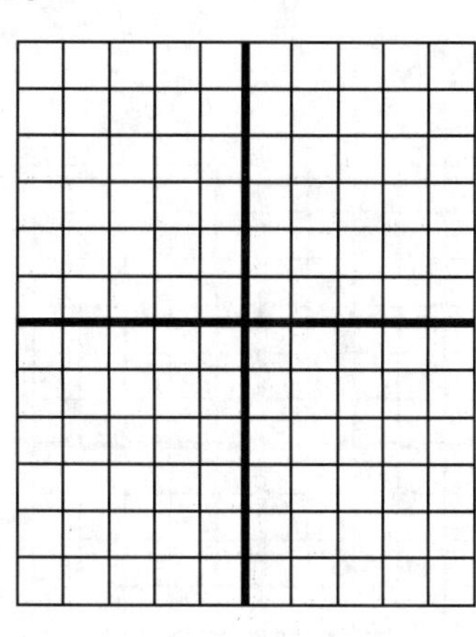

$b = 3 \quad m = -\frac{5}{2}$

y = ______________

9.

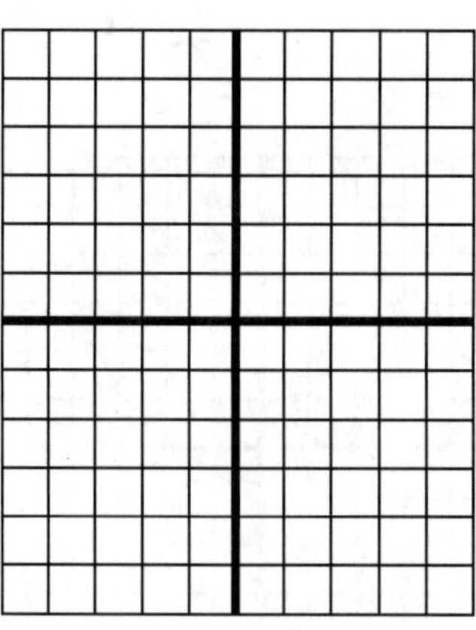

$b = -4 \quad m = -\frac{5}{2}$

y = ______________

10.

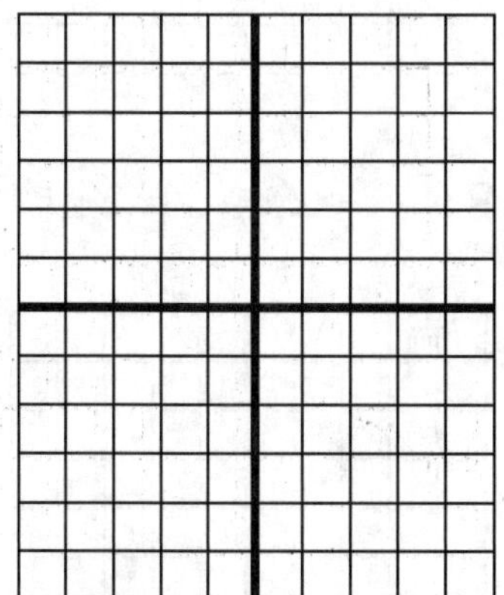

$b = 0 \quad m = 4$

y = ______________

11.

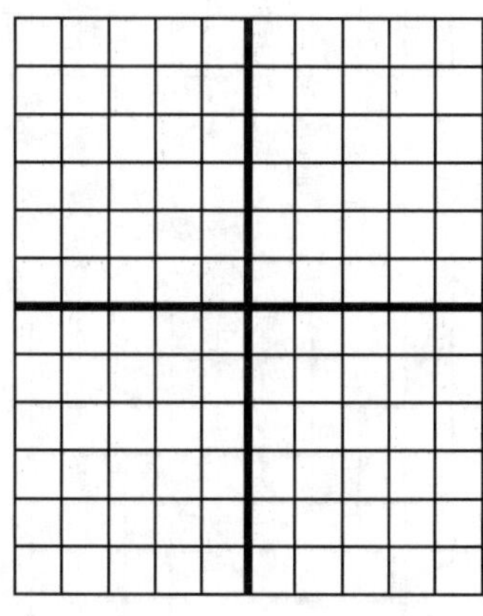

$b = -1 \quad m = -2$

y = ______________

12.

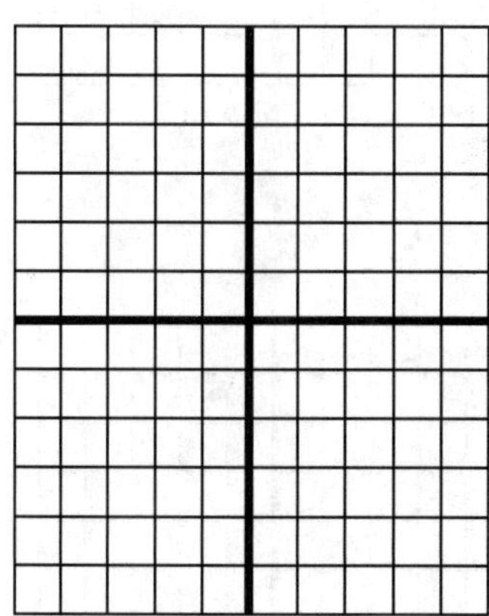

$b = 4 \quad m = -\frac{4}{3}$

y = ______________

Name ______________________________

Graphing 2

Directions: Graph each linear equation, and label the slope and the *y*-intercept.

1. $x + 3 = 0$

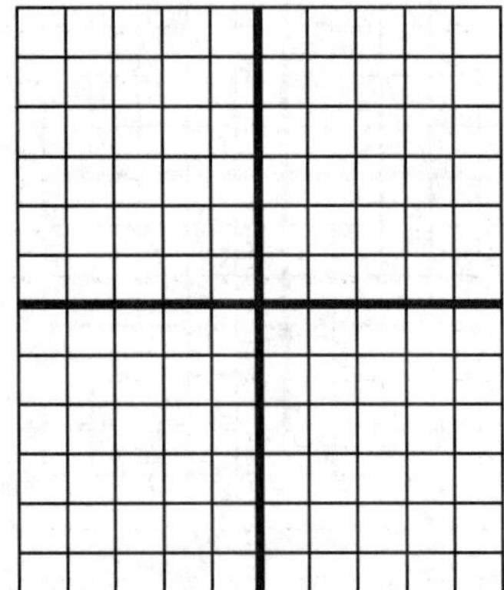

2. $y = -2$

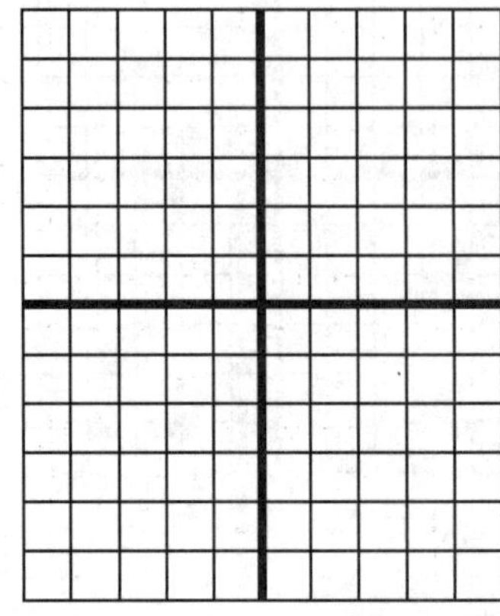

3. $x = 4$

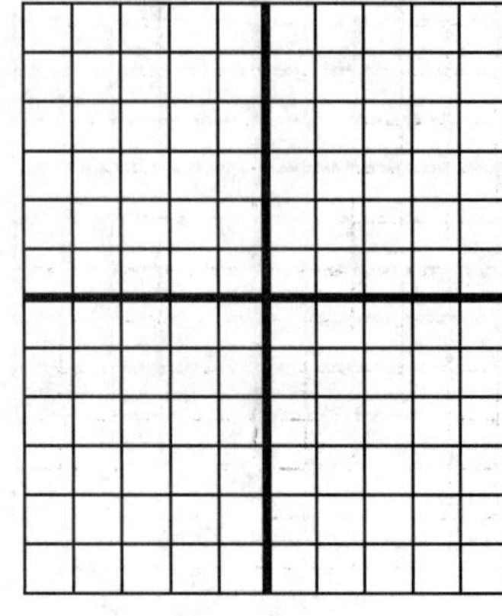

4. $y = 3$

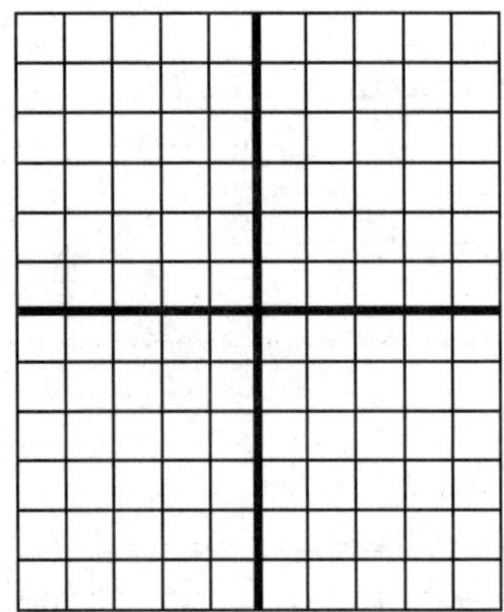

5. $y = \frac{1}{2}x - 3$

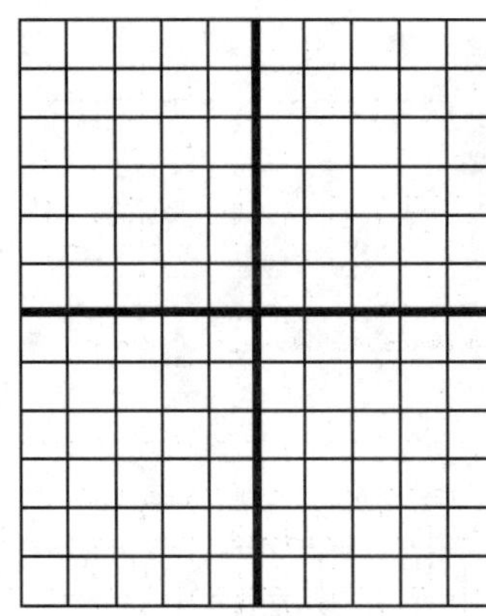

6. $y = -\frac{1}{4}x + 2$

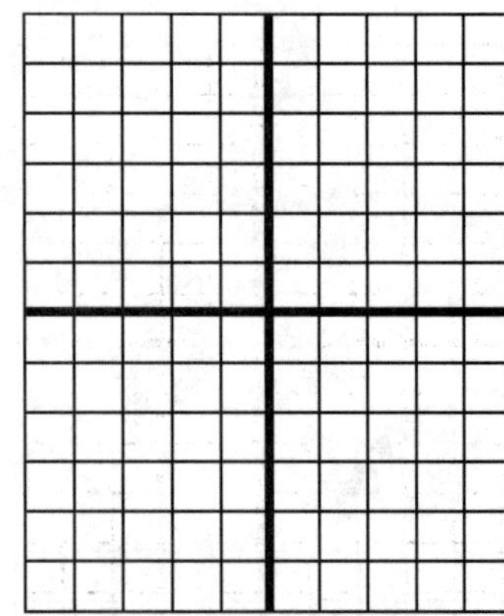

7. $y = 4x - 2$

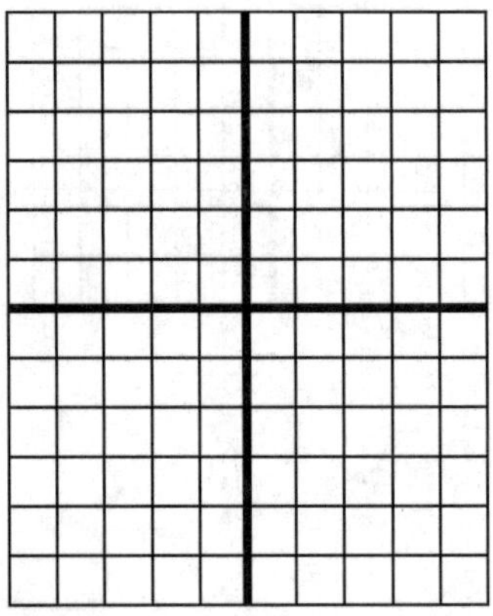

8. $y = \frac{5}{3}x$

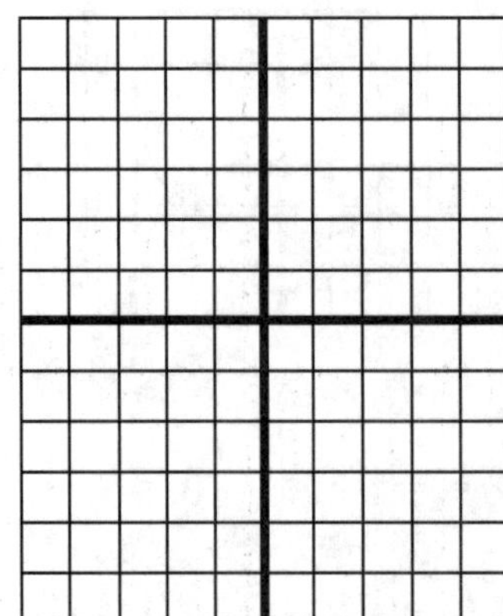

9. $y = 2x - 4$

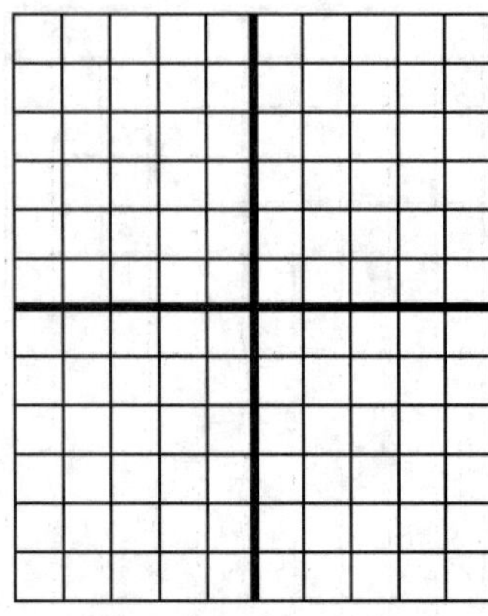

Graphing 2 *(cont.)*

Directions: Graph each linear equation, and label the slope and the *y*-intercept.

10. $-2x - 3 = y$

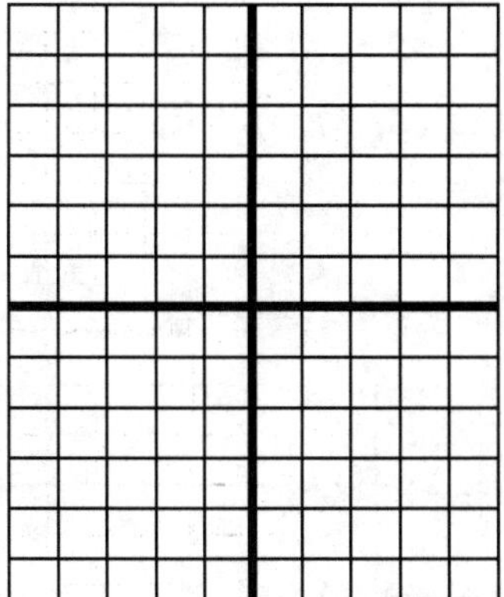

11. $-\frac{2}{3}x + 2 = y$

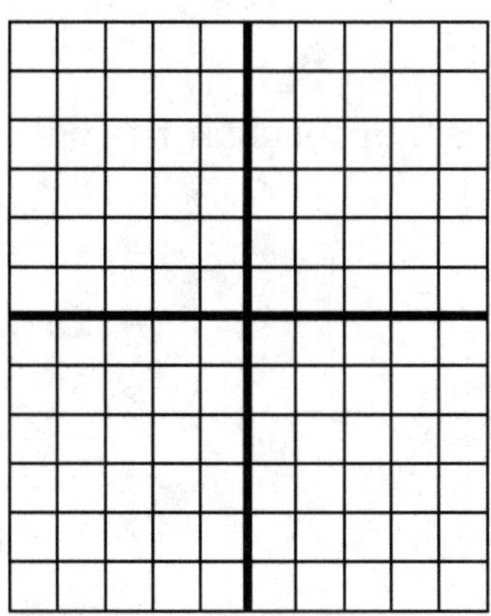

12. $-\frac{3}{4}x + 3 = y$

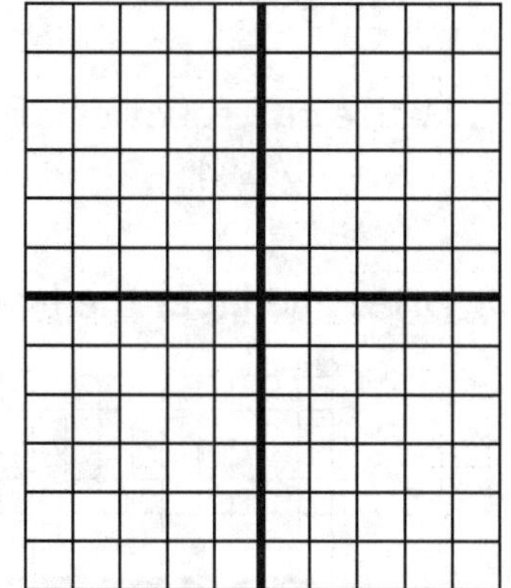

13. $\frac{3}{2}x + 1 = y$

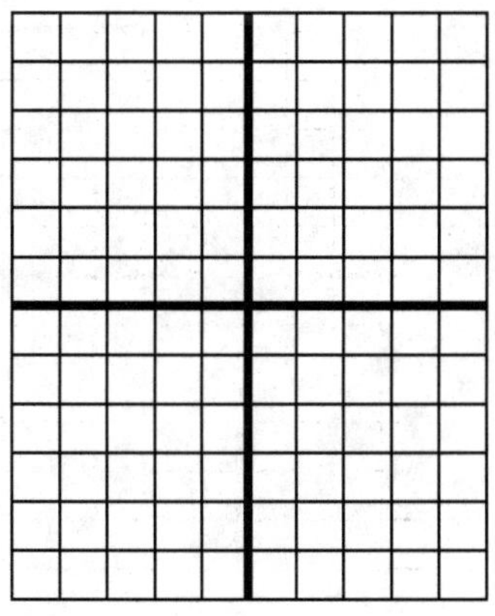

14. $3x - 1 = y$

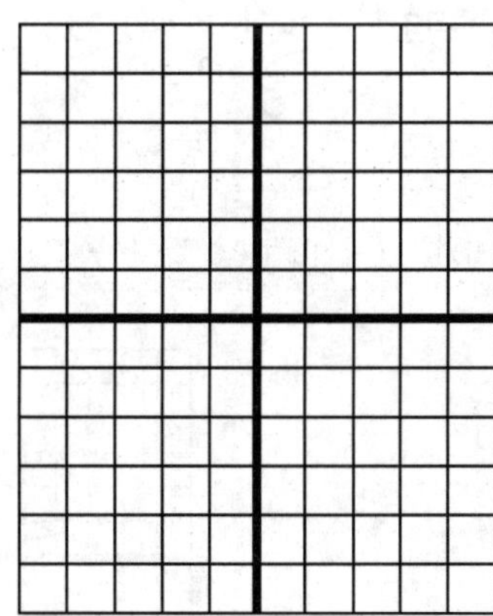

15. $-\frac{4}{3}x = y$

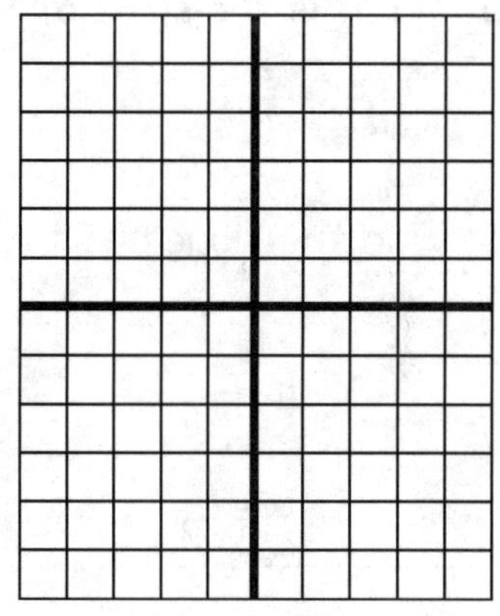

16. $\frac{6}{5}x + 4 = y$

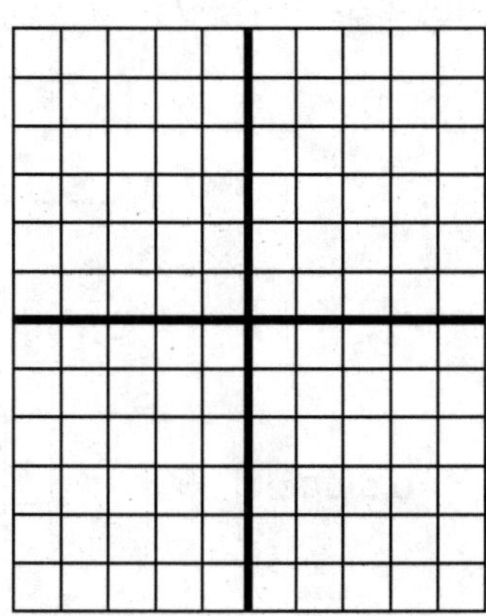

17. $\frac{1}{4}x - 2 = y$

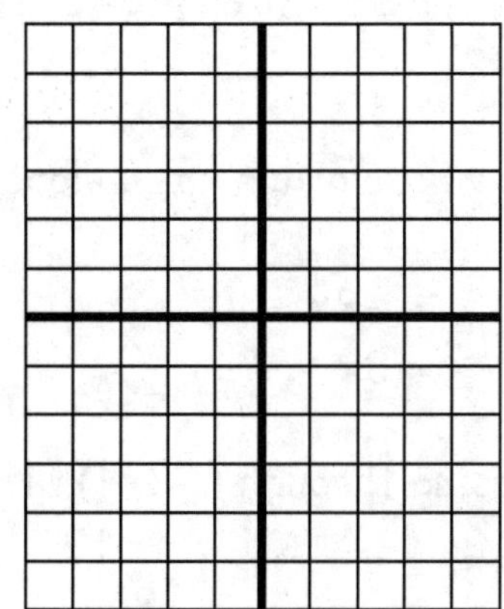

18. $x - 3 = y$

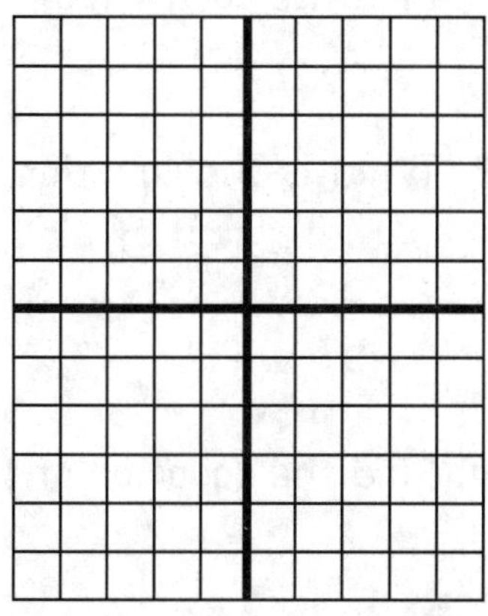

Name ____________________________________

Graphing Unit Review 1

Directions: Show your work neatly on another piece of paper.

1. Write the equation of the line passing through the points (2, 2) and (2, 5). 1. _____
   A. $y = 2$ B. $y = 3$ C. $x = 2$ D. $y = 5$

2. Write the equation of the line passing through the points (−1, 4) and (2, 4). 2. _____
   A. $y = 4$ B. $y = -1$ C. $x = 2$ D. $x = 4$

3. Draw and label the line $x = 3$.

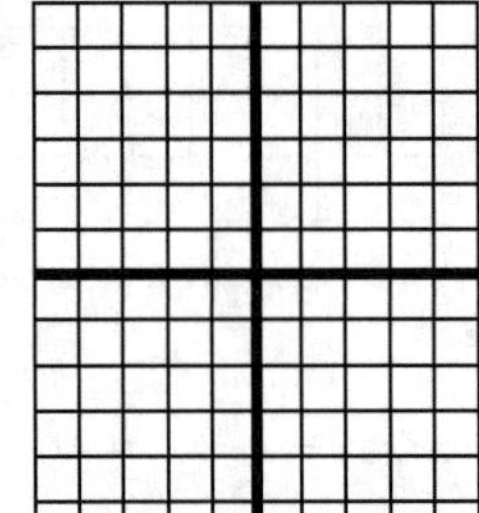

4. Draw and label the line $y = -2$.

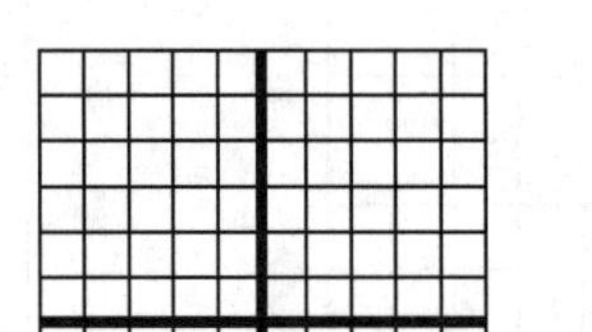

5. What is the slope of the line passing through (−2, 3) and (−3, 1)? 5. _____
   A. $-\frac{2}{5}$ B. -2 C. $\frac{2}{5}$ D. 2

6. Find the slope and the y−intercept of the line below. 6. _____
   A. $m = 1$, $b = \frac{1}{3}$
   B. $m = \frac{1}{3}$, $b = 1$
   C. $m = 3$, $b = 1$
   D. $m = 1$, $b = 3$

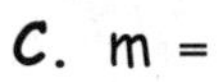

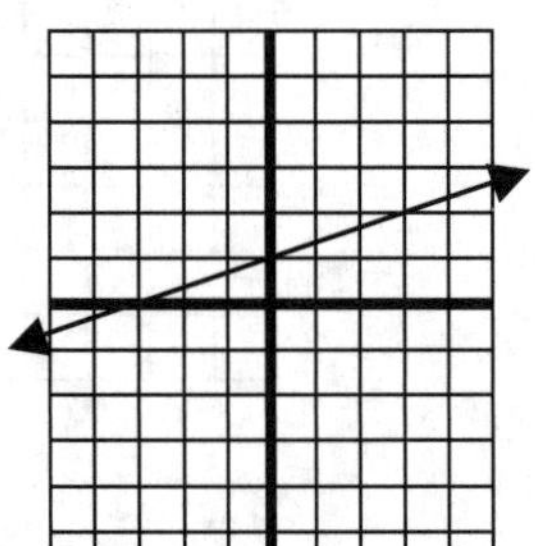

7. Find the equation of the line that passes through (−2, 1) with the slope of 0. 7. _____
   A. $y = 1$ B. $y = -2$ C. $x = -2$ D. $x = 1$

8. What is the equation of the line whose graph has a slope of −3 and a y-intercept of 2? 8. _____
   A. $y = -3x + 2$ C. $y = -2x + 1$
   B. $y = 2x - 3$ D. $y = 3x - 2$

9. Find the equation of the line passing through (−2, 4) with an undefined slope. 9. _____
   A. $y = -2$ B. $x = -2$ C. $x = 4$ D. $y = 4$

Graphing Unit Review 1 *(cont.)*

10. Find the equation of the line passing through (6, −3) with slope of $\frac{1}{2}$. **10.**______

A. $y = -\frac{1}{2}x$ **C.** $y = \frac{1}{2}x + 6$

B. $y = \frac{1}{2}x$ **D.** $y = \frac{1}{2}x - 6$

11. Find the equation of the line passing through (3, −4) and (−3, 5). **11.**______

A. $y = -\frac{3}{2}x + \frac{1}{2}$ **C.** $y = -\frac{1}{6}x - \frac{7}{2}$

B. $y = -\frac{1}{6}x + \frac{7}{2}$ **D.** $y = -\frac{3}{2}x - \frac{17}{2}$

12. Find the equation of the line parallel to the graph $y = -3x + 1$ and passing through the point (−2, −1). **12.**______

A. $y = -3x + 5$ **C.** $y = -3x + 2$

B. $y = x + 1$ **D.** $y = -3x - 7$

13. Which of the following is the graph of $y = -\frac{2}{3}x + 1$? **13.**______

A.

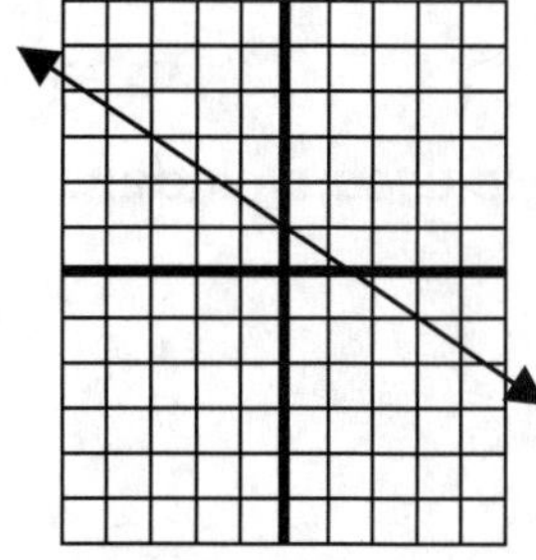

B.

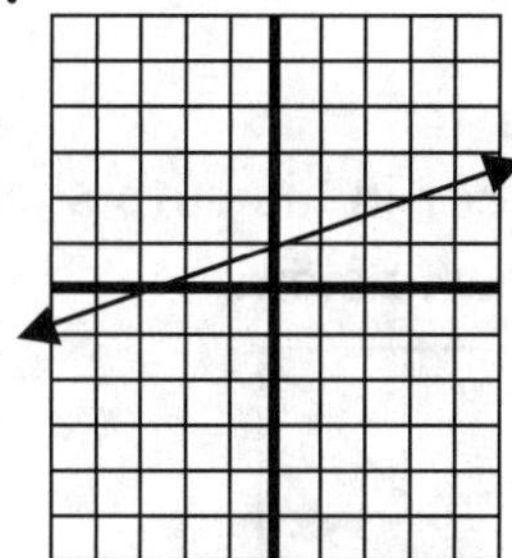

C.

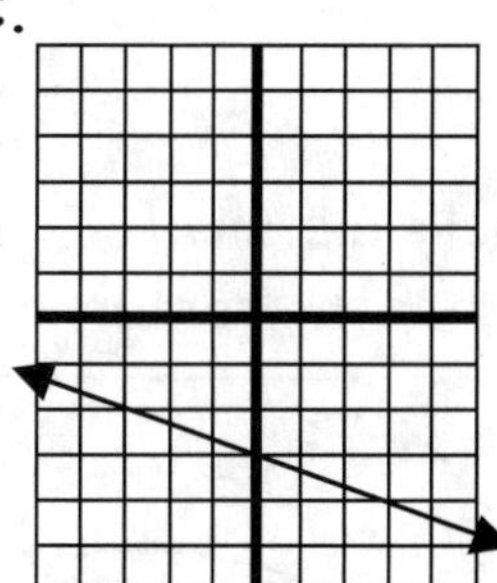

D.

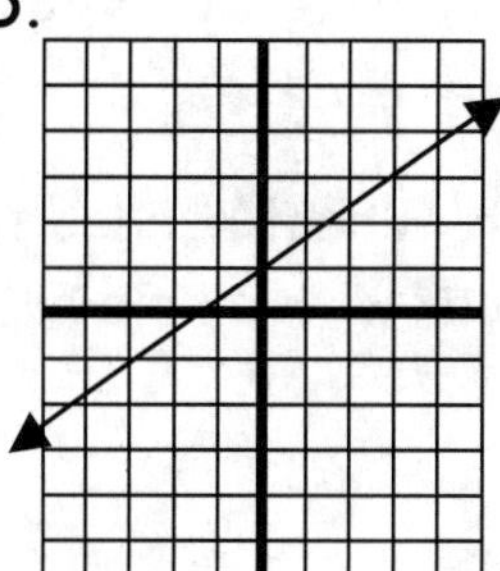

14. What is the equation of the line whose graph passes through the origin and has a slope of −3? **14.**______

A. $y = -3x$ **B.** $y = -3x + 2$ **C.** $y = 3x$ **D.** $y = x - 3$

15. What is the x-intercept of the graph of $-x + y = 2$? **15.**______

A. −2 **B.** 2 **C.** −1 **D.** 1

16. Which is the scatter plot for the data set (5, 1000), (7, 1200), (8, 1300)? **16.**______

A.

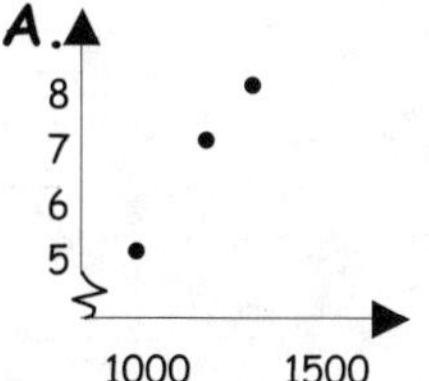

B.

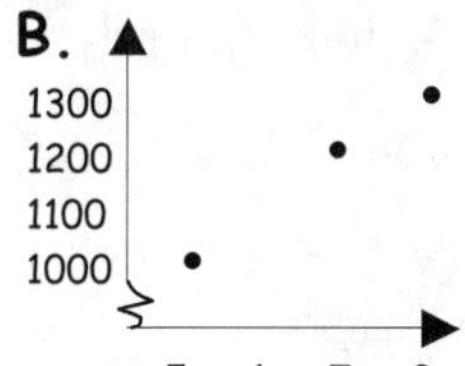

C.

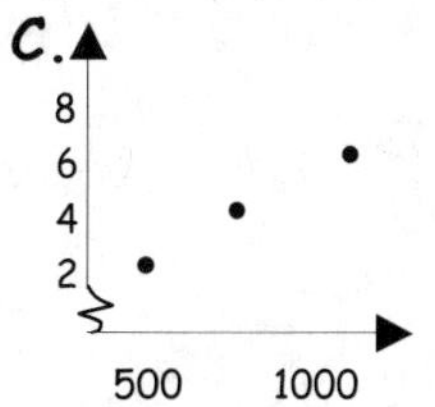

D.

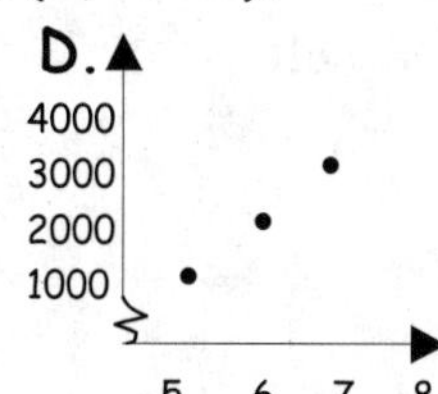

Graphing Unit Review 1 *(cont.)*
Measurement

17. Find the volume of the following shape. (Round to the nearest hundredth.)

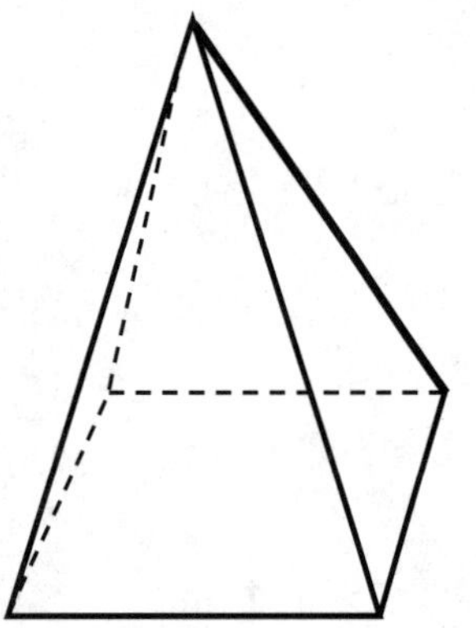

Side is 3.5 cm.
Height is 10.5 cm.

Volume = ____________________

18. Find the area of the following shape.

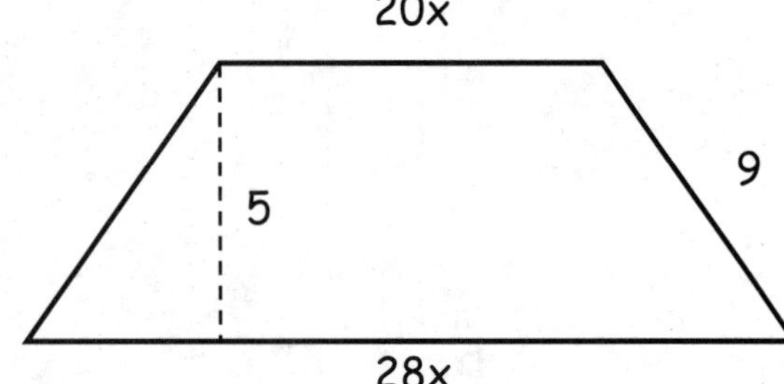

Area = ____________________

19. Mr. Wheat needed to make a stand for a project in his auto shop. He used a cinder block with a hole cut out of the center, as shown below.

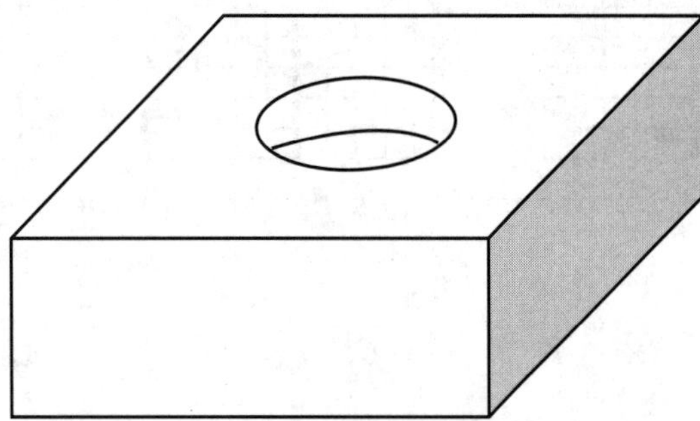

Which formula could be used to find the volume of the stand?

A. $V = lwh + \pi r^2h$

B. $V = lwh$

C. $V = \pi r^2h$

D. $V = lwh - \pi r^2h$

Graphing Unit Review 1 *(cont.)*
Measurement

20. Find the volume of the following shape. (Exclude the volume of the holes.)

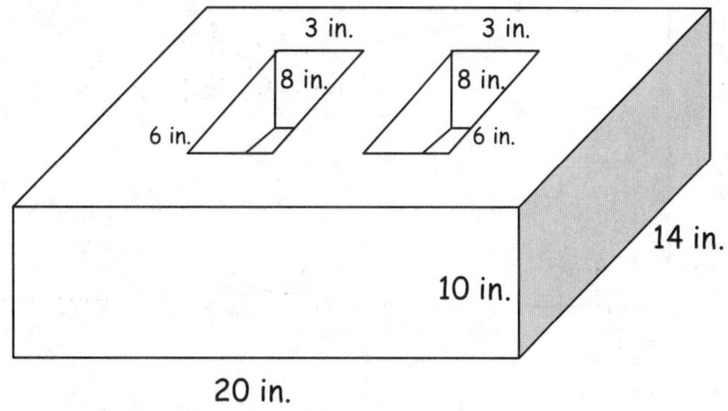

Volume = ____________________

21. Find the surface area of the following net of a square pyramid.

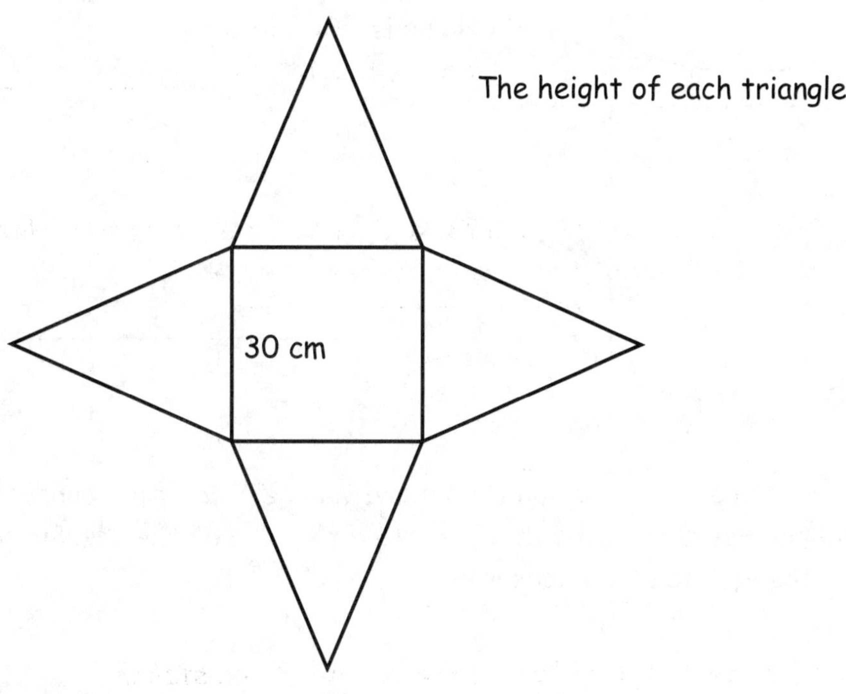

Surface Area = ________________

Graphing Unit Review 1 *(cont.)*
Measurement

22. Find the area of the given figure.

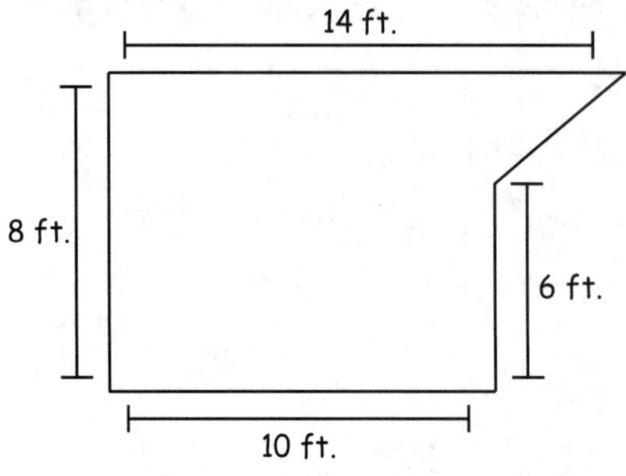

Area = ____________________

23. Find the missing measure. (Do not use 3.14 for π.)

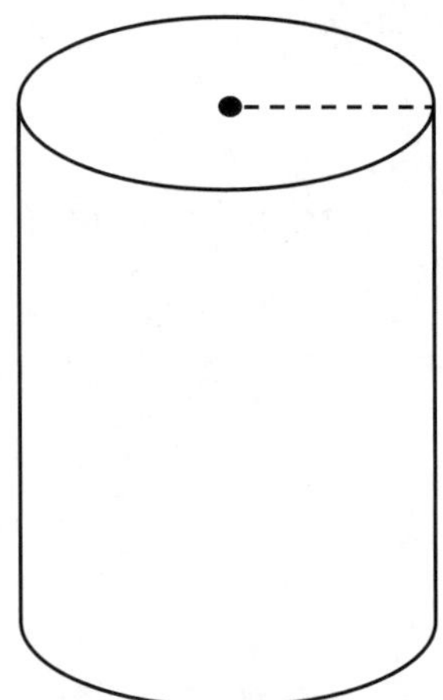

Radius is 10 in.
Volume is 500π in^3.
Find the height.

Height = ____________________

24. A cylindrical can of transmission fluid has a volume of 24 fluid ounces. A second cylindrical can has dimensions that are twice the size of the smaller can. Which is closest to the volume of the larger can?

A. 48 fl. oz.
B. 96 fl. oz.
C. 85 fl. oz.
D. 192 fl. oz.

Graphing Unit Review 1 *(cont.)*
Measurement

25. Find the missing measure. (Do not use 3.14 for π.)

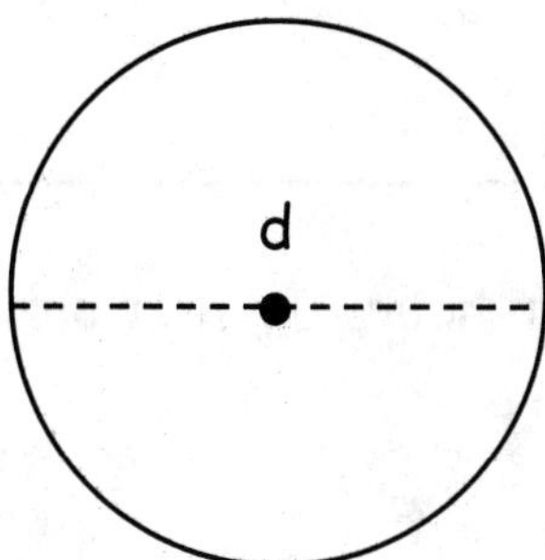

Area is 144π in^2.
Find the diameter.

Diameter = ____________________

26. Find the circumference of the following shape.

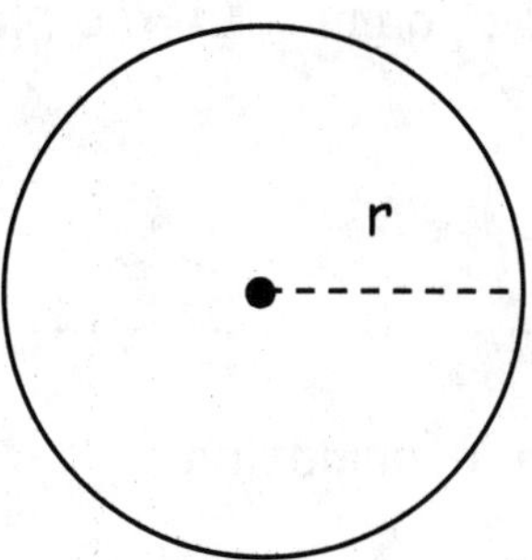

Diameter is 8 cm.

Circumference = ____________________

Graphing Unit Review 1 *(cont.)*
Formulas

Directions: Solve and label answers.

27. A jet travels 400 miles in 0.75 of an hour. How fast is the jet traveling? Round the nearest hundredth.

____

28. Manjit works at a bike store. He gets paid $8.00 per hour. If he worked 3.5 hours on Saturday, how much did he earn?

____

29. Tia drove 262.5 miles today. If she traveled an average of 70 miles per hour, how long did it take her?

____

30. To play the *Go Cars Go* arcade game it costs $0.75 per game. If you play the game 11 times, how much did you spend?

____

31. Write a problem to solve for distance with the given information. Be sure to include the answer.

Rate = 65 miles per hour

Time = 4.75 hours

____

32. The density of aluminum is 2.7 g/mL. If its volume is 50 mL, what is the mass? Round to the nearest thousandth.

____

Graphing Unit Review 1 *(cont.)*
Formulas

Directions: Graph and solve. Label the axes and use appropriate scales.

33. A boat can travel 25 mph for 7 hours before running out of gas. Graph how far it will have traveled after each hour.

34. Jon has to work two weeks before he can get a day of vacation. How many weeks would Jon have to work in order to take two weeks (10 days) off? Create a graph to solve the problem.

35. Kameko needs $300 for a new game. She has $14. She can earn $4 an hour babysitting. Graph it to find out how many hours Kameko must work to have the money she needs?

36. Explain the relationship among a table of values, a linear equation, and a graph. Use an example problem to explain your thinking.

____

____

____

____

____

____

Name ______________________________

Graphing Unit Review 2

Directions: Show your work neatly on another piece of paper.

1. Write the equation of the line passing through the points (3, 6) and (2, 6). 1.______
   A. $y = 3$ B. $y = 6$ C. $x = 2$ D. $y = 2$

2. Write the equation of the line passing through the points (−1, 4) and (−1, 5). 2.______
   A. $y = 4$ B. $y = -1$ C. $x = 2$ D. $x = -1$

3. Draw and label the line $y = -1$.

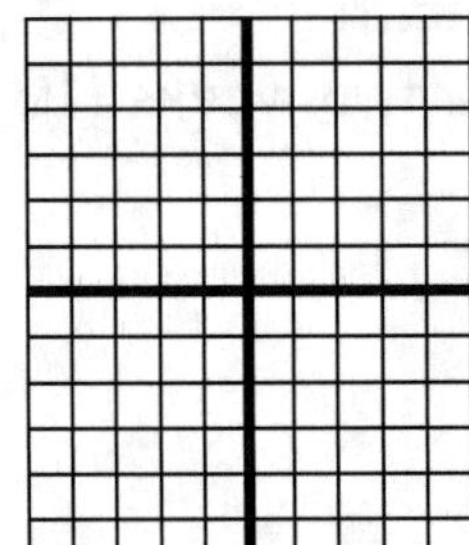

4. Draw and label the line $x = 3$.

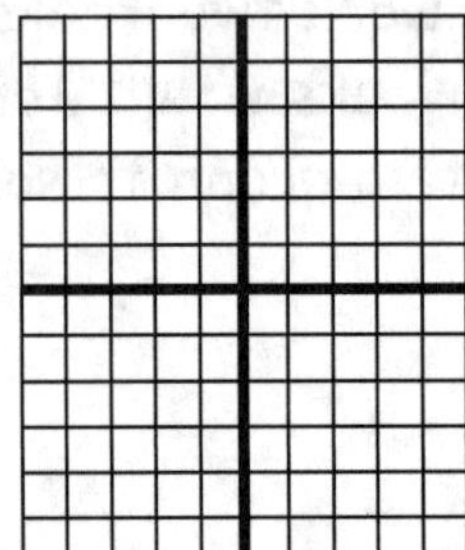

5. What is the slope of the line passing through (4, −2) and (−3, 1)? 5.______
   A. $\frac{3}{7}$ B. $-\frac{1}{7}$ C. $\frac{1}{7}$ D. $-\frac{3}{7}$

6. Find the slope and the y-intercept of the line below. 6.______

   A. $m = -2$, $b = -\frac{1}{3}$
   B. $m = -\frac{1}{3}$, $b = -2$
   C. $m = 3$, $b = -2$
   D. $m = -2$, $b = 3$

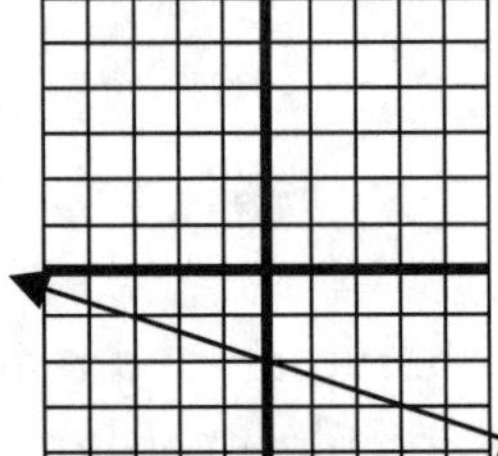

7. Find the equation of the line that passes through (−3, 1) with the slope of 0. 7.______
   A. $x = -3$ B. $x = -1$ C. $y = -1$ D. $y = 1$

8. What is the equation of the line whose graph has a slope of 2 and a y−intercept of −1? 8.______ 
   A. $y = 2x - 1$
   B. $y = -x + 2$
   C. $y = -2x + 1$
   D. $y = 2x + 1$

9. Find the equation of the line passing through (−2, 4) with an undefined slope. 9.______
   A. $y = -2$ B. $x = -2$ C. $x = 4$ D. $y = 4$

Graphing Unit Review 2 *(cont.)*

10. Find the equation of the line passing through (4, – 3) with slope of $\frac{2}{3}$. 10.______

A. $y = \frac{2}{3}x + 6$

C. $y = \frac{2}{3}x - \frac{17}{3}$

B. $y = \frac{2}{3}x - \frac{1}{3}$

D. $y = \frac{2}{3}x + 2$

11. Find the equation of the line passing through (3, – 4) and (– 3, 5). 11.______

A. $y = -\frac{3}{2}x + \frac{1}{2}$

C. $y = -\frac{1}{6}x - \frac{7}{2}$

B. $y = -\frac{1}{6}x + \frac{7}{2}$

D. $y = -\frac{3}{2}x - \frac{17}{2}$

12. Find the equation of the line parallel to the graph $y = 2x - 4$ and passing through the point (– 4, 3). 12.______

A. $y = -14x - 13$

C. $y = -4x + 19$

B. $y = 2x - 5$

D. $y = 2x + 11$

13. Which of the following is the graph of $-\frac{1}{3}x - 3 = y$? 13.______

A.

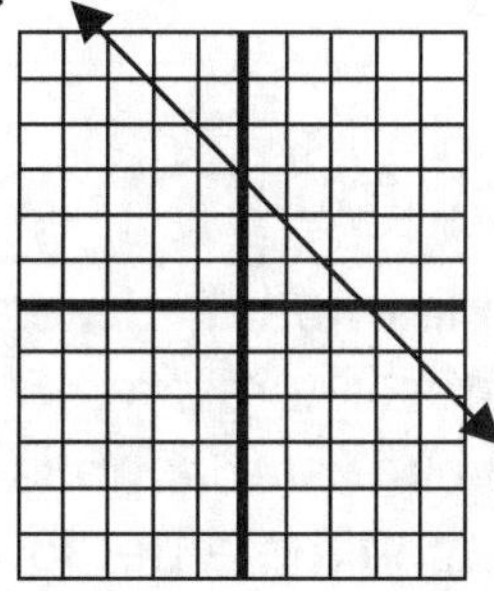

B.

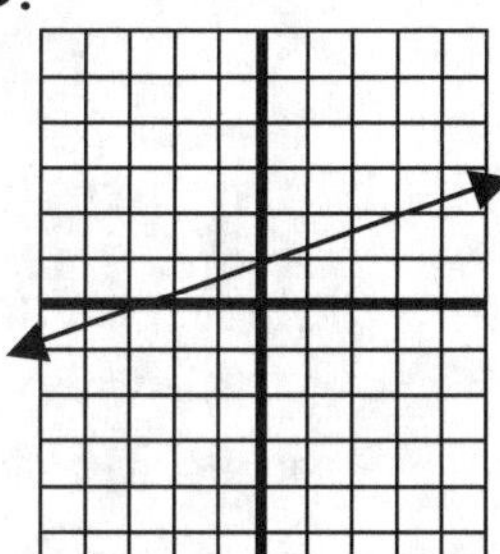

C.

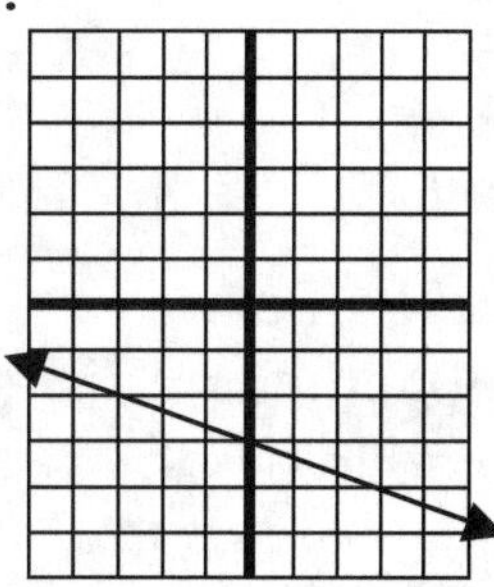

D.

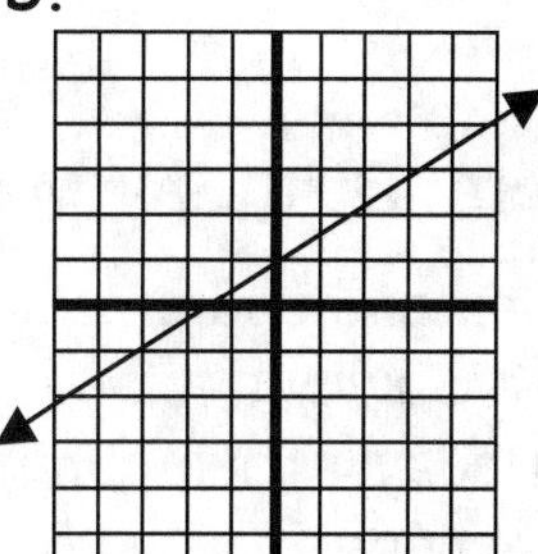

14. What is the equation of the line whose graph passes through the origin and has a slope of 4? 14.______

A. $y = x + 4$ B. $y = -4x$ C. $y = 4x + 3$ D. $y = 4x$

15. What is the x – intercept of the graph of $x + 2y = 2$? 15.______

A. –2 B. 1 C. 2 D. –1

16. Which is the scatter plot for the data set (500, 3) (600, 6) (800, 9)? 16.______

A.

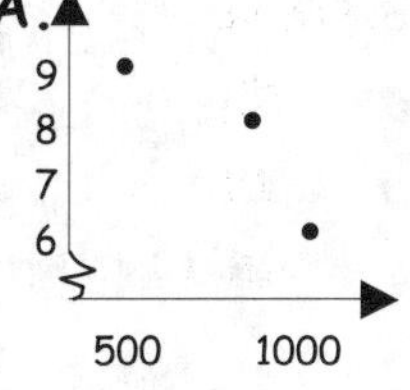

B.

800
700
600
500
6 7 8 9

C.

12
9
6
3
500 1000

D.

800
700
600
500
6 7 8 9

Part A Problem Solving Strategy Notes:

Acting It Out or Using Concrete Materials

Using objects or materials such as counters and blocks, to represent people, places, or things in a problem often helps you find a solution more easily.

These objects can be moved through the steps of the problem. By showing this movement, you keep track of what is happening as you solve the problem.

It can also be helpful to act out the roles of the different people or objects in the problem. Building a model will sometimes clarify questions that students have.

Read the following information to learn more about how and when to use objects or "act it out" to solve problems.

Act It Out!

Often, amounts of money or material things are exchanged among the people in a problem. This can be confusing. Acting out a problem can be very helpful and fun!

Problem: Birthday Money

- Their grandparents sent Nick, Sally, and Shirley a total of $160 for their birthdays. Their parents had to divide the money so that Nick was given $20 more than Sally and $30 more than Shirley. How much money was each grandchild given?

To solve this problem, you need three "actors" and $160 in play money. Start by giving Sally an estimated amount of $40. Next, give Nick $20 more ($60). Shirley should then receive $30 less ($30). This total is too low. So, start Sally with a higher amount ($50) and act out the same steps again to find a solution. (Sally gets $50, Nick gets $70, and Shirley receives $40.)

Use Concrete Materials

When a problem contains large numbers of objects or people or gives directions for building something, it may be better to use concrete materials rather than acting out the problem.

Problem: Impatient John!

- John is waiting in line to buy tickets at the movie theater. There are 45 people in front of him, and John is very impatient. Each time a person is served, John slips past two people. How many people will be served before John reaches the front of the line?

With so many people involved, this problem would be difficult to act out. However, you can use blocks or counters to simulate the problem. You can better visualize the movement of people in the problem by actually moving counters or blocks as John and the other people in line would be moving forward. (A total of 15 people will be served before John.)

Problem Solving Strategy Notes: Part B
Acting It Out or Using Concrete Materials *(cont.)*

Sample Problem

Fluffy the cat was lying asleep on the middle step. The dog, Milo, arrived and sat three steps above Fluffy. There were two steps between the dog and the top step. How many steps were there altogether?

Understanding the Problem

What do I know?

- Fluffy was lying on the middle step.
- Milo sat three steps above Fluffy.
- There were two steps between Milo and the top step.

What do I need to find out?

- How many steps were above Fluffy?
- How many steps were below Fluffy?
- How many steps were there altogether?

Planning and Communicating a Solution

First, you should draw a staircase or make one out of blocks. Use a counter to show Fluffy's position in the middle of the staircase. Place a second counter three steps above Fluffy, to represent Milo. Leave two steps empty. The third step above Milo should be the top step.

Count to find out how many steps there are above Fluffy and add the same number below Fluffy's position.

There are six steps above and six steps below the middle step, so there are thirteen steps altogether.

Source: Jiri Vaclavek/Shutterstock, Inc.

Reflecting and Generalizing

The problem is much easier to solve once steps are made or drawn. Then, you simply have to use markers for Fluffy and Milo. Count the steps above Fluffy and add the same number below, plus the step on which Fluffy is sitting.

(Note: You could also act out this problem on a real flight of stairs.)

Extension

The problem can be extended by including additional animals or by moving animals to different steps.

What if Fluffy's sister, Patty, decided to sit on the step second from the bottom? How many steps below Fluffy would she be?

Part A

Real-Life Problem Solving: Emergency!

Source: Harald Hoiland Tjostheim/Shutterstock, Inc.

When Cedar City was founded, the planners decided to be very organized. They planned the city in four quadrants, like a coordinate plane. This system has made it easy for emergency workers to answer calls. The Emergency Management Officer is especially grateful because she is able to know instantly where an emergency is happening so that she can make sure the right help gets there quickly.

Phones are ringing off the hooks! People are racing everywhere! Vehicles with flashing lights and sirens are screeching down the streets! What's going on? An emergency!

Every year many communities are faced with emergency situations. Storms and fires are two of the major hazards that cause emergencies. Sometimes train or automobile crashes involve large numbers of people and vehicles. Communities must be prepared to protect people and property within their areas. Fire departments, police departments, hospital emergency rooms—all must be coordinated to deal with an emergency. Cedar City has an office that provides this coordination. It is headed by the Emergency Management Officer.

Cedar City's Street Plan

There are 53 streets running north and south and 53 streets running east and west. When you know the naming and numbering system, it is easy to find your way around. Main Street runs north and south and is exactly in the middle of the north-south streets. State Street crosses Main Street and separates the city equally into north and south halves. So, Main Street separates the east side from the west side and State Street separates the north side from the south side. State Street and Main Street are the axes.

All of the east-west streets above State Street are named for presidents, and all of the east-west streets below State Street are named for states. The president names are in the order they served, starting with Washington for the street just north of State Street. The state names are in alphabetical order, starting just south of State Street. The streets running north and south on the east side of Main Street are numbered, starting just east of Main Street—First Street, Second Street, and so on, up to Twenty-sixth Street. The north-south streets west of Main Street are lettered from A to Z, starting just west of Main Street—A Street, B Street, etc.

On maps of the city, the northeast section of the city is labeled Quadrant I and the northwest section is labeled Quadrant II. The southwest section is Quadrant III and the southeast is Quadrant IV.

Real-Life Problem Solving: Emergency! *(cont.)* Part B

Directions: Use the information on page 164 and in the problems below to answer the questions. Before you begin, be sure to locate the key information you will need.

What Is the Problem?

You are the Emergency Management Officer for Cedar City. Wildfires are burning near the town. The wind is blowing fiercely, and hot embers are flying everywhere. Buildings in any section of the city could be on fire at any moment. You will need to send emergency workers to the sites of fires. You should draw a map of Cedar City before you try to solve any of these problems. Use that grid as you try to locate the sites listed in the problems below.

Problem-Solving Strategy: Acting It Out or Using Concrete Materials

Problem A

Fires are reported near the corners of:

D and Monroe
R and Buchanan
S and Lincoln

Into which section (quadrant) of the city should you send emergency workers? Which two fires are close together? How do you know?

Answer: ______________________________

____

____

____

Problem B

You have several teams of emergency workers available. One team is already in Quadrant II. New fires are reported near the corners of:

D and Alabama
S and Texas
Third and Hoover
First and Jefferson
B and Truman

Problem B *(cont.)*

Which fire should your Quadrant II team cover? Into which quadrants should you send new teams? Which section of the city has not had any fires yet?

Answer: ______________________________

____

____

Problem C

You have teams already in the sections of the city where fires were located in Problems A and B.

New fires break out at:

Second and Monroe
E and Jackson
M and Garfield
Fifth and Polk
Fourth and Arkansas
H and Hayes
10th and Michigan

You have two teams left. To what two quadrants of the city should you send them? How many fires total are in each quadrant?

Answer: ______________________________

____

____

Part A

Real-Life Problem Solving: Coordinate Map

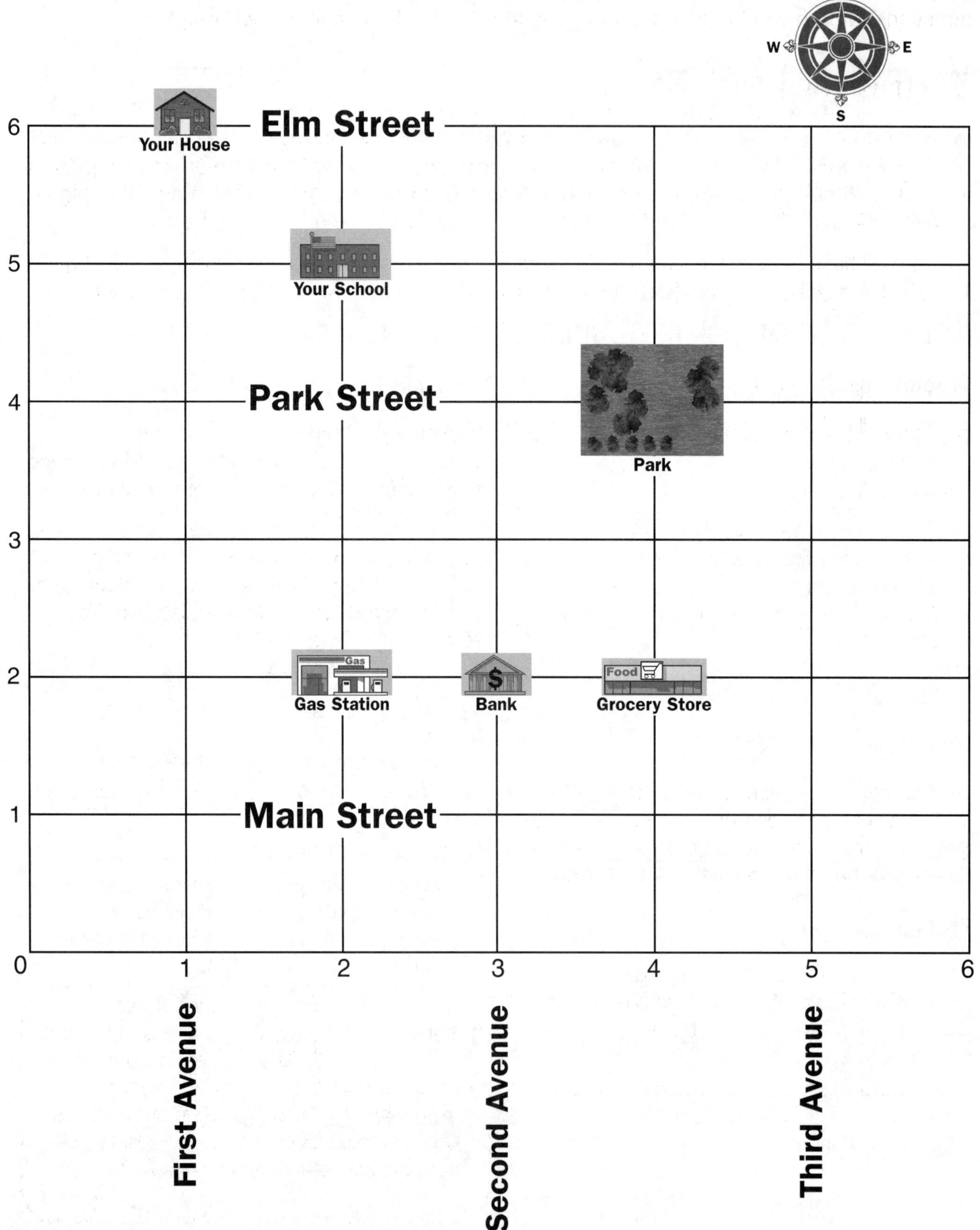

Real-Life Problem Solving: Coordinate Map (cont.)

Part B

Directions: Use the information on page 166 and in the problems below to answer the questions. Before you begin, be sure to locate the key information you will need.

What Is the Problem?

You live on Elm Street. Your grandma is visiting you and does not know her way around town. Your job is to use the map and coordinate grid to give directions and distances and help her get around town. For example, if your grandma wanted to visit with a friend at the park, her distance would be three blocks east and two blocks south.

Hint: If you have trouble planning ways to solve the problem, reread it and rethink your strategy. Think about how you will act out the problem or what concrete materials you will use to help you solve the problem.

Problem-Solving Strategy: Acting It Out or Using Concrete Materials

Problem A

Give compass directions and all line lengths to get from your house to the bank.

Answer: ______________________________

____

Problem B

Give compass directions and all line lengths for two different routes from your house to the grocery store. Have one route go east on Elm Street and the other go south on First Avenue.

Answer: ______________________________

____

____

____

Problem C

Your grandma wants to pick you up from school, go to the grocery store, and get gas before taking you home. Give compass directions and all line lengths for a route she can take. Your grandma starts at your house.

Answer: ______________________________

____

____

____

____

Class Challenge

Locate a map of your town. Plot your school and a grocery store on the map. Give compass directions to tell how to get from the school to the grocery store.

Name ______________________________

Real-Life Problem Solving:

Acting It Out or Using Concrete Materials

Directions: Use the strategy to solve each problem. Then, explain each answer.

The Problem

Jonah has a $20 bill. He exchanges the bill for two $10 bills. He takes one of the $10 bills and exchanges it for two $5 bills. He takes one of the $5 bills and exchanges it for five $1 bills. Jonah takes one $1 bill and exchanges it for four quarters. What bills and coins does Jonah now have?

Using the Strategy—Show Your Work

Explain Your Answer

Real-Life Problem Solving:
Acting It Out or Using Concrete Materials *(cont.)*

The Problem

Twelve people are on a bus. At the first stop, half of the people get off the bus. Half as many people (as the number of people remaining on the bus) get on the bus. At the second stop, one-third of the people get off. Half as many people (as the number of people remaining on the bus) get on the bus. At the third stop, one-third more people (as the number of people remaining on the bus) get on the bus. How many people are now on the bus?

Using the Strategy—Show Your Work

Explain Your Answer

Name ________________________________

One-Variable Inequalities

Directions: Circle all correct solutions for each inequality.

1. $x > -4$	A. 5	B. 0	C. −4	D. −6
2. $y < 3$	A. 0	B. 3	C. −3	D. −1
3. $a \geq 4$	A. −4	B. 0	C. 4	D. 6
4. $m \leq 12$	A. 5	B. −12	C. 0	D. −13
5. $c < -3$	A. 0	B. −3	C. −4	D. 3
6. $a \geq 0$	A. 3	B. −2	C. 0	D. −1

Directions: Graph each of the following inequalities on the number line provided.

7. $x > -4$

8. $m \leq 12$

9. $a \geq 0$

10. $a \geq 4$

11. $y < 3$

12. $c < -3$

13. $m \leq -2$

14. $g \geq -7$

15. $h < 0$

One-Variable Inequalities *(cont.)*

Directions: Write the inequality shown by each graph.

16. 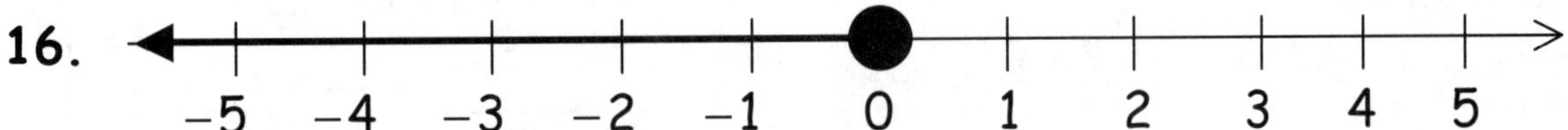

17. 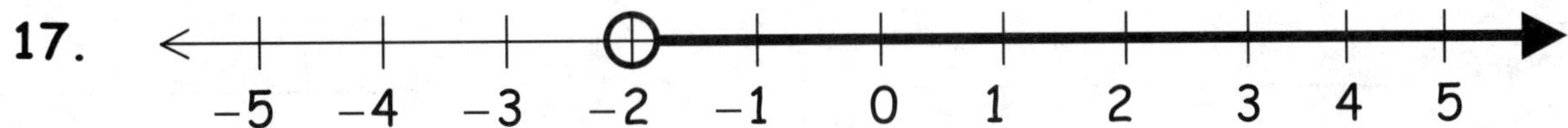

18. 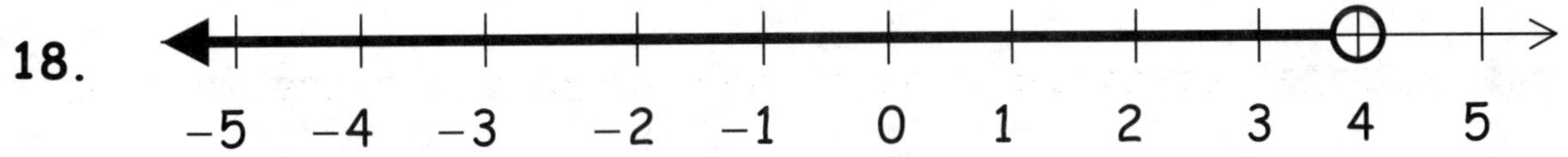

19. 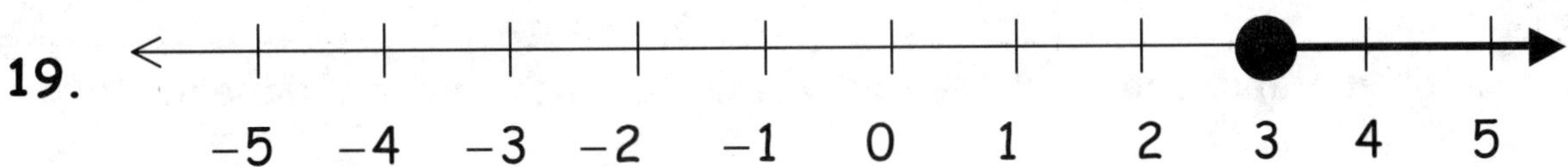

Name ______________________________

Solving Compound Inequalities ("ands")

Directions: Graph each of the compound inequalities, and write the solution set.

1. $5 < x$ and $x < 8$

______

______

$\cap$

Solution Set: ______________________

2. $-4 \le x$ and $x \ge -1$

______

______

$\cap$

Solution Set: ______________________

3. $0 \le x < 6$

______

______

$\cap$

Solution Set: ______________________

4. $x \le 2$ and $x > 5$

______

______

$\cap$

Solution Set: ______________________

Directions: Solve, graph, and write the solution set for each compound inequality.

5. $4 < x + 6 < 7$

______

______

$\cap$

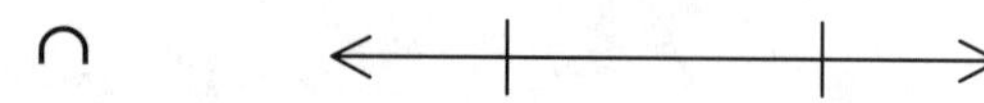

Solution Set: ______________________

6. $-25 \le 5x \le 20$

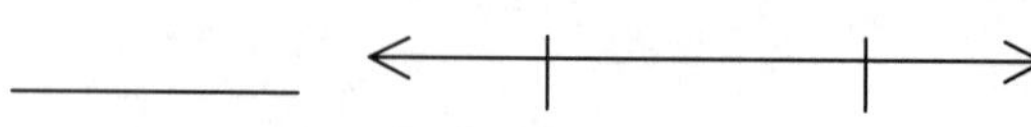

______

______

$\cap$

Solution Set: ______________________

Solving Compound Inequalities ("ands") *(cont.)*

7. $-9 \le 7x - 9 < 40$

______

______

$\cap$

Solution Set: ______________

8. $-3x - 6 > -6$ and $-3x - 6 > 9$

______

______

$\cap$

Solution Set: ______________

9. $-4 < x - 4 \le 2$

______

______

$\cap$

Solution Set: ______________

10. $-16 \le -4x \le 4$

______

______

$\cap$

Solution Set: ______________

Directions: Write the solution set of inequalities shown by each graph.

11. 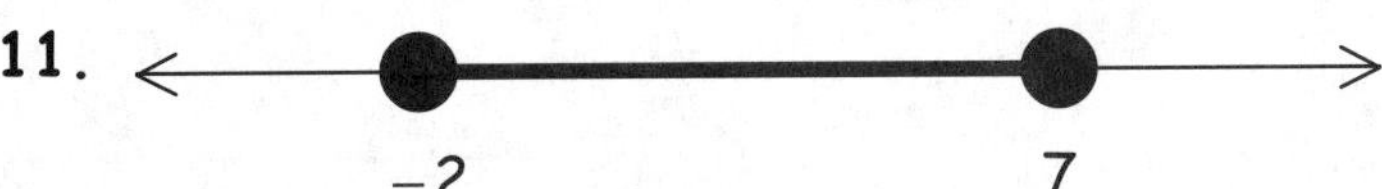

12. 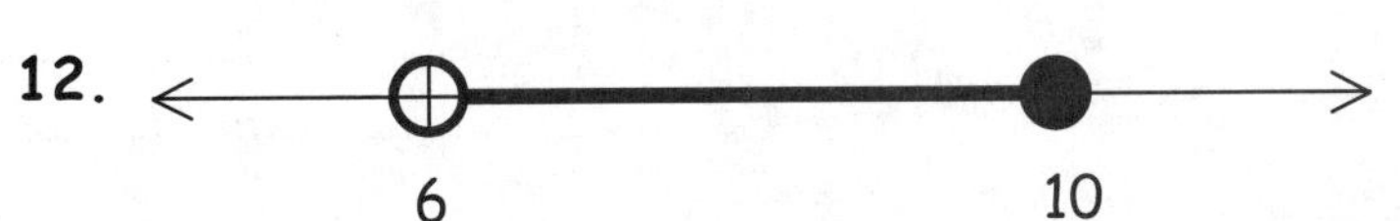

(Hint: nontypical)

13.

–12 0

Name ______________________________

Solving Compound Inequalities ("ors")

Directions: Graph each of the following compound inequalities, and write the solution set.

1. $x < 4$ or $x > 7$

____

____

$\cup$

Solution Set: ____________________

2. $-8 > x$ or $x < -2$

____

____

$\cup$

Solution Set: ____________________

3. $x > 1$ or $x \geq -3$

____

____

$\cup$

Solution Set: ____________________

4. $x > -2$ or $x \leq 4$

____

____

$\cup$

Solution Set: ____________________

Directions: Solve, graph, and write the solution set for each compound inequality.

5. $x + 9 < 6$ or $x - 5 > 3$

_______ 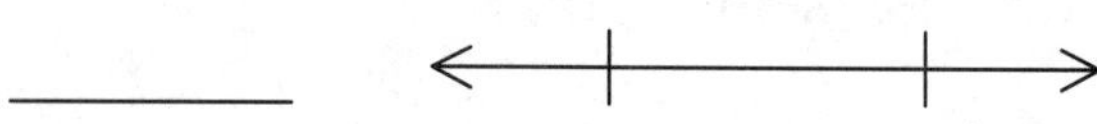

_______ 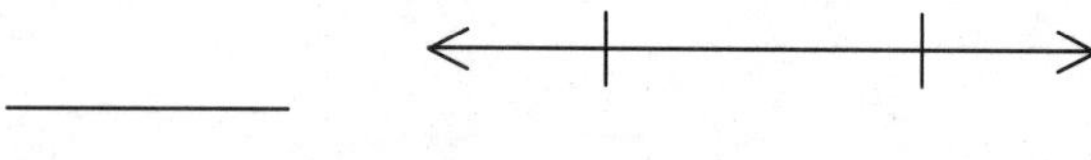

$\cup$ 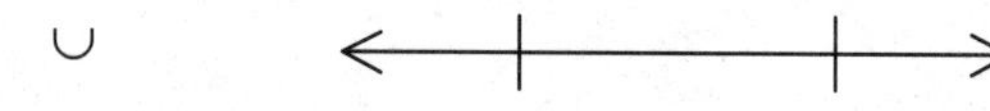

Solution Set: ____________________

6. $6x > 36$ or $4x \leq 16$

____

____

$\cup$

Solution Set: ____________________

Solving Compound Inequalities ("ors") *(cont.)*

7. $2x + 5 < 1$ or $4x - 7 \geq 9$

____

____

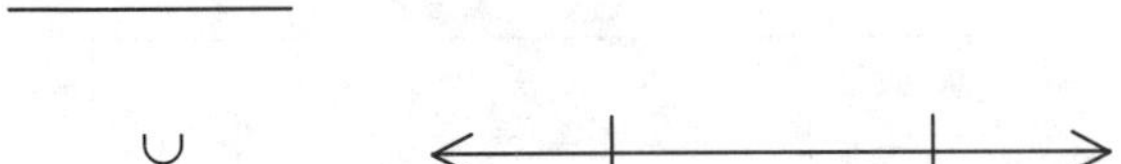

$\cup$

Solution Set: ______________________

8. $x + 2 \leq 0$ or $x - 5 \geq 3$

____

____

$\cup$

Solution Set: ______________________

9. $-2x < -16$ or $7x < 63$

____

____

$\cup$

Solution Set: ______________________

10. $3x + 8 < 29$ or $-3x - 10 > 5$

____

____

$\cup$

Solution Set: ______________________

Directions: Write the solution set of inequalities shown by each graph.

11.

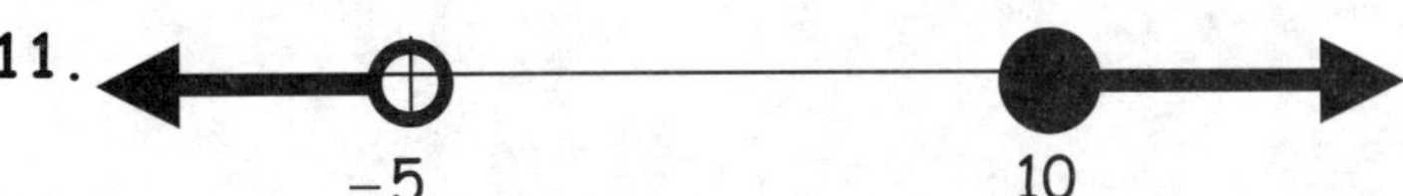

12.

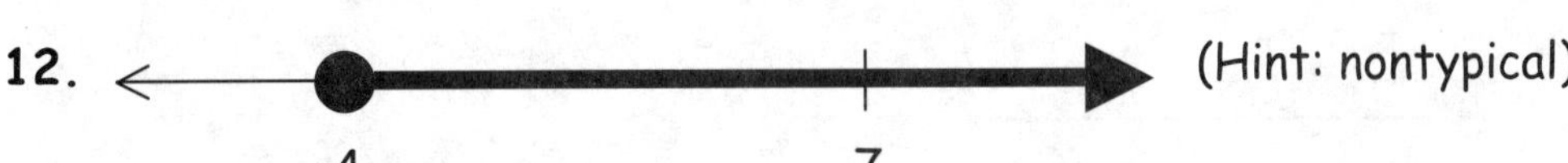

(Hint: nontypical)

13.

–15 0

Name ______________________

Compound Inequalities Review

Directions: Graph. Write the solution sets.

1. $x > 2$

$x \le 5$

$\cup$ ______________________

$\cap$ ______________________

2. $x \le 1$

$x > -2$

$\cup$ ______________________

$\cap$ ______________________

3. $x < 2$

$x \le 6$

$\cup$ ______________________

$\cap$ ______________________

4. $x > 2$

$x \le 7$

$\cup$ ______________________

$\cap$ ______________________

Compound Inequalities Review *(cont.)*

Directions: Graph. Write the solution sets.

5. $x > 2$

$x \geq 5$

$\cup$ ____________________

$\cap$ ____________________

6. $x < -3$

$x \geq 5$

$\cup$ ____________________

$\cap$ ____________________

7. $x < -3$

$x \leq 7$

$\cup$ ____________________

$\cap$ ____________________

8. $x > -2$

$x < 6$

$\cup$ ____________________

$\cap$ ____________________

Name ______________________________

Absolute Value Inequalities (Special Cases)

Directions: Solve each open sentence, and graph.

1. $|x + 4| \geq 3$

____

____

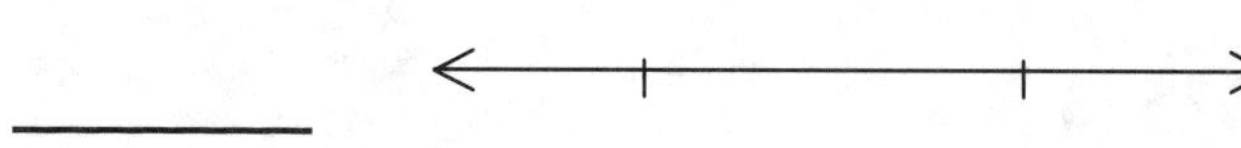

____

Solution Set: ____________________

2. $|4x + 4| < 8$

_______ 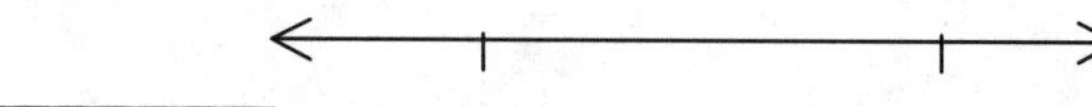

_______ 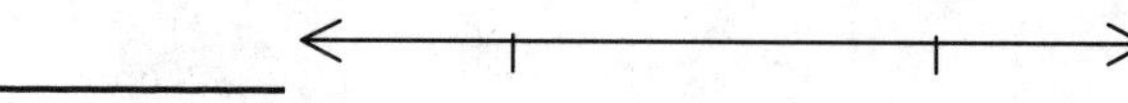

____

Solution Set: ____________________

3. $|2x - 4| < 0$

____

____

____

Solution Set: ____________________

4. $|x + 3| > -2$

_______ 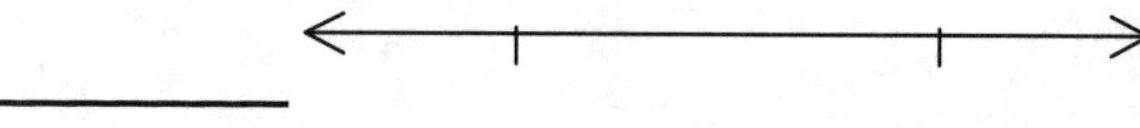

_______ 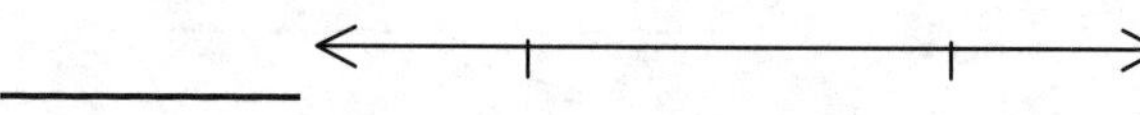

_______ 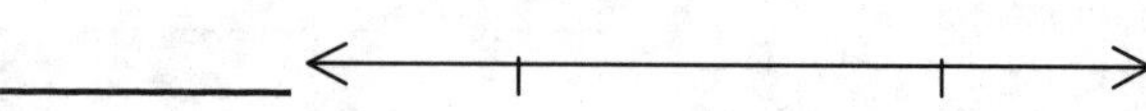

Solution Set: ____________________

Absolute Value Inequalities (Special Cases) *(cont.)*

Directions: Solve each open sentence, and graph.

5. $|x + 5| < -1$

______

______

______

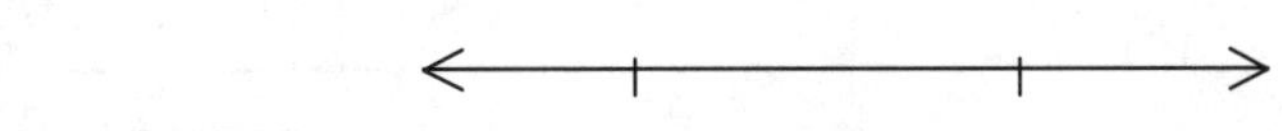

Solution Set: ______________________

6. $|x - 4| = -3$

______

______

______

Solution Set: ______________________

7. $|2x - 6| = 0$

______

______

______

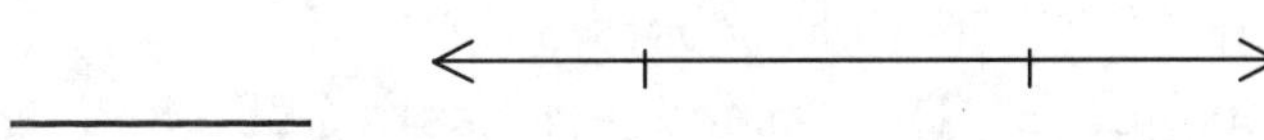

Solution Set: ______________________

8. $|2x + 8| > 0$

______

______

______

Solution Set: ______________________

Name ______________________________

Writing Systems of Equations 1

Directions: Assign two variables for each problem, and write the equations. **Do not solve.**

1. A store receives a shipment of VCRs and CD players. A shipment of 5 VCRs and 4 CD players costs $1,950. A shipment of 3 VCRs and 6 CD players costs $2,250. Find the cost of a VCR and the cost of a CD player.

Set up: | Equations:

Let ____ = ____________________ | ____________________

____ = ____________________ | ____________________

2. A basketball team stopped at a fast-food restaurant after a game. They divided into two groups. One group bought 5 chicken sandwiches and 7 hamburgers for a cost of $24.90. The second group spent $28.80 and bought 5 chicken sandwiches and 9 hamburgers. How much does a hamburger cost?

Set up: | Equations:

Let ____ = ____________________ | ____________________

____ = ____________________ | ____________________

3. A travel agent offers 2 package vacation plans. The first plan costs $400 and includes 3 days at a hotel and a rental car for 2 days. The second plan costs $550 and includes 4 days at a hotel and a rental car for 3 days. The daily charge for the room and the car is the same under each plan. Find the cost per day for the room and for the car.

Set up: | Equations:

Let ____ = ____________________ | ____________________

____ = ____________________ | ____________________

Writing Systems of Equations 1 *(cont.)*

4. The Math Club is having their end-of-the-year party. Natasha found that the cafeteria usually makes 200 cups of pineapple-ginger ale fruit punch. The cook told her that if she doubles the pineapple and triples the ginger ale, she will have a total of 420 cups of punch. How many cups of each are needed to make 420 cups of fruit punch?

Set up: Equations:

Let ____ = ______________________ ______________________

____ = ______________________ ______________________

5. A cruise ship has 680 rooms. Those with a view rent for $160 per night, and those without a view rent for $105 per night. On a night when the ship was completely occupied, revenues were $92,500. How many rooms of each type are on the ship?

Set up: Equations:

Let ____ = ______________________ ______________________

____ = ______________________ ______________________

6. A pair of boots and a pair of tennis shoes cost $196.12. The difference in their cost is $44.38. Determine the cost of each type of footwear.

Set up: Equations:

Let ____ = ______________________ ______________________

____ = ______________________ ______________________

Writing Systems of Equations 1 *(cont.)*

7. Two different types of batteries are needed to run Joshua's remote-controlled jeep. The two batteries produce a total voltage of 6.5 V. The difference in their voltage is 2.5 V. Determine the voltages of the two batteries.

Set up: Equations:

Let ____ = ____________________ ____________________

____ = ____________________ ____________________

8. In the Alice High School band, the number of trumpet players is 4 times the number of French horn players. There are 35 trumpet and French horn players in the band. How many people play the trumpet?

Set up: Equations:

Let ____ = ____________________ ____________________

____ = ____________________ ____________________

9. Jason, a vendor at the baseball park in Houston, sells two sizes of drinks. One costs $1.00 and the other costs $1.50. He knows he sold a total of 230 drinks for a total of $285.00. How many small drinks did he sell?

Set up: Equations:

Let ____ = ____________________ ____________________

____ = ____________________ ____________________

Name ______________________________

Writing Systems of Equations 2

Directions: Assign two variables for each problem, and write the equations. **Do not solve.**

1. Al has a $12 gift certificate to Aqua-land. He can buy 3 fish and 1 frog, or he can buy 2 frogs. Find the cost of each type of animal.

   Set up: Equations:

   Let ____ = ____________________ ____________________

   ____ = ____________________ ____________________

2. An electric guitar costs $781 more than an acoustic guitar. If 13 electric guitars and 12 acoustic guitars were sold, revenues would be $72,628. Find the cost of each guitar.

   Set up: Equations:

   Let ____ = ____________________ ____________________

   ____ = ____________________ ____________________

3. On the PSJA North tennis team, there are 9 more boys than girls. If there is a total of 21 players, how many boys are on the team?

   Set up: Equations:

   Let ____ = ____________________ ____________________

   ____ = ____________________ ____________________

4. Tashika went to Frosty's and bought fruit slushies for .75 cents each and cones for $1 each. She spent a total of $12.75 and she bought 15 total items. How many fruit slushies did she buy?

   Set up: Equations:

   Let ____ = ____________________ ____________________

   ____ = ____________________ ____________________

5. The cost of a movie on DVD is 2 times that of the VHS version. If 1 DVD and 2 VHS tapes cost $23.85, find the cost of a DVD and the cost of a VHS tape.

   Set up: Equations:

   Let ____ = ____________________ ____________________

   ____ = ____________________ ____________________

Writing Systems of Equations 2 *(cont.)*

6. Mr. Lege's third-period class collected $60 more this week than they did last week for the homeless shelter. Altogether, they collected $340. How much did they collect last week?

Set up: Equations:

Let ____ = ______________________ ______________________

____ = ______________________ ______________________

7. The basketball team has 20 more players than the baseball team does. There are 100 players total. How many basketball players are there?

Set up: Equations:

Let ____ = ______________________ ______________________

____ = ______________________ ______________________

Directions: Assign two variables, and write the equations. For an extra challenge, solve these systems of equations.

8. For a fund-raiser, a Boy Scout troop sold two sizes of popcorn boxes—small for $3 and large for $6. If 302 boxes were sold with a cash receipt of $1,803, how many large boxes were sold?

Set up: Equations:

Let ____ = ______________________ ______________________

____ = ______________________ ______________________

SOLVE:

Writing Systems of Equations 2 *(cont.)*

Directions: Assign two variables for each problem, and write the equations. For an extra challenge, solve these systems of equations.

9. Together, 1 small package of gum and 1 large package of gum cost \$1.10. If you bought 2 small packages of gum and 1 large package of gum, they would cost \$1.45. How much did the large package of gum cost?

Set up: Equations:

Let ____ = ______________________ ______________________

____ = ______________________ ______________________

SOLVE:

10. The Key Club is selling T-shirts and key chains. Its members sold a total of 261 items. Twice as many T-shirts were sold as key chains. How many items of each type were sold?

Set up: Equations:

Let ____ = ______________________ ______________________

____ = ______________________ ______________________

SOLVE:

Name ________________________________

Inequalities and Systems Unit Review

Directions: Solve. Show your work neatly on another sheet of paper.

1. Solve $m + 4 < -16$.
   A. $\{m|m > -20\}$ B. $\{m|m < -12\}$ C. $\{m|m < -20\}$ D. $\{m|m < 20\}$ 1.______

2. Solve $-24 \le w - 3$.
   A. $\{w|w \ge 21\}$ B. $\{w|w \le -21\}$ C. $\{w|w \ge 8\}$ D. $\{w|w \ge -21\}$ 2.______

3. Solve $-3a \le 9$.
   A. $\{a|a \ge -3\}$ B. $\{a|a \le -3\}$ C. $\{a|a \ge 3\}$ D. $\{a|a \ge 12\}$ 3.______

4. Solve $4c > -16$.
   A. $\{c|c < -4\}$ B. $\{c|c > -4\}$ C. $\{c|c > -20\}$ D. $\{c|c > 20\}$ 4.______

5. Solve $3 \ge 2x - 4$.
   A. $\{x|x \ge -\frac{7}{2}\}$ B. $\{x|x \ge -\frac{1}{2}\}$ C. $\{x|x \ge \frac{7}{2}\}$ D. $\{x|x \le \frac{7}{2}\}$ 5.______

6. Solve $4y - 3 \le 6y + 5$.
   A. $\{y|y \le \frac{4}{5}\}$ B. $\{y|y \le -4\}$ C. $\{y|y \ge -4\}$ D. $\{y|y \ge 4\}$ 6.______

7. Solve $-4(3x + 2) \ge 4x + 8$.
   A. $\{x|x \le 0\}$ B. $\{x|x \le -1\}$ C. $\{x|x \ge 0\}$ D. $\{x|x \ge 1\}$ 7.______

8. Solve $-\frac{2}{3}c \le 8$.
   A. $\{c|c \ge -12\}$ B. $\{c|c \ge 12\}$ C. $\{c|c \le -12\}$ D. $\{c|c \ge 4\}$ 8.______

9. Solve $3.2n - 4 \le 12.48$.
   A. $\{n|n \ge 3.91\}$ B. $\{n|n \le 3.91\}$ C. $\{n|n \le 5.15\}$ D. $\{n|n \ge 5.15\}$ 9.______

10. Solve $|4x - 3| = 16$.
    A. $\{5, -\frac{7}{2}\}$ B. $\{-\frac{19}{4}, \frac{13}{4}\}$ C. $\{-5, \frac{7}{2}\}$ D. $\{\frac{19}{4}, -\frac{13}{4}\}$ 10.______

11. Solve $|3p - 6| \le 12$.
    A. $\{p|-2 \le p \le 2\}$ C. $\{p|-2 \le p \le 6\}$ 11.______
    B. $\{p|0 \le p \le 2\}$ D. $\{p|-6 \le p \le 6\}$

Inequalities and Systems Unit Review *(cont.)*

12. Solve $|4w + 2| > 6$.

A. $\varnothing$

B. $\{w \mid w < -2 \text{ or } w > 1\}$

C. $\{w \mid w > 2 \text{ or } w > 1\}$

D. $\{w \mid w > -2 \text{ or } w < 2\}$

12._____

13. Solve $|2p + 1| < 0$.

A. $\varnothing$ **B.** $\{p \mid p > -\frac{1}{2}\}$ **C.** $\{p \mid p > \frac{1}{2}\}$ **D.** $\{p \mid p > 1\}$

13._____

14. Which of the following is the graph of the solution set of $2w < 6$ and $6 < w$?

A. $\varnothing$

B. 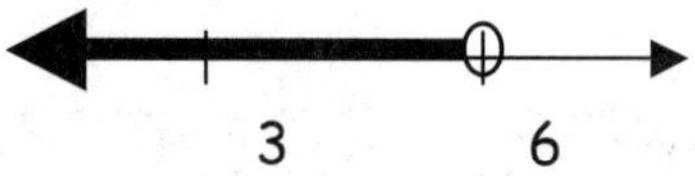 [number line: shaded left, open circle near 6; labels 3, 6]

C. 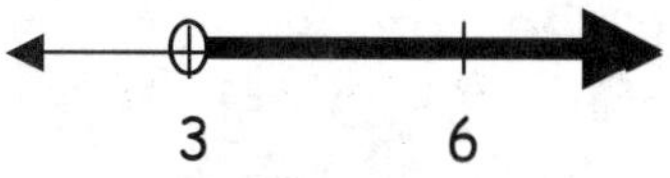 [number line: open circle at 3, shaded right; labels 3, 6]

D. 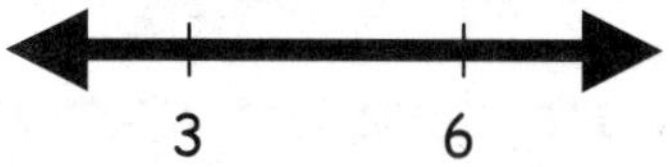 [number line: entire line shaded; labels 3, 6]

14._____

15. Solve $-6 \le n + 3 \le 9$ and choose the graph of the solution set.

A. $\varnothing$

B. 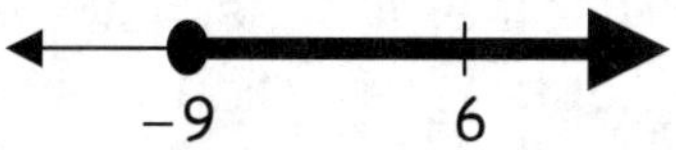 [number line: closed circle at −9, shaded right; labels −9, 6]

C. [number line: closed circles at −9 and 6, shaded between; labels −9, 6]

D. [number line: closed circles at −3 and 12, shaded between; labels −3, 12]

15._____

16. Solve $3x + 4 \le 16$ or $2x - 8 \ge 12$ and choose the graph of the solution set.

A. $\varnothing$

B. 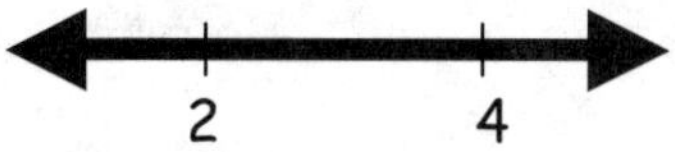 [number line: entire line shaded; labels 2, 4]

C. 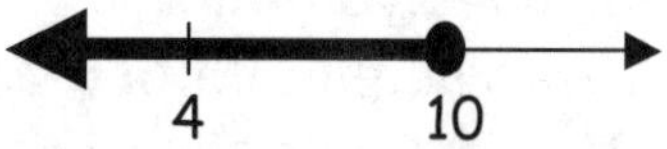 [number line: shaded left to closed circle at 10; labels 4, 10]

D. 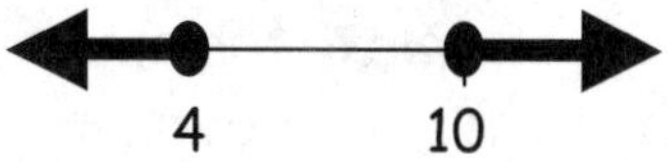 [number line: shaded left to closed circle at 4 and right from closed circle at 10; labels 4, 10]

16._____

17. Which of the following is the graph of the solution set of $x \le -3$ or $x \ge 4$?

A. $\varnothing$

B. 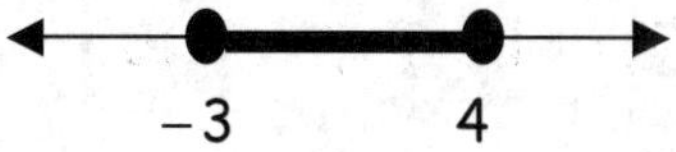 [number line: closed circles at −3 and 4, shaded between; labels −3, 4]

C. 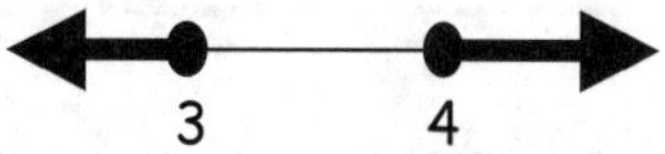 [number line: shaded left to closed circle at 3 and right from closed circle at 4; labels 3, 4]

D. 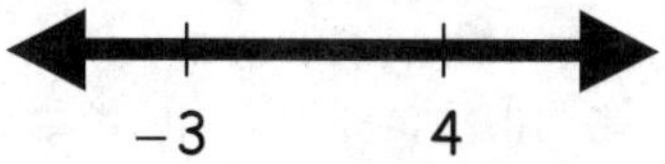 [number line: entire line shaded; labels −3, 4]

17._____

18. Which of the following is the graph of the solution set of $m \ge 6$ and $m < 9$?

A. $\varnothing$

B.  [number line: entire line shaded; labels 6, 9]

C. 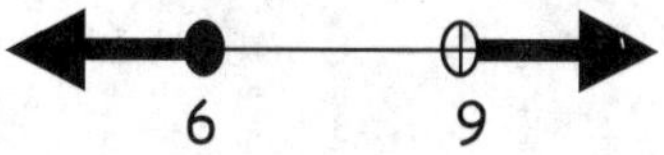 [number line: shaded left to closed circle at 6 and right from open circle at 9; labels 6, 9]

D. 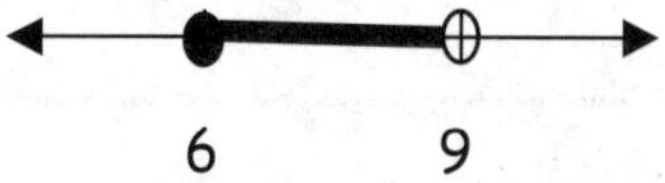 [number line: closed circle at 6, open circle at 9, shaded between; labels 6, 9]

18._____

Part A

Problem Solving Strategy Notes:
Analyzing and Investigating

Having a group of people analyze and investigate can solve many problems. The first step in this process is to analyze what is known and what you need to know. Working with a group allows you to rely on the information everyone in the group knows to solve the problem.

The second step in the process is to investigate the problem to gather more information to solve it. The group uses their pooled information to solve the problem.

Problems that require analyzing and investigating are often complex. Usually, more information must be gathered before a solution can be found.

The following information will help you solve mathematics problems using analyzing and investigating.

Estimation and Quick Mental Computation

Estimation can be used when beginning to solve a complex problem. Estimation allows the members of the group to begin with a rough estimate of the answer. If you have begun with a rough estimate, you will quickly know if your answer is far off from the original estimate. This is especially important when solving complex problems that require additional gathering of data.

Planning an Approach to Gather Information

Consider whether the task involves measurement, observation, a survey, or other information. Explore the different methods that can be used to gather information and decide how you want to display the information you discover. Once you gather the information the group can work together to solve the problem.

If you wanted to put in a new floor in your classroom, how many floor tiles would be required? Before taking exact measurements, estimate the length and width of the room. Then, estimate the size of the floor tiles. This information can be used to solve the problem.

Estimate: 20 foot x 20 foot room = 400 square feet
12 inch x 12 inch floor tile = 1 square foot
So, 400 tiles would be needed to cover the room.

Problem Solving Strategy Notes: Analyzing and Investigating *(cont.)* Part B

Sample Problem

Each day, many cars drive past your school. How long will it take for a million cars to pass?

Understanding the Problem

What do I know?

- Cars rush past the school each day.
- Eventually one million cars will pass.

What do I need to find out?

- How long will it take for a million cars to pass?
- What processes or strategies will I use to solve the problem?

Planning and Communicating a Solution

One Possible Solution: Students believe there are two peak traffic times, from 8:00–9:00 A.M. and 3:00–4:00 P.M. During the remainder of the day, cars do not pass very often.

Plan: Survey the traffic during the peak hours and at at least two other times during the day. Tally the number of cars that pass during a ten-minute period and multiply by six to get the number of cars per hour.

Peak Hours

8:00–9:00 A.M.—250 cars in a ten-minute period
250 x 6 = 1,500 cars/hour

3:00–4:00 P.M.—275 cars in a ten-minute period
275 x 6 = 1,650 cars/hour

Other Times

10:00–11:00 A.M.—10 cars in a ten-minute period
10 x 6 = 60 cars/hour

Other Times *(cont.)*

1:00–2:00 P.M.—12 cars in a ten-minute period
12 x 6 = 72 cars/hour

9:00–10:00 P.M.—It would be quiet. Estimate 25 cars per hour during this time.

12:00–6:00 A.M.—It would be very quiet. Estimate 5 cars per hour during this time.

The flow of traffic in one 24-hour period can be recorded as follows:

Peak Hours = 3,150 cars

12:00–6:00 A.M. = 5 cars/hour
5 x 6 hours = 30 cars

6:00–8:00 A.M. and 9:00 A.M.–12:00 P.M. = 60 cars/hour
60 x 5 hours = 300 cars

12:00–3:00 P.M. and 4:00–6:00 P.M. = 72 cars/hour
72 x 5 hours = 360 cars

6:00–12:00 P.M. = 25 cars/hour
25 x 6 hours = 150 cars

Total Cars in One Day =
3,150 + 30 + 300 + 360 + 150 = 3,990

1,000,000 divided by 3,990 cars/day =
250.63 days until one million cars pass.

Reflecting and Generalizing

In the process of the investigation, you used the strategy of observation (tallying the peak and average traffic flow times). You also used generalization by applying these tallies to other peak and non-peak times. When you made an assumption for the low traffic flow time, you used estimation. These strategies are useful for solving many types of word problems.

Extension

It is important to develop different methods for solving problems. Solve the same problem in a different way. Explain your methods clearly.

Part A Real-Life Problem Solving: A Stockbroker?

Source: David Davis/ Shutterstock, Inc.

It is career day at a local elementary school. Mr. Wilson, one of the guest speakers, is a stockbroker. He briefly explains to the students how to invest in a company. He uses a movie company as an example of how the stock market works. First, he defines a few words to help explain the process.

stock—shares in a company

share—a part of ownership in a company or corporation

profit—the amount earned when a stock is sold for more than its purchase price

loss—the amount lost when a stock is sold for less than its purchase price

Mr. Wilson shared this scenario. If you purchase 20 shares of a movie company stock at \$80 each, the purchasing price is \$1,600 (20 x \$80 = \$1,600).

Once you have made a purchase, you should keep track of how your stock is doing. This can be done by looking online or in the newspaper. One day, the cost of the shares is \$80.25. If you sell your shares on that day, you will have made a profit of \$5. To calculate the profit:

1. Multiply \$80.25 by 20 shares (\$1,605).
2. Your purchasing price was \$1,600.
   Your selling price was \$1,605.
   You made a profit of \$5.

Suppose that on another day, the cost of the shares was \$78. If you sell your shares on that day, you will have incurred a loss of \$40. To calculate the loss:

1. Multiply \$78 by 20 shares (\$1,560).
2. Your purchasing price was \$1,600.
   Your selling price was \$1,560.
   You lost \$40.

Real-Life Problem Solving: A Stockbroker? *(cont.)* Part B

Directions: Use the information on page 190 and in the problems below to answer the questions. Before you begin, be sure to locate the key information you will need.

What Is the Problem?

After listening to Mr. Wilson, the stockbroker, you decide to invest in Nickey. You purchase 20 shares of Nickey at $90 per share. Calculate the purchase price for your Nickey shares. You will need this information for the problems below. The line graph shows the closing price for Nickey each day for a week.

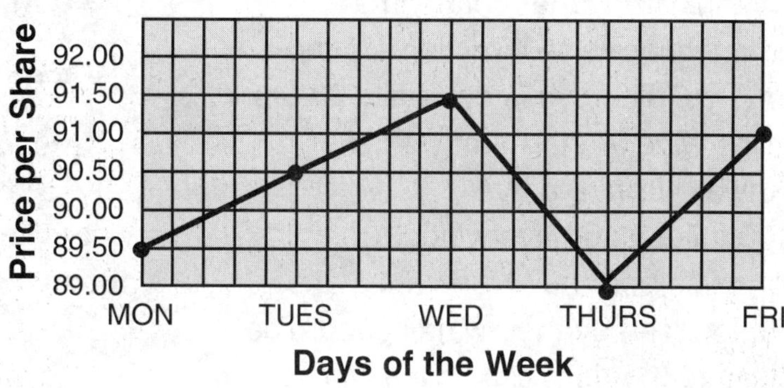

Problem-Solving Strategy: Analyzing and Investigating

Problem A

On which day were Nickey shares the highest? On which day were Nickey shares the lowest? If you sold your shares of Nickey on Friday, would you have made a profit or loss? By how much?

Answer: ______________________

____

____

Problem B

On which day would you have made the highest profit by selling your shares? How much is the profit? On which day would you have had the greatest loss by selling your shares? How much is the loss?

Answer: ______________________

____

Problem C

What are the mean, median, and mode for the closing prices of Nickey?

Answer: ______________________

____

____

Class Challenge

Using any day's closing price for two companies listed on the New York Stock Exchange (NYSE), pretend to purchase 35 shares from each company. Calculate the purchase price for each company. Then, record the closing prices for the companies over the next 5 days. Use the information to create a line graph for each company.

Part A

Real-Life Problem Solving: Hurricanes

Hurricanes are tropical storms that form over the southern Atlantic Ocean, Caribbean Sea, Gulf of Mexico, and the eastern Pacific Ocean. Hurricanes rotate in a counterclockwise direction around an "eye." The eye is generally 20–30 miles wide. A storm may extend outward from the eye 400 miles and have winds over 74 miles per hour. Hurricanes are categorized by their wind speed. The chart to the right shows the wind speed ranges for each category.

Category 1—74 to 95 miles per hour

Category 2—96 to 110 miles per hour

Category 3—111 to 130 miles per hour

Category 4—131 to 155 miles per hour

Category 5—more than 155 miles per hour

Meteorologists label a category 3, 4, or 5 hurricane as a major hurricane.

Source: Ingrid E Stamatson/ Shutterstock, Inc.

Source: Robert A. Mansker/ Shutterstock, Inc.

Hurricanes are given names to identify the storms as well as to track them as they move across the ocean. At any time during hurricane season, June 1 through November 30, more than one hurricane can be in the ocean. In 1953, the United States National Weather Service, which is a federal agency that tracks hurricanes, began using female names for storms. By 1979, both women's and men's names were used. One name for each letter of the alphabet (except for Q, U, and Z) is selected each year by the World Meteorological Organization. The organization uses six lists in rotation. If a hurricane is very deadly or costly, its name is retired. Then, a new name is added. In 2005 alone, five names were retired.

Because hurricanes can be costly or deadly, hurricane watches (hurricane possible within 36 hours) and hurricane warnings (hurricane expected within 24 hours) should be taken seriously. If you live in a hurricane area, you should read a preparedness pamphlet to learn about how to prepare for these severe storms.

Real-Life Problem Solving: Part B
Hurricanes *(cont.)*

Directions: Use the information on page 192 and in the problems below to answer the questions. Before you begin, be sure to locate the key information you will need.

What Is the Problem?

The National Weather Service keeps track of all the hurricanes that strike the United States. Their National Hurricane Center website includes a chart showing each hurricane. In one century (1901–2000), 167 hurricanes struck the United States. The chart to the right shows these hurricanes, organized by category.

As you complete the problems below, round each answer to the nearest hundredths. You will need to write each category as a fraction of the total to find the percent.

Category	Number
Category 1	66
Category 2	39
Category 3	47
Category 4	12
Category 5	3
Total	**167**

Problem-Solving Strategy: Analyzing and Investigating

Problem A

What percentage of the hurricanes in the twentieth century were classified as Category 1? If a total of 200 hurricanes struck the United States in the same century, how many hurricanes would be Category 1?

Answer: ______________________

____

Problem B

What percentage of the hurricanes in the twentieth century were classified as Categories 1 and 2? If a total of 200 hurricanes struck the United States in the same century, how many hurricanes would be Categories 1 and 2?

Answer: ______________________

____

Problem C

What percentage of the hurricanes in the twentieth century were classified as major hurricanes? If a total of 200 hurricanes struck the United States in the same century, how many would be major hurricanes?

Answer: ______________________

____

Class Challenge

Research to find ten retired names for past hurricanes. Determine the category when each struck the mainland. Create a pie chart that shows the percentages of retired hurricanes by categories.

Name ______________________________

Real-Life Problem Solving:
Analyzing and Investigating

Directions: Use the strategy to solve each problem. Then, explain each answer.

The Problem

Find at least ten 2- or 3-dimensional shapes in your classroom. Using these objects, create a geometric pattern and state the rule for your pattern.

Using the Strategy—Show Your Work

Explain Your Answer

Real-Life Problem Solving:
Analyzing and Investigating *(cont.)*

The Problem

1. Roll two dice. Write the largest and smallest two-digit numbers that can be made. For example, if 3 and 6 are rolled. The largest two-digit number is 63 and the smallest is 36.
2. Then, find the difference between the two numbers.
3. Repeat this process a minimum of 10 times. Make a chart to record the numbers and their differences.
4. What do you notice about the differences?

Using the Strategy—Show Your Work

Explain Your Answer

Name ______________________________

Adding and Multiplying Monomials 1

Directions: Simplify.

1. $2x + 3x$ __________
2. $-5m + 6m$ __________
3. $-4y - 7y$ __________
4. $-5a + 6a - 3a$ __________
5. $2x - 3y + 4x - 6y$ __________
6. $-3x + 4y + 3x - 5y$ __________
7. $3a^2b - 2ab^2 - 5a^2b$ __________
8. $-6mn + 4mn - 3m$ __________

9. $3x(4x^2)$ __________
10. $-2m(3m)$ __________
11. $-6k(4y)$ __________
12. $-2a(-3x^2)$ __________
13. $-6(3x - 4)$ __________
14. $-3x(2x^2 - 5y)$ __________
15. $-2m(3m^3 - 4m^2)$ __________
16. $-2xy^3(3xy^5)$ __________

17. $-5y - 8y$ __________
18. $6k(-2y)$ __________
19. $3m^2n(6mn)$ __________
20. $-5(2x - 6)$ __________
21. $-6m + 4m - 2m^2$ __________
22. $-2x + 5y - 6x + 4y$ __________
23. $-5m^2(3m^3n + 4m)$ __________
24. $2m^3(-5mn)$ __________

25. $-6xy^2 - 5xy + 6xy^2$ ____________________
26. $-3x + 4 - 6x(2x - 3) + 4(2x - 3) + x$ ____________________

Name ______________________________

Adding and Multiplying Monomials 2

Directions: Simplify.

1. $12x + 3x$ __________
2. $6p - 8p$ __________
3. $-4k - 6k$ __________
4. $-3m + 6m - 4m$ __________
5. $3p - 6x - 5p + 4x$ __________
6. $-6m + 8n + 6m - 10m$ __________
7. $-4x^2y - 6xy^2 + 3x^2y$ __________
8. $-3ab - 6ab + 5b$ __________

9. $4m(2m^2)$ __________
10. $-6p(-3p^3)$ __________
11. $-6x(3y)$ __________
12. $-6a(4x^2)$ __________
13. $-3(2x + 4)$ __________
14. $-6p(3p^2 - 6p)$ __________
15. $-5x(3x + 4)$ __________
16. $-3xy^3(2x^2y^5)$ __________

17. $-6y + 3y$ __________
18. $-8y(2y^3)$ __________
19. $4m^2n(3mn^2)$ __________
20. $-3(2x - 6)$ __________
21. $-8p + 4 - 6p$ __________
22. $-p + 5n - 6p + 3n$ __________
23. $-6p^2(3p^2 - 6n)$ __________
24. $5x^2(3xy^2)$ __________

25. $-6pm^2 - 4p^2m - 8pm^2$ ______________________

26. $-3p - 4p(3p - 5) - 6p(2p + 1)$ ______________________

Name ______________________________

Simplifying Radicals 1

Directions: Simplify the following. Assume that all variables are nonnegative.

1. $\sqrt{32}$ ____________
2. $\sqrt{12}$ ____________
3. $\sqrt{20}$ ____________
4. $\sqrt{8}$ ____________
5. $\sqrt{25}$ ____________
6. $\sqrt{50}$ ____________
7. $\sqrt{48}$ ____________
8. $\sqrt{9}$ ____________
9. $\sqrt{10}$ ____________
10. $\sqrt{x^2}$ ____________
11. $\sqrt{x^4}$ ____________
12. $\sqrt{9p^4}$ ____________
13. $\sqrt{20x^2}$ ____________
14. $\sqrt{32x^6}$ ____________
15. $\sqrt{m^4n^6}$ ____________
16. $\sqrt{50x^4y^{10}}$ ____________
17. $\sqrt{13x^2}$ ____________
18. $\sqrt{75}$ ____________
19. $\sqrt{45}$ ____________
20. $\sqrt{300}$ ____________
21. $\sqrt{49}$ ____________
22. $\sqrt{125}$ ____________
23. $\sqrt{28}$ ____________
24. $\sqrt{200}$ ____________
25. $\sqrt{4}$ ____________
26. $\sqrt{100}$ ____________
27. $\sqrt{80}$ ____________
28. $\sqrt{12m^4}$ ____________
29. $\sqrt{100x^4}$ ____________
30. $\sqrt{45m^8}$ ____________
31. $\sqrt{49x^{10}y^{12}}$ ____________
32. $\sqrt{28p^2q^6}$ ____________
33. $\sqrt{25m^6n^{12}}$ ____________
34. $\sqrt{19p^{10}}$ ____________

Name ________________________________

Simplifying Radicals 2

Directions: Simplify the following. Assume that all variables are nonnegative.

1. $\sqrt{98}$ ____________
2. $\sqrt{80}$ ____________
3. $-\sqrt{12}$ ____________
4. $3\sqrt{8}$ ____________
5. $\sqrt{121}$ ____________
6. $\sqrt{40}$ ____________
7. $4\sqrt{64}$ ____________
8. $\sqrt{10}$ ____________
9. $\sqrt{196}$ ____________
10. $\sqrt{x^4}$ ____________
11. $3\sqrt{x^7}$ ____________
12. $\sqrt{16p^6}$ ____________
13. $\sqrt{-75x}$ ____________
14. $\sqrt{32x^8}$ ____________
15. $4\sqrt{m^3n^9}$ ____________
16. $\sqrt{144x^4y^9}$ ____________
17. $-5\sqrt{13x^3}$ ____________
18. $\sqrt{500}$ ____________
19. $2\sqrt{54}$ ____________
20. $\sqrt{225}$ ____________
21. $\sqrt{150}$ ____________
22. $\sqrt{-150}$ ____________
23. $\sqrt{6}$ ____________
24. $\sqrt{45}$ ____________
25. $\sqrt{9}$ ____________
26. $5\sqrt{81}$ ____________
27. $\sqrt{90}$ ____________
28. $\sqrt{8m^5}$ ____________
29. $-2\sqrt{49x^4}$ ____________
30. $\sqrt{45m^{11}}$ ____________
31. $\sqrt{36x^8y^{12}}$ ____________
32. $-\sqrt{28p^5q^3}$ ____________
33. $3\sqrt{25m^7n^{14}}$ ____________
34. $\sqrt{19p^9}$ ____________

Name ______________________________

Simplifying Rational Expressions 1

Directions: Simplify. Assume that no denominator has a value of zero.

1. $\frac{x^2(x+2)}{6x^5}$ ______________

2. $\frac{(x+2)(x-3)}{x+2}$ ______________

3. $\frac{5m^2n(n-3)}{10m(n-3)}$ ______________

4. $\frac{2x^3y^3(x-2)}{6x^5y(2-x)}$ ______________

5. $\frac{2(x-3)}{2x+7}$ ______________

6. $\frac{3(x-2)}{6(x+2)}$ ______________

7. $\frac{x-1}{1-x}$ ______________

8. $\frac{3(m+6)}{2(m-4)}$ ______________

9. $\frac{4(m+8)}{6m}$ ______________

10. $\frac{3x(2x+5)}{6x^4(x+5)}$ ______________

11. $\frac{3(6x+5)}{3x+2}$ ______________

12. $\frac{4x(2x-1)}{5x(3x-1)}$ ______________

13. $\frac{2m^2n^5}{6m^5n}$ ______________

14. $\frac{8(k-3)}{6k}$ ______________

Name ______________________________

Simplifying Rational Expressions 2

Directions: Simplify. Assume that no denominator has a value of zero.

1. $\dfrac{2x^2(x+4)}{6x^8}$ ______________

2. $\dfrac{(x+6)(x-5)}{x-5}$ ______________

3. $\dfrac{5v(2x+3)}{10v^2}$ ______________

4. $\dfrac{-6x^5y^2(x-2)}{3x^5y(x-2)}$ ______________

5. $\dfrac{h-2}{2-h}$ ______________

6. $\dfrac{2(x-9)}{4(x+9)}$ ______________

7. $\dfrac{(x+1)(x-1)}{x+1}$ ______________

8. $\dfrac{x+2}{x+2}$ ______________

9. $\dfrac{3(a+4)(4-a)}{9a(a-4)}$ ______________

10. $\dfrac{x(2x+3)}{2x^3(x+3)}$ ______________

11. $\dfrac{8(2x+5)}{3x+5}$ ______________

12. $\dfrac{4x(3x-1)}{6x(2x-1)}$ ______________

13. $\dfrac{4x^7y^3(x-2)}{12x^5y(2-x)}$ ______________

14. $\dfrac{7(a-6)}{21a}$ ______________

Part A — Problem Solving Strategy Notes: Creating a Tree Diagram

A tree diagram can be used when there are different combinations or permutations possible in a problem. For example, if you had one scoop each of chocolate, vanilla, and strawberry ice cream on a cone, in how many different orders could you put the ice cream?

You can draw a tree diagram using simple pictures or words. Using a tree diagram helps a problem solver see the different combinations more easily.

Before you begin using tree diagrams, read the following information to learn more about how and when to use tree diagrams to solve problems.

Source: Thomas M Perkins/Shutterstock, Inc.

Listing All the Names or Options

The first step in making a tree diagram is to list all of the options. The three ice cream flavors are:

chocolate
vanilla
strawberry

Pairing or Connecting Information Using Lines or Brackets

Now show all of the different orders. Build on the list of ice cream flavors by writing the other two flavors next to each flavor. Then draw two lines linking each flavor to the other two flavors. Now add the flavor that hasn't been linked to each second flavor yet. By doing this you will have a tree diagram showing every possible order.

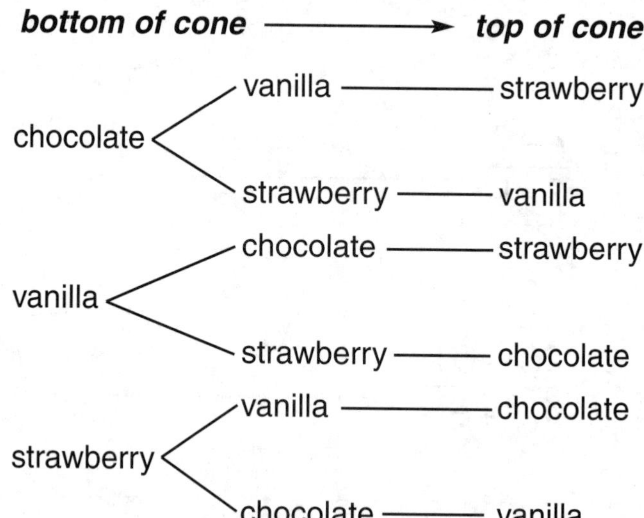

So, there are six different orders in which the ice cream scoops could be placed on the cone. By drawing a tree diagram like this one, it is easy to see how many combinations are possible.

Problem Solving Strategy Notes: Creating a Tree Diagram *(cont.)*

Part B

Sample Problem

There are eight basketball teams playing in a tournament. Once a team loses, they leave the tournament. How many games will be played during the entire tournament?

Understanding the Problem

What do I know?

- There are eight basketball teams. Teams that lose leave the tournament.

What do I need to find out?

- How many games will be played during the tournament?

Planning and Communicating a Solution

Begin by writing a list of every team in the competition (Team 1 through Team 8).

Then, pair each team with another team by drawing lines.

Next, write the name of the winning team for each pairing. (You can choose who will be the winners.)

Keep pairing the teams and writing the winners until you are left with just one team.

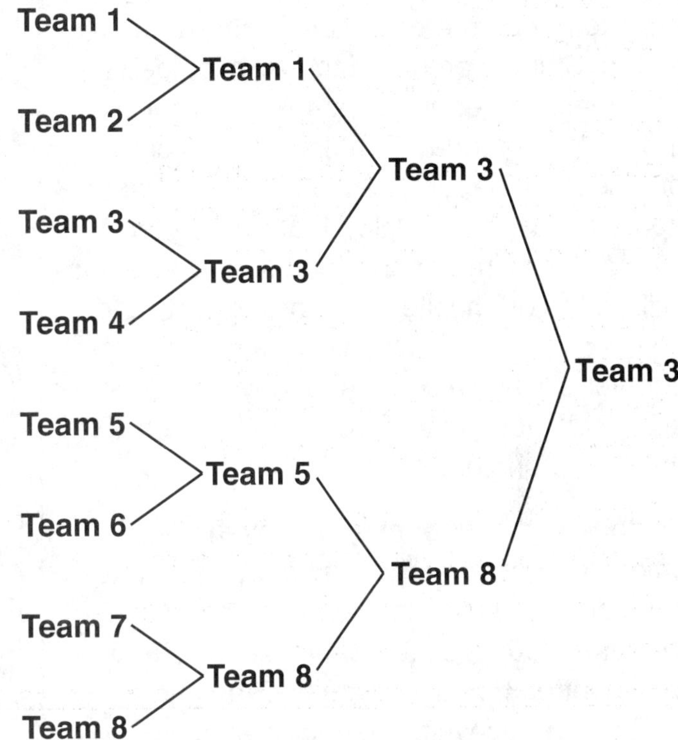

So, seven games of basketball will be played during the tournament.

Reflecting and Generalizing

By listing the teams and working methodically through each stage of the basketball tournament, you can count how many games were played.

It would be easy to forget a team with broad problems like this, but by creating a tree diagram, you can see the parts of the problem and make sure nothing is forgotten.

Extension

This strategy can also be used for problems with high numbers. What if there were 16 teams in the competition? How many games would be played then?

Part A

Real-Life Problem Solving:
Stamps, Stamps, Stamps!

Have you ever sent someone a letter? You had to write his or her address and your address on the envelope. What else did you have to put on the envelope? That's right, a stamp. Stamps are used to pay postage on your mail. The original stamps were not like the stamps of today. The first stamps came on sheets of paper. The stamps had to be cut apart. It wasn't until 1857 that perforated stamps were introduced. At that time, stamps still had to be moistened in order to stick to an envelope. Today, we have stamps that are self-adhesive, which means they work like a sticker. All you have to do is peel and stick the stamp on your envelope.

Postage is the amount of money the post office charges to mail an item. Postage rates have changed over the last two centuries. In the mid-1800s it cost 3 cents per ounce to mail a letter. Postage remained the same until the 1950s when postage was raised to 4 cents per ounce. Then postage rates began to rise every four to seven years. In 1975, postage was 10 cents per ounce. In that same year, the post office began to charge a smaller amount for each additional ounce per item. In the 1980s, postage rates began at 21 cents per ounce and increased to 29 cents by the end of the decade. Today, the postage rate is set at 39 cents for the first ounce and 24 cents for each additional ounce. But, you always have to be on the lookout for additional rate increases.

To meet the demands of the changing postal rates, stamps have been made with different values. This allows the sender to send mail that weighs more than one ounce without wasting stamps.

Source: Jasenka Luksa/Shutterstock, Inc.

Stamps are necessary for mailing letters, but did you know they are also like little works of art? Many of us have bought stamps that have the United States flag on them, but the United States post office also has stamps with pictures of important people, places, and things. These stamps honor past events and people. There have even been stamps with cartoon characters on them. All this variety has created a hobby known as stamp collecting.

The next time you are mailing a letter, think about all the history behind that stamp you are sticking on the envelope.

Real-Life Problem Solving: Part B

Stamps, Stamps, Stamps! *(cont.)*

Directions: Use the information on page 204 and in the problems below to answer the questions. Before you begin solving the problems, be sure to locate the key information you will need.

What Is the Problem?

Letters are a great way to keep in touch with people around the world. You have to use stamps to send letters. Stamps come in different values to help you spend the right amount of money when sending a letter. Some available values of stamps are shown in the chart to the right.

Hint: Make a tree diagram to solve each problem. Keep track of the total value of the stamps you are using on each branch. Write your final number of combinations on the lines below.

Postage Stamp Values	
39 cents	4 cents
37 cents	3 cents
24 cents	2 cents
10 cents	1 cent
5 cents	

Problem-Solving Strategy: Creating a Tree Diagram

Problem A

Pick three of the stamps from the chart above. How many different postage amounts can you make with two stamps?

Answer: ____________________

Problem B

Pick four of the stamps from the chart above. How many different postage amounts can you make with two stamps? What is the sum of each combination of stamps?

Answer: ____________________

____

____

Problem C

Pick five of the stamps from the chart above. How many different postage amounts can you make with two stamps? What is the sum of each combination of stamps? Using all five stamps, how many ounces could you mail with today's postage rates?

Answer: ____________________

____

Class Challenge

Pick a weight (in ounces) for a package you want to mail. Figure out how much it would cost to ship. Using the stamp values above, are there multiple stamp combinations that you could use to send your package?

Part A

Real-Life Problem Solving:
Let's Have a Party

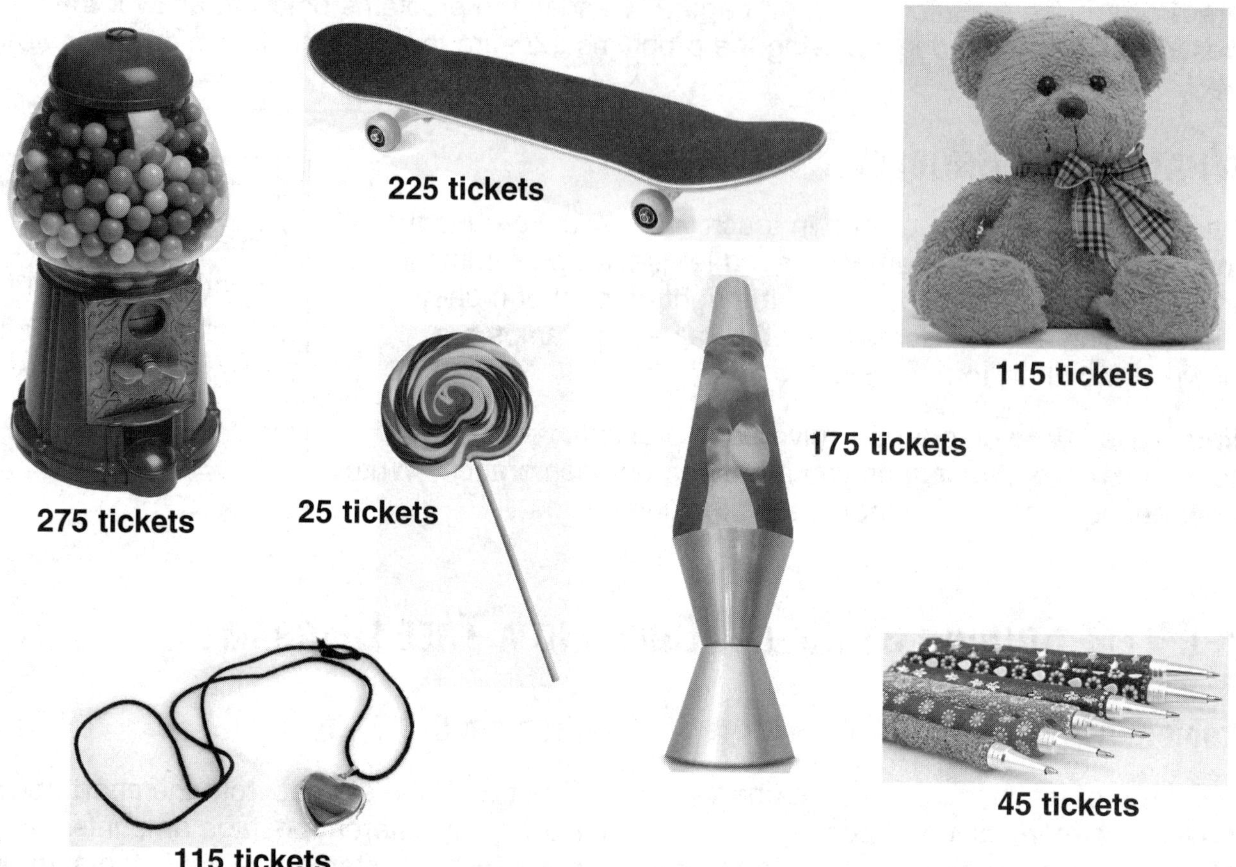

Fantastic Fun is Sam's favorite place to eat and have fun. They have video games, activity games, and rides. When you win a game, a machine gives you tickets. The more tickets you win, the more prizes you can buy.

This year Sam's parents told him he could have his thirteenth birthday party anywhere he wanted. Sam, of course, chose Fantastic Fun. It's a great place to have a party! They have tasty pizza and more games than you can imagine. He invited his entire math class. All 20 of his classmates were able to come to the party. Sam was very excited to have all his friends there to celebrate his birthday.

Everyone had a great time. They ate pizza and birthday cake. Then, everyone played games and rode the rides. By the end of the party, they had all won many tickets. Sam won 175 tickets.

Before leaving, the partygoers had to make big decisions about whether to spend their tickets on one or two large prizes or get several smaller ones. After much thinking and figuring, all the tickets were spent.

Sam thanked everyone for coming to his birthday party. They all thanked him back and said what a good time they'd had. It was really a happy birthday!

Real-Life Problem Solving: Let's Have a Party *(cont.)*

Part B

Directions: Use the information on page 206 and in the problems below to answer the questions. Before you begin solving the problems, be sure to locate the key information you will need.

What Is the Problem?

You went to Sam's party. Now, it's your turn to figure out how you want to spend your tickets. The prizes are shown on page 206. Use these prizes and their amounts to answer the problems below.

Hint: Creating a tree diagram will help you make your prize selections. Remember to keep track of the number of tickets you have left after you add each selection to your tree diagram. Write your final choices on the lines below. You may want to use rounding to estimate what you can buy before creating each tree diagram. This will save you time as you work through the problems.

Problem-Solving Strategy: Creating a Tree Diagram

Problem A

You won 246 tickets. You know you want the necklace. What else can you afford? List at least two possible combinations of what you can buy.

Answer: ______________________________

____

Problem B

You won 498 tickets. You decide to get a skateboard and give it to Sam as his birthday present. About how many tickets do you have left to spend on yourself? What other prizes could you choose with your remaining tickets? List at least two possible combinations of what you can buy.

Answer: ______________________________

____

____

Problem C

You won 249 tickets. You and Sam decide to combine your tickets and share the prizes you can buy. About how many tickets do you and Sam have to spend together? He wants the gumball machine 275 tickets. What other prizes could you buy? List at least two possible combinations of what you can buy.

Answer: ______________________________

____

____

____

Class Challenge

You earned 333 tickets at Fantastic Fun. Two of those tickets are red tickets and they are worth ten times as much as a regular ticket. What prizes could you choose? Draw a tree diagram to list all the possible choices.

Name ______________________________

Real-Life Problem Solving:
Creating a Tree Diagram

Directions: Use the strategy to solve each problem. Then, explain each answer.

The Problem

Gabriel is designing his own car. He has the choice of three body styles—two-door, four-door, and convertible; four exterior paint choices—red, blue, green, and black; and four interior color choices—yellow, brown, white, and orange. How many different car combinations does Gabriel have to choose from?

Using the Strategy—Show Your Work

Explain Your Answer

Real-Life Problem Solving:
Creating a Tree Diagram *(cont.)*

The Problem

Create a play-off schedule (quarter-finals, semi-finals, and finals) for the following teams: Stingers, Kings, Stars, Galaxies, Bulls, Bears, Squids, and Hollows. If a team leaves the tournament once it loses, how many games are played?

Using the Strategy—Show Your Work

Explain Your Answer

Name ______________________________

Practice Using the Home Screen Method

Directions: Check the following answers on the Home Screen using the Home Screen method. Place a check beside the answers that are correct.

1. 132,000 = $\boxed{1.32 \times 10^5}$

2. 1.4×10^{-3} = $\boxed{.00014}$

3. Use the Pythagorean theorem, $a^2 + b^2 = c^2$, with the following values, $a = 7$; $b = 24$; $c = 25$, to solve the problem below.

In the figures below, the sides of squares can be used to form triangles. The areas of the squares that form right triangles have a special relationship.

Using the given lengths of the sides of the squares, can the set of squares form a right triangle? Explain your answer.

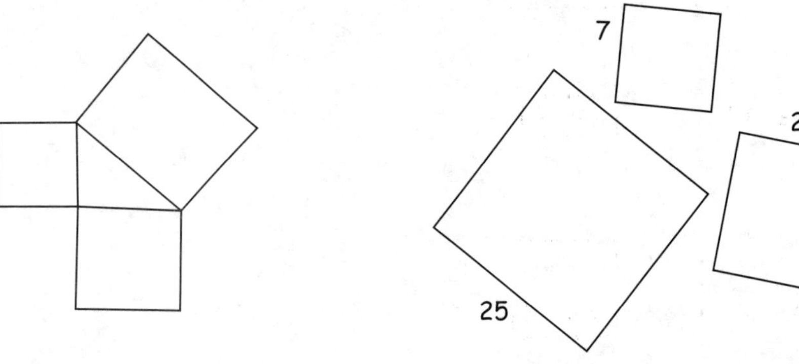

4. $(x + 2)(x - 3)$ = $\boxed{x^2 - x - 6}$

5. $2x^2 - 7x + 5$ = $\boxed{(2x + 5)\ (x + 1)}$

Name ______________________________

Practice Using the Store Before Method

Directions: Check the following solutions by storing your answer on the Home Screen using the Store Before method. Place a check beside each answer that is correct.

1. $3(x - 2) = 18$ $\boxed{x = 6}$

2. $12p - 7 = -3p + 8$ $\boxed{p = 1}$

3. $x^2 - 10x = -24$ $\boxed{x = 6, 4}$

4. $a^2 + 2a = 2$ $\boxed{a = -1 \pm \sqrt{3}}$

5. $\frac{3}{x} + \frac{1}{2} = 6$ $\boxed{x = \frac{6}{11}}$

6. $3 + 4\sqrt{2x} = 11$ $\boxed{x = 2}$

7. $x + y = 1$

$4x - y = 9$

$\boxed{x = 2}$ $\boxed{y = -1}$

8. $y = 4x + 5$

$3x + 7y = 35$

$\boxed{x = 0}$ $\boxed{y = 4}$

Name ___________________________________

Practice Using the Trace Method

Directions: Check the following solutions using the Trace method. Place a check beside each answer that is correct.

1. $x^2 - 10x = -24$ $\boxed{x = 6, 4}$

2. $a^2 + 2a = 2$ $\boxed{a = -1 \pm \sqrt{3}}$

3. Find the range of $y = 2x + 4$ when the domain is {–3, 0 ,2}. $\boxed{R = \{-2, 4, 8\}}$

Name ____

Practice Using the Table Method

Directions: Use the Table method to work the following problems.

1. Which equation represents the relation given in the table below?

x	y
−2	−2
−1	0
0	2
1	4
2	6

a. $y = -2x + 2$

b. $y = 2x - 2$

c. $y = 2x + 2$

d. $y = -2x - 2$

e. None of the above

2. Find the range of $\mathbf{y = x^2 + 6x - 8}$ when the domain is **{−4, −1, 2, 3}**.

3. Find the domain of $\mathbf{y = 3x - 1}$ when the range is **{−7, −1, 5}**.

4. Find the value of x in $\mathbf{y = x^2 - x}$ when $\mathbf{y = 6}$.

5. Find the missing value, if $\mathbf{3x + y = 0}$ and $\mathbf{(3, y)}$.

6. Find the missing value, if $\mathbf{2x - y = 7}$ and $\mathbf{(x, -3)}$.

Name ______________________________

Practice Using the Truth Table Method

Directions: Use the Truth Table method to check the following solutions. Place a check beside each answer that is correct.

1. $12p - 7 = -3p + 8$ | $p = 1$

2. $3(x - 2) = 18$ | $x = 8$

3. $x^2 - 10x = -24$ | $x = 6, 4$

4. $a^2 + 3a = 2$ | $a = -1 \pm \sqrt{2}$

5. $3 + 4\ \ 2x = 11$ | $x = 1$

6. $\frac{2}{x} = \frac{\sqrt{3}}{8}$ | $x = \frac{22}{5}$

Name ______________________________________

Practice Using the Graphing One-Variable Inequalities Method

Directions: Use the graphing calculator to graph the following inequalities using the Graphing One-Variable Inequalities method. Then, graph the inequalities by hand on the number line.

1. $6x + 3 \leq 9$

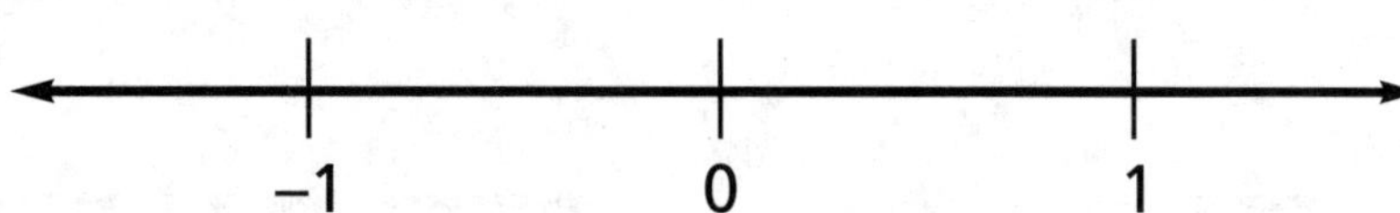

2. $5x - 2 < 8$

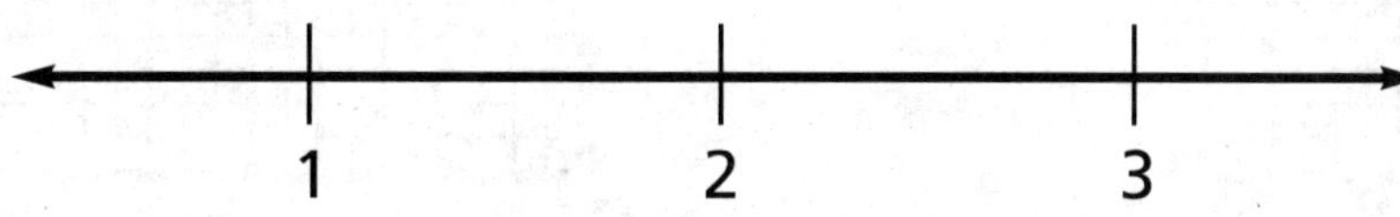

Name ______________________________

Practice Using the Graphing Two-Variable Inequalities Method

Directions: Use the graphing calculator to graph the following inequalities, and then graph them by hand on the grid below each problem.

1. $6x + 3 \leq 9$

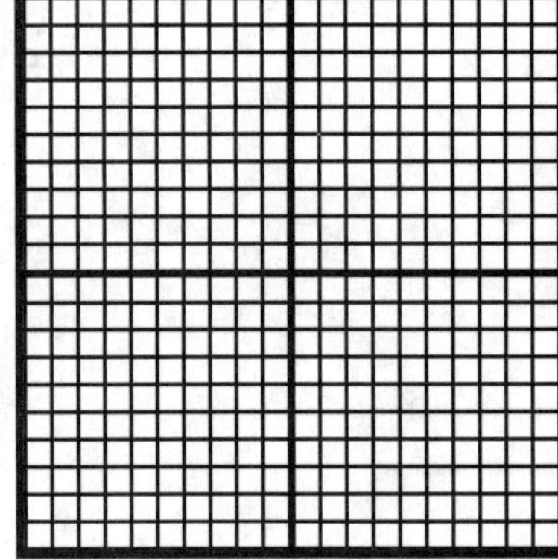

2. $y \geq -5x + 3$

$y \leq 3x + 2$

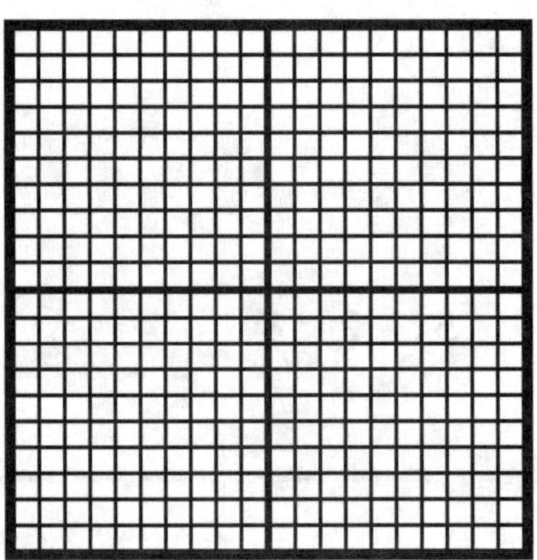

3. $y \geq 4x + 1$

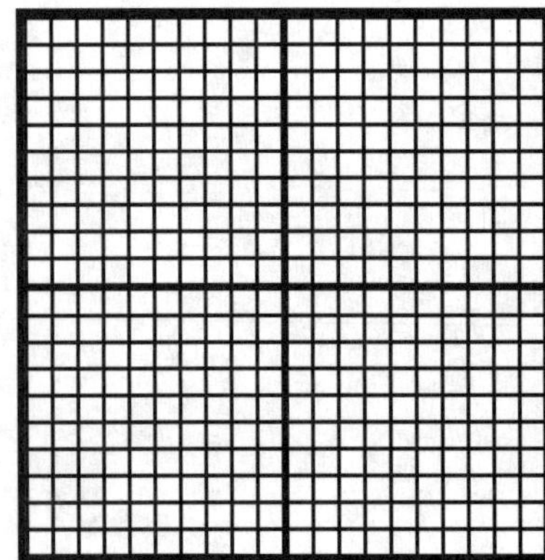

4. $y > 4x - 1$

$y \leq 2x + 3$

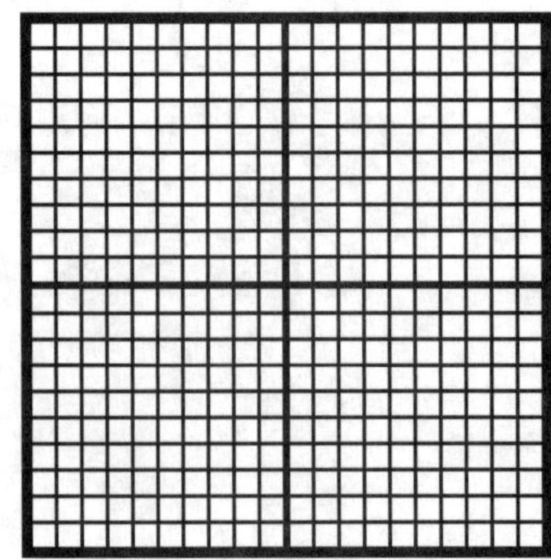

Mathematical Terms Glossary

absolute value—the distance of a number from 0 on the number line; always a positive number

acting out or using concrete materials—a problem-solving strategy in which objects, materials, or people are moved through the steps of the problem to more easily find a solution

addend—a number that is added in an addition problem

addition—an operation that puts numbers together; the opposite of subtraction; answer is called the *sum*; *altogether*, *increase*, and *total* indicate to add

algebraic expression—any term, or combination of terms, using variables that express an operation or series of operations

analyze and investigate—a problem-solving strategy in which what is known and what needs to be known are determined and then more information is gathered to solve the problem

area—the number of square units needed to cover a two-dimensional surface

associative property—the sum or product stays the same when the grouping of addends or products changes; $(a + b) + c = a + (b + c)$ or $(ab)c = a(bc)$, where *a*, *b*, and *c* stand for any real numbers

axis of symmetry—a line that passes through a figure so that half of the figure on one side of the line is a mirror reflection of the half on the other side of the line

base (of an exponent)—the number, or term, that is multiplied; for example, in 5^2, the base is 5

base (of a triangle)—the side of the triangle that contains one end of the altitude

binomial—a polynomial with the sum or difference of two terms; for example, $5x - 3$

cancel—To remove equal factors from both sides of an equation or from the numerator and denominator of a fraction

circle—a shape where all points are equally distant from the center

circumference—the measurement of the outer boundary of a shape, usually a circle

coefficient—a number in front of a variable; for example, in $9x^2 - 7x + 1$, the coefficient of x^2 is 9 and the coefficient of x is -7

collecting like terms—when working with an expression, adding or subtracting terms that have the same variable and are raised to the same power

column—in a table or chart, these are the vertical sections

combination—a collection of objects where the order of the objects does not matter

common denominator—in fractions, a number divisible by all the denominators; for example, 12 is a common denominator of $\frac{1}{4}$ and $\frac{5}{6}$

common factor—a number that divides evenly into all the given terms; for example, 3 is a common factor of 9 and 12

commutative property—the sum or product remains the same when the order of addends or products changes; $a + b = b + a$ or $a \cdot b = b \cdot a$, where *a* and *b* are any real numbers

complementary angles—two angles where the sum of the measures is 90°

composite number—a number with more than two factors

compound inequalities—two inequalities that are combined by the word *and* or the word *or*

cone—a solid with a circular base and sloped sides that meet at one point

Mathematical Terms Glossary *(cont.)*

congruent—having the same size and shape

consecutive numbers—numbers that follow one another in order; for example, 11, 12, 13, and 14

constant—a quantity that always stays the same

coordinate pair—*See ordered pair.*

coordinate plane—the plane determined by a horizontal number line, called the *x*-axis, and a vertical number line, called the *y*-axis; the *x*-axis and *y*-axis intersect at a point called the origin; an ordered pair (x, y) of numbers represents each point in the coordinate plane

creating a table—a problem-solving strategy that is used to organize information in a problem, identify relationships and patterns among values, and determine missing or unknown information

creating a tree diagram—a tree diagram is used to identify combinations (order does not matter) and permutations (order matters) in a problem; the combinations or orders branch off one central value or item; each part of the diagram is linked by a line segment to another part

cube—a solid figure with six congruent square faces

curve—a continuous line that bends without angles

cylinder—a solid figure with two circular bases connected by a curved face; like a can

data—facts, statistics, or sets of information

decimal number—a number with one or more digits to the right of the decimal point; each decimal place has ten times the value of the place to its right

denominator—a term or expression written below the fraction line; it represents the number of equal parts the whole is divided into; for example, 3 is the denominator of the fraction $\frac{2}{3}$

density—the mass of a substance per unit volume

dependent variable—a variable in a function whose value is affected by the value of the related independent variable

digits—any of the numerals 0–9

dimensions—measurement in length, width, and thickness

direct variation—an equation in the form of $y = kx$

distributive property of multiplication—property stating that the product remains the same whether one adds two or more terms enclosed in parentheses and then multiplies the results by a factor or multiplies each term alone by a factor and adds the results; for example, $a(b + c) = ab + ac$

dividend—a quantity to be divided

division—operation tells how many times a number can go into another number; opposite operation is multiplication; verbs include *divide*, *split*, *separate*, and *break apart*; answer is called the *quotient*; *into* often indicates to divide

divisor—the quantity by which another quantity is to be divided

domain—the possible values for x in a function; the set of values for the independent variable of a given function

equality—a statement in which two quantities or mathematical expressions are equal; for example, $x - 8 = 12$ means that $x - 8$ must have the same value as 12

equation—a mathematical statement where the left side of the equal sign has the same value as the right side

equivalent—equal in value; for example, $4 + 6$ is equivalent to $5 \cdot 2$; *equal* is a synonym for equivalent

Mathematical Terms Glossary *(cont.)*

estimate—to make an approximate judgment or opinion about a calculation

evaluate—to find the value of a mathematical expression

expanded form—writing a number showing the full form of each digit; for example, 285 is 200 + 80 + 5

exponent—the number of times a term is multiplied by itself; for example, in 3^4, the exponent is 4

exponential expression—terms that include an exponent

exponential form—a way to write a number using exponents

face—surface of a three-dimensional figure

factor—an integer or term that divides into another with no remainder; for example, 7 is a factor of 21

factoring or factorize—to determine the factors of a number or expression; to write a number or expression as a product of its factors

figure—a closed shape in two or three dimensions

formula—mathematical statement, equation, or rule using variables; for example, $A = \pi r^2$ is the formula for the area of a circle

fraction—a number that identifies part of a whole or part of a group

function (of *x*)—a relation in which every value for the variable *x* has only one value for the variable *y*; for example, the total sales are a function of the number of products sold

generalize—to state understanding of a mathematical idea, concept, or procedure; to state a mathematical conjecture or theory

geometry—the mathematics of the properties and relationships of points, lines, angles, surfaces, and solids

graph—a pictorial representation of a numerical relationship among two or more terms or sets of data

greatest common factor (GCF)—the highest number that divides into all of the given numbers or terms

grid—a pattern of horizontal and vertical lines, usually forming squares

height—the difference between the highest and lowest points on a vertical line

hypotenuse—the longest side of a right triangle, opposite the right angle

identity property—the sum or product of any real number combined with 0 is the original number; for example, $a + 0 = a$ or $a \cdot 1 = a$, where *a* stands for any number

improper fraction—fraction with a larger numerator than denominator

inequality—a mathematical statement that uses the symbols $<$, $>$, $\leq$, $\geq$, to compare two expressions; for example, $6 > 4$ or $x \leq 9$

infinite—unlimited or unbounded

integers—positive and negative whole numbers; for example, –3, –2, –1, 0, 1, 2, 3

intersection—the point where a set of lines meet or cross

inverse operations—a pair of operations that are opposite of each other and undo each other; for example, + and –

isosceles triangle—a triangle with at least two congruent sides (equal length and equal angles)

least common multiple (LCM)—the smallest number, or term, that is a multiple of all the given numbers or terms

leg—one of the two sides that form a right angle

length—a measured distance along a line or figure from one end to the other

Mathematical Terms Glossary (cont.)

like terms—terms that have exactly the same variables with the same corresponding exponents; for example, $3x^2$ and $4x^2$

line—straight path extending in both directions with no endpoints

line of best fit—a line, segment, or ray drawn on a scatter plot that estimates the relationship between two data sets; also called a linear regression

line segment—part of a line; includes a defined length with endpoints and all the points between the endpoints

linear equation—a first-degree equation with two variables whose graph is a straight line; for example, $y = x + 5$

logical reasoning—a problem-solving strategy in which given information is regarded as pieces of a puzzle that need to be put together in order to find a solution to the problem

lowest common denominator (LCD)—the smallest number that is a common denominator of a given set of whole numbers or fractions; also called the least common denominator

mean—a mathematical average; the sum of a set of numbers divided by the number of members in the set

measure—a unit or standard of measurement

median—the middle number in a set of numbers that are in ascending order; if there is no single middle number, it is the mean of the two middle numbers

mixed number—a number with a whole number amount and a fraction or decimal amount; also called a mixed fraction or mixed decimal

mode—in a list of data, it is the number that occurs most often

monomial—an algebraic expression with one term that is a product of constants and multiples; for example $15a^5b^2$

multiples—a number that results from multiplying a given number by the set of whole numbers, for example, some multiples of 5 are 5, 10, 15, and 20

multiplication—an operation that simplifies adding the same number many times; the opposite of division; verbs are *multiply* and *times*; answer is called the product; the word *of* often indicates to multiply

net—the figure formed when a solid shape is unfolded into a two-dimensional shape

no solution—no value of a variable makes an equation true or there are no points of intersection on a graph; for example, the lines in a problem are parallel

nonrepeating/nonterminating decimal—the digits in a decimal do not end and do not have a repeating pattern

number line—line with numbers along it; the same positive and negative numbers are equal distances from zero

numeral—a word, letter, symbol, or figure representing a number

numerator—the number or expression written above the fraction line; represents the number of equal parts of a total number of parts; for example, 2 is the numerator of the fraction $\frac{2}{3}$

operations—the various ways of manipulating numbers; addition, subtraction, multiplication, and division

opposite—a number that is the equal distance from zero in the other direction on a number line; for example, 2 and –2

opposite operations—*See inverse operation.*

order of operations—rules describing the order to use when evaluating expressions; parentheses, exponents, x and ÷, + and –

Mathematical Terms Glossary *(cont.)*

ordered pair—a pair of numbers that describes the location of a point on a grid, given in the following order, (horizontal coordinate, vertical coordinate) or (x, y)

origin—in a coordinate plane, the intersection of the x-axis and y-axis; represented by the ordered pair (0, 0)

parallel lines—lines that are always the same distance apart and do not intersect; lines that have the same slope

pattern—a form or model by which elements can be arranged so that what comes next can be predicted

percent—a part of a whole expressed in hundredths

perimeter—the distance around a figure

period—a group of three places in a place value chart, separated by a comma; for example, thousands, millions, and billions

permutation—an arrangement of objects in which the order of items counts as a different arrangement

perpendicular lines—lines that intersect at a 90° angle; lines that have a negative reciprocal slope

pi (π)—the ratio of the circumference of any circle to its diameter, approximately equal to 3.14 or $\frac{22}{7}$

place value—the value of a number is determined by its placement in the whole number; each place has a value of ten times the value of the place to its right

plotting—placing points on a grid or a number line

point—an exact location in space that has no length, width, or thickness

polynomial—an algebraic expression with two or more terms (monomials) that are added, subtracted, multiplied, or divided

power—*See exponent.*

powers of ten—the numbers produced by multiplying 10 by itself; for example, $10^1 = 10$, $10^2 = 100$, $10^{-1} = 0.10$

prime factorization—using only prime numbers as factors of composite numbers

prime number—a whole number that has only two factors, itself and one

prism—a solid having bases or ends that are parallel, congruent polygons and sides that are parallelograms

probability—measure how likely an event or outcome is

proportion—an equation that states that two ratios are equal; for example, $\frac{2}{5} = \frac{8}{20}$

pyramid—a solid figure with a base and steeply sloping sides meeting at a point

Pythagorean theorem—the theorem that the square of the hypotenuse of a right triangle is equal to the sum of the squares of the length of the legs

Pythagorean triples—any set of positive integers that satisfy the relationship $a^2 + b^2 = c^2$

quadrants—the four regions of a coordinate plane that are divided by the intersection of the x-axis and y-axis; numbered counterclockwise from the upper right—I, II, III, IV

radical ($\sqrt{\ }$)—a symbol that specifies that the root is to be taken

radical expression—an expression with a number or term (radicand) in front of a radical symbol, which is placed over a number that signifies the square root should be calculated; for example $3\sqrt{9}$

radius—the distance from the center to a point on a circle

random—a process of selection where each item of a set has an equal probability of being chosen

Mathematical Terms Glossary *(cont.)*

range—difference between the greatest number and the least number in a set of data

rate—a ratio that compares two unlike kinds of quantities

ratio—a comparison of two measures or numbers by means of division; for example, $\frac{4 \text{ cats}}{5 \text{ dogs}}$

rational expression—an algebraic expression that represents a quotient of two polynomials; for example, $\frac{8x}{16x^2}$

rational numbers—a number that can be expressed as the ratio of two integers; in other words, a fraction

reciprocals—two numbers that have a product of 1; for example, $\frac{3}{2}$ is the reciprocal of $\frac{2}{3}$

rectangle—a quadrilateral with two pairs of parallel sides and four right angles

reduce (a fraction)—to make an equivalent fraction with smaller numbers by dividing the numerator and the denominator by the greatest common factor

reflect (problem-solving)—to think about a math problem and determine if the solution to the problem is reasonable

region—a part of a plane

regroup—in place value, to shift part of the value from one place to another place to make addition and subtraction easier

relation—a set of ordered pairs

remainder—the quantity that remains after subtracting one number from another

represent—to use symbols, pictures, or objects in place of words; to use symbols, pictures, or objects to make a mathematical statement

right angle—an angle that makes a square corner; it measures exactly 90°

rise—the change in *y* when determining slope

rounding—a strategy in which an exact number is changed to another number that is close to its value; numbers can be rounded to any place value

row—in a table or chart, these are the horizontal sections

run—the change in *x* when determining slope

scales—the numeric value assigned to the axes of a graph

scatter plot—a graph with one point representing each item measured; two coordinates for each point represent two different attributes of the measured item

scientific notation—a form of writing numbers as a product of the power of 10 and a decimal number greater than or equal to one but less than 10

set—a collection of objects or elements classed together

simple interest—rate of interest determined by multiplying the principal times the annual rate of interest times the number of years

simplest form—way of writing a fraction so that the numerator and the denominator have no common factors other than 1

simplify—combine like terms and apply properties to an expression to make calculations easier

simplify a fraction—reduce a fraction until the common factor of the numerator and denominator is 1 or –1

slope—the steepness of a line from left to right, which can be calculated by finding two points on the line and dividing the change in the *y*-values over the change in the *x*-values; if a line slants upward, it has a positive slope; if a line slants downward, it has a negative slope

solution—any value for a variable that makes an equation or inequality true; the answer to a problem

Mathematical Terms Glossary *(cont.)*

solution set—the set of values for an equation that makes the equation true

sphere—a round, solid shape whose surface is at all points the same distance from the center

square—a parallelogram with four equal sides and four right angles

square root—one of the two identical factors of a given number

squared number—the product of two identical factors

standard form—a number written with one digit for each place value; for example, the standard form for the number five hundred fifty-seven is 557

statement—in math, sentences that often take an *if, then* form; the *if* part is the hypothesis and the *then* part is the conclusion

straight angle—an angle with a measure of 180°

strategy (problem-solving)—a way in which to approach a problem

substitution—replacing a variable with a number

subtraction—an operation that takes away numbers; it is the opposite of addition; the verb is *subtract*; the answer is called the *difference*; words that indicate the operation are *fewer, decreased, minus*

supplementary angle—an angle where the sum of the measures is 180°

surface area—includes the total area of the faces of a solid figure (including the base)

symbol—a letter, figure, or mark that represents an object, quantity, operation, or function

symmetrical—a geometric property that means two sides of a figure match exactly

system of equations—a collection of two or more equations with a same set of unknowns; to solve a system of equations, values are found for each of the unknowns that will satisfy every equation in the system

table—a column listing of x-values of a function and the corresponding y-values of the function

term—each of the members of an algebraic expression that is a number, variable, product, or quotient, but not a sum or a difference; for example, $2x$, $8y^2$, 7, $9ab$

trapezoid—a quadrilateral with one pair of parallel sides

trend—a general pattern that develops in a set of data

triangle—a polygon with three angles and three sides

trinomial—a polynomial with three terms; for example, $3x^2 - 4x + 3$

undefined—indefinite in form or extent

union—the set consisting of elements each of which is in at least one or more given sets

unit—the smallest positive integer

unlike terms—terms in an algebraic expression whose variable parts are not exactly the same; for example, $4x^2$ and $4x$

using simpler numbers—a problem-solving strategy in which smaller numbers are substituted for larger numbers or in which a problem is broken into smaller parts

variable—a symbol, usually a letter, used to represent different values

vertex—the point at which two line segments, lines, or rays meet to form an angle

vertical angle—the congruent angles formed when two lines intersect

Mathematical Terms Glossary *(cont.)*

vertical-line test—a vertical line drawn on the graph of any function will not intersect the graph at more than one point

volume—the number of cubic units it takes to fill a figure

whole numbers—a counting number from zero to infinity

width—horizontal measurements taken at right angles to the length

working backwards—a problem-solving strategy in which a problem is solved by starting with the information at the end of the problem and going back to the beginning to determine any missing or unknown information; opposite operations are used

***x*-axis**—the horizontal axis on a coordinate plane

***x*-coordinate**—the first value in the ordered pair that indicates the horizontal distance from the origin on a coordinate plane; for example, in (4, –3), 4 is the *x*-coordinate

***x*-intercept**—the point at which a line intersects the *x*-axis; for example, (5, 0)

***y*-axis**—the vertical axis on a coordinate plane

***y*-coordinate**—the second value in the ordered pair that indicates the vertical distance from the origin on a coordinate plane; for example, in (4, –3), –3 is the *y*-coordinate

***y*-intercept**—the point at which a line intersects the *y*-axis; for example, (0, 6)

zero pairs—any pair of numbers whose sum is zero

zero property of multiplication—a rule stating that the product of zero and any number equals zero